Using Technology in Physical Education

Third Edition

Bonnie S. Mohnsen, Ph.D.
Orange County (CA) Department of Education

Bonnie's Fitware
Cerritos, California

Library of Congress Cataloging-in-Publication Data

Mohnsen, Bonnie S., 1955-
Using technology in physical education, 3rd / Bonnie S.
Mohnsen

ISBN 1-893166-51-1
1. Physical education and training–Computer-assisted instruction.
2. Educational technology. 3. Media programs (Education)

I. Title.
GV364.M64 2001

ISBN 1-893166-51-1

Copyeditor: Carol A. Bruce.

Printed in the United States of America

Bonnie's Fitware
18832 Stefani Avenue
Cerritos, California 90703
(562) 924-0835
http://www.pesoftware.com/

Dedication

To Carolyn Thompson for her constant professional

and personal support.

Reviewers

Liz Aurbach
Software Developer
Aurbach & Associates, Inc.

Rick Aurbach
Software Developer
Aurbach & Associates, Inc.

Debra A. Ballinger, Ph.D.
Associate Professor
University of Rhode Island

Dr. Deborah Callaway
HPER Department Chairperson
No. Carolina A&T State University

Greg Comfort, Ed.D.
Assistant Professor
Wichita State University

Daniel Frankl, Ph.D.
Associate Professor
CSU, Los Angeles

Dr. Cheri Halderman
Director, Instructional Technology
Dallas Independent School District

Dr. Joanne Hynes-Dusel
Assistant Professor
Towson University

Dr. Pat Jordan
Pedagogy , HPE Dept.
Tennessee Technological University

Shaunna McGhie, Ed.D.
Associate Professor
Southeast Missouri State University

Sarah Menke-Fish
Teacher in Residence
American University

Dr. Ruth Morey Sorrentino
Post Doctoral Fellow
University of Calgary

Roberta Stokes
Professor
Miami-Dad Community College

Paula Summit
Elementary Physical Educator
Winslow Elementary School

Table of Contents

Chapter 4

Chapter 5

Chapter 6

Chapter 7

Chapter 8

Chapter 9

Chapter 10

Chapter 11

Chapter 12

Appendix A

Appendix B

Appendix C

Preface

*U*sing *Technology in Physical Education, Edition 3* is designed to help you to accomplish more of your teaching responsibilities in less time. Technology can assist you with your paperwork and help you individualize instruction for large, heterogeneous classes. Now is the time for you to harness the power of that technology—use this book to get started. Here's what you'll find.

Chapter 1 describes the growth and variety of technology available and how to incorporate the most recent technological advances into your physical education program. Choosing the best computer and peripherals, such as printers and monitors, can seem overwhelming. Chapter 2 will show you how to identify your needs, consider your budget, and make those choices. This chapter also looks at notebook, handheld, and palm computers that make it easy to record grades, fitness test results, and data on teaching effectiveness when you're out in the field where a desktop computer is not readily accessible.

Technology can be as commonplace as an overhead projector for enlarging visual aids or as futuristic as a hologram demonstration of the correct technique for a skill or game strategy. Chapters 3 and 4 introduce the many ways you can capture and display audio and video segments in physical education.

Chapter 5 focuses on devices that can assist in the learning process—especially in the area of fitness. You'll learn how to enhance a physical fitness unit with easy-to-operate blood pressure monitors, spirometers, and heart monitors.

Chapter 6 looks at software. It shows you how to manage fitness scores and grades effectively and efficiently. It also provides examples: using word processing software to create study guides, data base software to create a locker system, spreadsheet software to create an inventory and budget, and desktop publishing software to create your own newsletter to keep parents and community members informed about your programs.

Chapters 7 and 8 introduce telecommunications and the Internet in physical education. Whether you're sharing information with colleagues or reviewing lesson plans with a student teacher, electronic mail can help you make more efficient use of your time and abilities. Chapter 7 targets selecting an Internet Service Provider (ISP), electronic mail, listservs, newsgroups, chats, telephony, and videoconferencing. Chapter 8 focuses on the many uses of the World Wide Web—the world's largest library.

In the classroom or the gym, computers can help you instruct and improve your students' understanding of physical fitness, motor skills, and social skills. They can help you individualize instruction for your students, allowing them to progress at their own rates. Chapter 9 shows how computers can help students understand cognitive concepts, develop skills, and create their own fitness plans. Chapter 10 focuses on evaluating student learning using project-based assessment and electronic portfolios.

Chapter 11 focuses on you and how you can become an even more effective teacher. For example, you can use video technology and special software to watch yourself teach, analyze your own performance, and enhance your teaching skills.

The final chapter takes a look at the future of technology and provides possible scenarios that will help you keep your students motivated and physically educated.

A companion web site is located at http://www.pesoftware.com/ UseTech.html. Here you will find links to additional web resources, updates on this book, and additional learning opportunities. In addition, for those using this as a course textbook, you will find sample syllabi and course outlines, along with additional reflection questions and projects.

I hope this book will help you find the justification and leverage you may need to begin or increase your use of technology in physical education. It's a wide open field with continual innovations. Our challenge is to learn to use these innovations to best meet our needs and the needs of our students.

Let's begin our journey…

Other Books by Bonnie Mohnsen

Teaching Middle School Physical Education

Concepts of Physical Education:
What Every Student Needs to Know, editor

The New Leadership Paradigm in
Physical Education: What We Need to Lead, editor

Chapter 1

Introducing Technology in Physical Education

The year is 2008. The place is the gymnasium of Middle School USA, where a group of students is about to begin physical education class. The teacher, speaking into a microphone on a palm computer, quickly takes attendance and begins the warm-up/fitness phase of the lesson. The students perform flexibility, muscular strength, and muscular endurance exercises in their cooperative learning groups. They have been in the tumbling unit for the past three weeks, and most have already met the performance criteria for a variety of forward and backward rolls, headstands, cartwheels, and handstands. Today they will learn the roundoff, review the skills already covered, and create a routine that combines all the skills. There are eight stations, or learning centers, set up around the room for tumbling and cardiorespiratory endurance activities. Each group rotates from one station to the next.

At Learning Center 1, a DVD player shows sample floor exercise routines from the 2004 Olympics. Learning Center 2 is a review station, where the more skilled students help others in their group who have not yet met the minimum performance standards or who wish to strive for higher marks. When a student achieves a higher standard during the period, another student alerts the teacher, who verifies and records the accomplishment. Learning Center 3 is an aerobic station where students choose an activity that will improve cardiorespiratory endurance. The students wear heart monitors to record their heart rates and gauge where they are in their target heart rate zones.

1

Learning Center 4 focuses on the new motor skill—the roundoff. Students take turns recording one another's attempts to perform the skill and then view their attempts for immediate feedback. Learning Center 5 is a computer station where the students create their own routines. They input the names of their stunts in the order they wish to perform them, and the computer displays graphic representations of their routines. The students edit and fine-tune their routines, then perform them at Learning Center 6, where the routines are recorded for immediate playback and review.

Learning Center 7 is a fitness station. Four times a year, the students measure their blood pressure and percent of body fat. A body composition analyzer and an electronic blood pressure device allow students to take their measurements and record their scores. At Learning Center 8, a software program provides students with information on the biomechanical principles of a roundoff. The program has multi-language audio and visual tracks.

The data collected at each station are entered into a networked computer. All networked computers in the school are connected to a server where student work is stored in a separate folder for each student. The teacher or the student can check that folder at any time from any computer station to monitor progress.

Some of what I've just described can be seen in some physical education classes today, although generally not to the extent described in the scenario. However, once a school acquires the technology, its applications for physical education are limited only by the imagination of the user. Some skeptics may say that the promise of technology has been around for decades and, as yet, much of it is still mere promise. However, one has only to remember that the television did not catch on for 29 years after its invention. The zipper required 32 years, and the ball point pen was around for 50 years before it was mass produced

(Thornburg 1992). The lesson here is that many innovations develop slowly. However, it is a certainty that the future holds many new ideas and innovations for our daily lives as well as for instruction in physical education.

Growth of Technology

Webster defines technology as "a scientific method of achieving a practical purpose." The inventions noted in the highlight box below, which have advanced the enjoyment and safety of various sporting events, can be included in that definition. The 19th century chalkboard and the 20th century computer, videocassette recorder/player, digital camera, and personal digital assistant also fit the definition. Of course, no one can be entirely certain about the tools of the 21st century. However, in order to gain insight into where we are going, it is important to know where we have been.

History

The first "computer revolution" in education occurred in the 1960s, when school districts installed computer terminals in

Technological Developments

1860	Heel bindings added to skis. The bindings added comfort and speed.
1876	First spoke tension wheel for a bicycle developed by Archibald Sharp. It improved the bicycle's stability and balance.
1895	First bicycle derailleur patented by Huret. It assisted with uphill cycling (gears did not become popular until the 1950s).
1928	Invention of the wet suit. It made cold water swimming bearable.
1960	First steel tennis rackets became commercially available.
1975	The original Nordic Track was created. It consisted of a simple flywheel and a few cables and pulleys.

special rooms in their schools. The computers were linked to a mainframe system (master computer) located at the district office or some other central location. Teachers signed up for times when they could take their classes to the computer room. This first effort didn't last long, because the machines were too expensive and they often broke down. Few physical educators were involved in the first computer revolution.

The second "computer revolution" in education began in the late 1970s. It coincided with the appearance of the personal computer. Personal computers made it possible to bring computers into classrooms, gymnasiums, and even our homes. During the early 1980s, physical educators at the university level began to experiment with the computer and to develop software (computer programs) for various specialty areas such as exercise physiology. In the K-12 public education setting, the first computers were used primarily for fitness reports. Then, physical educators began to see the need for other types of application software. Eventually, some of us began to use the few available computer-assisted instruction programs with our classes.

Current Status

Today, there are computers, videos, compact discs, and other new technologies everywhere we look. The use of the Internet has literally exploded. Many physical educators now have e-mail addresses, and they have moved beyond using a computer only for fitness reports. Elementary, middle school, and high school physical educators in pockets across the United States— and around the world—are exploring the effects of instructional software, the Internet, heart monitors, video analysis of performance, electronic portfolios, and multimedia development on student learning. For physical educators, the 1990s was an era of exploration and of promises to come.

Studies show that when computer programs are used learning

time can be shortened by 50 percent, retention can be increased by 80 percent, and costs can be cut in half (Levin & Meister, 1986; Niemiec, Blackwall, & Walberg, 1986; Gu, 1996). And, the costs continue to decline and the number of components in an integrated circuit doubles every 18 months (see highlight box below). The federal government and many states have earmarked funding to help bring new technologies into K-12 classrooms. Physical educators need only desire, know how, and vision to bring these technologies into their gymnasiums.

Future of Technology

In this century, the true power of technology will become a reality. Futurists are predicting that we will no longer have to worry about finding a computer to use, since we will actually be wearing one. Voice input will replace keyboarding, storage will become so compact that everything we can read in a lifetime will fit into an object the size of a marker, and smart machines will learn from their interactions with us (i.e., the coffee machine will learn how we like our coffee and continue to improve the coffee it produces based on our preferences).

Emerging technologies will continue to have an impact on

The Growth of Technology				
	1986	1996	2000	2009
RAM	1MB	8MB	51MB	3,251MB
Storage	40MB	500MB	3,175MB	203,187MB
Speed	15mhz	100mhz	635mhz	40,637mhz
Cost	$2,500	$1,500	$240	$10
Power		1x	6x	665x

education. Evidence of this trend is seen in the appearance of companies such as the Discovery Channel, Turner Broadcasting, and Microsoft in the K-12 market. These companies are purchasing and developing educational materials with the idea of distributing them on a pay-per-use basis to home schools and public schools alike.

Virtual reality will have the greatest impact on instruction in physical education. Virtual reality technology allows the user to transcend the barriers of keyboard and screen and to have an immersive interactive experience. As an early example, consider the experience of the programmer who, in 1985, developed a virtual reality system so that he could learn to juggle. With virtual goggles over his eyes and virtual gloves on his hands (both goggles and gloves were connected to the computer), the programmer picked up the virtual balls and began to practice juggling. He altered the physics of his new artificial world so the balls moved in slow motion, giving him more time to react. Because the computer responded to the force and release angle of each throw, however, each of his tosses and catches needed to be accurate. The more proficient the programmer got, the more he speeded up the balls until the speed matched that of reality. Eventually, he removed the virtual equipment and began juggling three "real" balls.

What To Expect in the Next 10 Years

1. Virtual reality in education.
2. Three-dimension fax (objects will have depth).
3. Personal robots.
4. A 500 "phone number" that tracks you for life.
5. Cellular phones in earrings, rings, and glasses.
6. Smart machines (capable of learning).
7. Affordable "flat screen" high definition television.
8. Six-language instantaneous translators.
9. Holograms.
10. Wearable computers (clothing, rings).

In the next decade, we will see students using virtual reality to learn motor skills and prosocial skills. They may even have their own personal trainer in the form of a hologram or a robot.

Types of Technology

Technology is defined as anything that achieves a practical purpose. In physical education, then, technology is anything that helps students improve their physical performance or cognitive understanding of physical education concepts. It is well known that people learn through three modalities—visual, aural, and kinesthetic. The greater the number of learning modalities that are engaged, the greater the learning that can occur. The types of technology used in physical education, therefore, can be organized into the following categories: auditory, visual, manipulative, and multi-modal devices.

Auditory Devices

Auditory devices include tape players, radios, MP3 players, and compact disc players. The content for these devices includes classical music for relaxation, a variety of music to accompany different movement experiences (e.g., exercising or tumbling routines), and recordings that explain specific concepts, such as those published by SyberVision. It is important to have a good sound system when using auditory devices. Be sure to purchase or select one with a cassette player and a compact disc player, and good speakers so all students can hear clearly. In addition, a remote microphone can save your voice when you must talk over music or give instructions to large groups. Chapter 3 addresses the use of auditory devices.

Visual Devices

Visual devices (text and pictures) provide learners with additional information to help them better understand the

7

concepts of a lesson. Pictures, charts, graphs, and diagrams are fairly common in physical education, but have you ever used models? Models are three-dimensional representations of real-life events. For example, playing fields can be made from plywood or particle board, and small dolls can be used to depict players. This allows you to demonstrate how players move during a real game. Chapters 3 and 4 focus on the selection and use of visual aids.

manipulative Devices

A manipulative device is one that students can handle and control. In the K-12 school system, these devices tend to be low-end models of sophisticated machinery. Digitized blood pressure machines, body composition analyzers, heart monitors, and printout stopwatches are examples of devices that provide students with hands-on opportunities to learn the scientific side of fitness and exercise physiology. Although these instruments don't compare with the more sophisticated (and expensive) models in terms of accuracy, they do serve to motivate students and to teach them about the relationship between bodily functions and exercise. Chapter 5 addresses manipulatives.

multi-modal Devices

Video and audio technology—television, cable television, satellite dish, videotape, laser disc, computer software, DVD, or the Internet—can bring model performances of trained athletes along with accurate explanations to your students during the initial stages of learning new motor skills. Students also can use video cameras to record and replay their performances for feedback and to monitor their own progress. Chapters 2, 3, 4, 6, 7, 8, 9, 10, 11, and 12 address different aspects of multi-modal devices and software, including those found on the Internet.

Considering Instructional Strategies for a Variety of Learning Outcomes

Learning Outcome	Instructional Strategies
Organization Skills	Brainstorming Outlines Overviews Prior reading
Attention	Familiar music Novelty Size of print Use of color Volume of audio
Comprehension	Collecting data Examples Connection with prior knowledge Modeling Organization of content
Creativity	Independent projects Interactive multimedia Problem-solving Virtual reality
Mastery	Making presentations Problem-solving activities Projects
Motivation	Challenging Encouraging Intrinsic value Related to real world
Transfer	Application Simulations Solving "real" problems

Incorporating Technology

It has taken time for all new technologies, including the chalkboard, to be accepted by teachers and to become integral parts of the education environment. If a new technology gets in our way, we won't use it. The technology must support what we are already doing, and we must have access to it where we work and live.

Making Technology Happen for You

The first step to integrating technology into the physical education environment is to learn how to use it to deal with the paperwork (attendance, grades, locker assignments, inventories, budgets, etc.) that we face daily. You will need to read, take classes, or complete tutorials on using your operating system, word processing, data base, and spreadsheet programs. No matter which method you use to learn a software program, be prepared to invest some time in it. The time invested up front will pay dividends in the time you save once you start using the computer to complete your daily tasks. Many software programs come with on-screen tutorials or manuals that explain how to use them. For software packages that don't include either of these types of assistance, support can usually be purchased separately.

Obviously, you must have access to a computer for practice if you are to truly benefit from any of these learning experiences. Many districts allow educators to borrow computers over weekends and during vacations. You also should consider purchasing your own computer, especially as prices continue to drop and discounts for educators become available.

Once you have learned to use the computer for yourself, the next step is to learn how to use the computer, videos, the Internet, and other technologies for teaching and assessing students. You can do this by reading (this book is a great start), attending inservices (whether or not they are specifically

10

Essential Computer Skills

1. Navigate desktop environments in Macintosh and Windows operating systems.
2. Load and install software.
3. Use word processing, data base, and spreadsheet programs in Macintosh and Windows operating systems.
4. Use test generators, gradebooks, and management systems.
5. Connect, disconnect, and use peripheral devices (modems, scanners, printers, projection systems).
6. Make products in draw, paint, and animated graphics.
7. Create a product with desktop publishing.
8. Send and receive e-mail.
9. Access, transfer files, and search the World Wide Web.
10. Participate in one-way and two-way interactive classes.
11. Search CD-ROMs for specific information.
12. Create a presentation using a presentation software program (i.e., PowerPoint).
13. Create a product in an authoring program (i.e., HyperStudio).
14. Compile compressed video sequences and use a time base corrector (i.e., DVI, QuickTime).
15. Identify computer software and video programming available and appropriate for K-12 physical education.
16. Videotape someone performing a motor skill and play it back.
17. Program a video cassette recorder to record a show.
18. Take a picture using a digital camera and print it out.
19. Program, use, download, and print out a graph showing target heart rate for an exercise period.
20. Record an individual's fitness level using the latest technological devices.
21. Create a web page.

designed for physical education), and taking classes through the local college or adult education program. Once you have learned to use these technologies, you must determine the roles they will play in helping you to be more productive in the physical education of your students. You will need to determine these roles for yourself, but this book will describe a wide variety of possible applications.

Suggested Computer Book Series

Dummie Series (Dummie Press)
Visual Start Series (Peachpit Press)
Bible Series (Addison-Wesley)

Finding Funds for Buying Equipment

Regardless of which technology you would like for your department, you will need money to purchase it. Many state departments of education allocate money specifically for the purchase of technology. Private grants also are available. For example, in 1989, Apple Computer began awarding money annually to educators and schools with innovative ideas for using technology in education. In 1989, IBM formed a partnership program with the State of California and gave $20 million to provide IBM computers to schools in the state. Some of the money was used for competitive grants, which were awarded to 42 educational programs throughout the state. One of these was in the area of physical education.

Grant information can be found on the World Wide Web, in computer magazines, and through your school administrators. However, more important than finding money is having the vision to creatively use and implement technology in physical education. Only new and innovative ideas have the potential to be funded through competitive grants.

Justifying Technology

Administrators evaluate teachers in four different areas: environment, curriculum, instruction, and assessment. To justify technology, physical educators must demonstrate how it will make them better teachers in each of these areas. For example, computer-generated newsletters that provide parents with up-to-date information on the physical education program, and computer-generated bulletin boards that create an energizing and engaging instructional climate can help to establish a positive learning environment. The use of a data base during the curriculum development process can ensure that all standards for both scope and sequence are addressed. Computer-assisted instruction software, heart monitors, and video feedback are but a few of the technology-based instructional resources that can help improve student learning. Grading programs and electronic portfolios are technology's answer to assessment. Chapters 3 through 12 will provide you with additional examples of how you can justify technology to your administrators.

Do's and Don'ts of Grant Writing

Do:
Start with a real need.
Develop an innovative project idea that is fundable.
Be realistic and honest about what you put in writing.
Review copies of funded proposals.
Search the Internet for potential funders.
Read Requests for Proposals (RFPs) very carefully.
Follow the directions in the RFP.
Make sure that you fit the eligibility criteria noted in the RFP.
Develop a timeline to assemble the grant application.
Allow time for review and final editing before submission.
Double check everything—especially spelling.
Include a table of contents.

Don't:
Contact a funding source without reviewing all information.
Invent a need.
Exaggerate your objectives.
Inflate the value of in-kind contributions.
Use creative writing skills—stick to the facts and be concise.
Submit incomplete applications.
Submit poorly assembled applications.
Turn a proposal in late.
Take rejection personally.
Give up.

Skeleton Grant Proposal

The Problem
Cardiovascular disease is the number one killer in the United States. Lack of exercise is noted in the Surgeon General's report on physical activity as one of the major risk factors for heart disease—it clearly states, "physical inactivity is hazardous to your health." About 25 percent of adults report no physical activity at all in their leisure time. Only about one-half of our young people (ages 12-21 years) regularly participate in vigorous physical activity. One-fourth report no vigorous physical activity. In addition, research shows that 90 percent of children who fail to exercise adequately in their teenage years also do not exercise adequately when they become adults. The result is that in the United States, cardiorespiratory fitness continues to decline, percent body fat continues to increase, and risk factors for heart disease are now known to exist in nearly half of the elementary children in this country. It is no wonder that it is costing this country nearly $130 billion a year to treat cardiovascular disease!

The Solution
This proposal strives to improve the quality of life for students, staff, parents, and community members through a lifelong practice of physical activity. Our students will work and live in the 21st century— maybe! It is up to schools and community programs to keep our students fit. In order to educate and motivate people to be concerned about their health and fitness, we will use a high-tech fitness and wellness system called the HealthFirst "TriFit." This state-of-the-art technology provides clients with valuable data (text, charts graphs) about their personal well being, suggests options for improving their quality of life, teaches them the importance of activity, provides them with the opportunity to design their own exercise program, and monitors their implementation of the program and their improvement.

Objectives
1. 300 participants assess their personal fitness using the HealthFirst "TriFit" system.
2. 300 participants design their own personal exercise programs.
3. 275 participants implement their exercise programs.
4. 250 participants improve their physical fitness.
5. 50 participants provide community service as "technicians" for the HealthFirst "TriFit" system.

continue next page

Budget
Total: $10,955
HealthFirst "TriFit" 520: $7,000
•Windows-based computer/printer
•Fitness Testing Equipment
Bike Ergometer: $1,000
Freight and Handling: $1,430

"TriFit" Software: $1525
•Health risk appraisal software
•Fitness assessment
•Exercise planning
•Meal planning

Activities
XYZ High School will offer its students, staff, parents, and community members a free "high tech" fitness/wellness evaluation along with free access to its Fitness/Wellness Center. The Fitness/Wellness Center and "TriFit" System will be available before and after school, at lunch, and on the weekends. During the school day, the center and system will be used by ninth grade students during a fitness unit in their physical education classes. The students will not only utilize the center and system for fitness assessment and implementation of a personal fitness program, but they also will learn how to set up the system and assist with the administration of the assessment and monitoring protocols for others.

During an individual's first visit to the Fitness/Wellness Center, he or she will participate in the fitness/wellness evaluation using the "TriFit" System. The data collected will include health risks, resting heart rate, muscular flexibility, muscular strength and endurance, blood pressure, percent body fat, lung capacity, nutritional needs, and cardiorespiratory endurance. Based on the results, the participant will be provided with individualized guidance (via the "TriFit" System) for setting up a personalized exercise/wellness/nutrition program.

During subsequent visits to the Fitness/Wellness Center, the participants will implement and monitor their personalized exercise/wellness programs. Periodical assessments, using the "TriFit" System, will be conducted to document each participant's improvement and to serve as a personal source of motivation. The "TriFit" System will be supervised at all times by students under the direction of a certificated physical educator.

Evaluation
1. A log listing all participants utilizing the system will be maintained.
2. Copies of each personal wellness program will be maintained.
3. Participation logs will be maintained.
4. Before and after data will be maintained and analyzed to document changes in participants' fitness levels.
5. A log listing student participation as technicians will be maintained.

Ergonomics

As we begin to use technology, we also must be aware of the potential hazards associated with it. Ergonomics is the study of the effects of computer use on humans. According to Walter J. Zinn, O. D., at least half of the people working with video display terminals (VDTs) experience vision and physical side effects (Zinn 1994). Similarly, almost two decades ago, a panel of vision experts assembled by the Research Council of the National Academy of Science estimated that more than 50 percent of VDT users experienced visual discomfort (National Academy of Science 1983). Headaches, eye strain, back pain, and shoulder or arm pain all are common complaints of VDT users. As physical educators interested in the health and well-being of our students, we can play an important role in modeling healthy behaviors when using technology.

Position of Monitor

The monitor and source material should be placed so that the user's head is in a comfortable and relaxed position to reduce the chance of neck and shoulder pain. The OSHA (1991) Guidebook notes that the preferred viewing distance to the monitor ranges between 18 and 24 inches. Current thinking places the monitor directly in front of the user and at least 20 inches from his or her eyes. The top of the monitor should be at or below eye level, with the center about 10 to 20 degrees below the line of sight.

Posture

In addition to proper positioning of the monitor, the user also must have the appropriate posture. Place your chair so that you can sit directly facing the monitor and make sure the chair is adjusted so your feet rest flat on the floor with your knees at a ninety degree angle to help your circulation. When you sit against the back of your chair, make sure there is clearance between the seat and the back of your legs. Adjust your back rest to support the small of your back. If possible, occasionally lean back in your chair to relax your back. Also, stand up and stretch periodically.

When you're seated at your desk and are in the typing position, your hands and wrists should be straight and your elbows should not be lower than your wrists. The keyboard should be positioned so that a 90-degree angle is formed between the upper arms and the forearms. Keep your elbows close to your sides with the forearms parallel to the floor. Keep the mouse close to the keyboard. When typing, use a light touch—don't arch fingers up to hit the keys, don't type with wrists resting on the desktop, and don't pound the keyboard. The use of palm or wrist rests (foam or rubber devices placed in front of the keyboard) and an angled keyboard can eliminate pain and stress, and can prevent Carpal Tunnel Syndrome, a soreness caused when muscles rub against each other in a small wrist passage called the Carpal Tunnel.

Preventing Eye Strain

The number one VDT-related health complaint is eyestrain. Red, sore, and dry eyes, blurred vision, headaches, and more develop with extended use of computers. Overly bright lighting or windows can cause glare on the screen and can increase eye strain. This occurs because your optic system is confused— your pupils are shrinking to accommodate the bright room or window light while you are simultaneously trying to focus on the relatively dim screen.

The best solution is to move the monitor away from the window in order to minimize or eliminate the bright light and glare. In overly bright areas, one solution is to remove half of the florescent bulbs in the overhead fixtures. Other solutions include lowering background lighting, adjusting the position of the

Do's and Don'ts of Computer Set Ups

Do:
Maintain a good rest position.
Take two "minute-long" breaks per hour.
Stretch at least twice per hour.
Use a chair with armrests that support your elbows.
Avoid monitor glare.
Keep your arms and hands suspended above the keyboard.
Purchase adjustable chairs.
Keep your feet flat on the floor.
Keep knees bent at just over a 90-degree angle.
Press your back against the backrest so the chair's lumbar support fits snugly into the small of your back.
Use a wrist rest.
Purchase keyboards which are simple, colorful, and smaller for children.

Don't:
Overextend your reach.
Strain your shoulders.
Let the seat press into the back of your knees.
Lay your wrists flat on the desk in front of the keyboard.
Let your wrists absorb the weight of the arms.
Overdo it.

monitor, and checking your posture. You should look away from the screen every few minutes and blink more often than normal in order to lubricate your eyes. Computer glasses, specially designed for the working distance from the eyes to the monitor based on desk setup, posture, etc., also can help to eliminate tired, red eyes and blurry vision.

Summary

Technology is changing the way we teach physical education— from its early uses in creating fitness reports to the future use of holograms as personal trainers. Technology, however, is not a means unto itself. It is a process and a tool for increasing student learning and teacher productivity. It can provide visual, aural, and kinesthetic input. As physical educators, we must access it, learn it, and use it. We also must be cautious of the potentially negative side effects of technology and counter those elements under our control: we must ensure that our students practice the proper ergonomics when using computers.

Reflection Questions

1. Is your personal computer setup ergonomically correct?
2. What kind of technology have you used or heard of in each of the categories?

Projects

1. Write a one-paragraph letter to an administrator describing why you need a computer (you will update this letter in chapter 12).
2. Investiage grant opportunities in your district.
3. Create your own scenario for a 2008 physical education class.

Chapter 2

Selecting a Computer and Basic Peripherals

Sara Jones has decided to buy a computer for her physical education department. She has attended several conferences and has learned that computers can be used effectively to teach students cognitive concepts and motor skills. In addition, she knows that a computer can help a physical education teacher be more productive. Now she must decide which computer to purchase and which peripherals she needs.

Once you have decided to use a computer in your physical education classes, you will need to answer a number of questions:

- What am I going to do with a computer?
- What brand should I select?
- What model should I buy?
- How much RAM do I need?
- What size hard drive do I need?
- What kind of printer and monitor will best serve my needs?
- How much money should I spend?

Walking into a computer store with these and other questions and seeing all the choices can be overwhelming. Identifying your needs, goals, and personal preferences ahead of time will help you make more informed decisions when you are presented with the many options that are available.

There are four components in a computer system: processor, memory, input device(s), and output device(s). A keyboard and a mouse are both input devices, but an input device also can be a storage device or a modem. A file is the information to be processed, and software is the set of instructions the computer follows when processing the data in the file. For example, a list of your students is data in a file, and the software contains the directions for the computer to alphabetize the list. When the file and program are brought into the memory of the computer, the processor manipulates the data according to the software's instructions. The processed data are then sent out of the computer via one or more output devices. Output devices include monitors, printers, and—again—storage units and modems.

Casing and Operating System

There are three sizes of computers that will be of interest to physical educators: desktop, notebook (2 to 10 pounds), and handheld PCs (H/PCs) or palm PCs (P/PCs). In the ideal world, we would have one of each for the various tasks we perform, but most of us are limited to one or two. If I had to choose between a desktop and a notebook for a first computer, I would select a notebook. It provides me with mobility; I can access and manipulate information regardless of where I am. In addition, notebook computers are very powerful and can meet the needs of most physical educators. The one place where it is not convenient to use the notebook computer is out on the field. In this setting, the palm computer is ideal. For students, the desktop computer is most appropriate for the indoor setting, while the notebook or sub-notebook is best for the outdoor setting.

Desktop

The term desktop (see Figure 2.1) is used here to refer to a stationary computer used at a desk or work station. It may be tall, narrow, and designed to sit upright on the floor (often

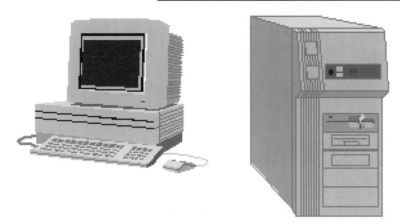

Figure 2.1   Desktop Computers

referred to as a tower), or it may be the more traditional configuration that sits on a desk, often with the monitor on top, or an all-in-one monitor and case. The advantages of the desktop computer are the number and variety of ports, the lower cost, and the amenities—such as a large monitor. Desktops typically contain sufficient ports (see Figure 2.2) to meet the needs of physical educators—ports for connecting a modem, printer, external hard drive, printer, scanner, tape backup drive, Zip drive, and CD-ROM/CD-R/CD-RW drives. Historically these ports were either serial or parallel ports, or (in the case of an external monitor or projection system) a video port, and (in the case of a network) an ethernet port.

Two relatively new ports are the USB (Universal Serial Bus) and IEEE1394 (FireWire). Both of these ports are faster than the older ports. The USB's data rate is 12 megabits per second). It is excellent for low-cost applications such as keyboards, mouse devices, joysticks, game controllers, and printers. The FireWire connection is more expensive and intended for ultra-high-performance peripherals such as digital video camcorders, DVD players, and high-speed disk drives. The data rate of the FireWire Bus is 200 megabits per second, and soon will be 400 megabits per second.

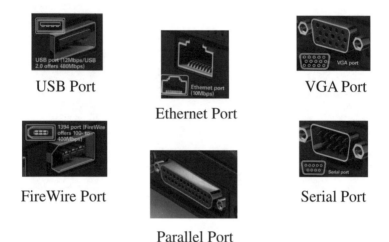

USB Port

Ethernet Port

VGA Port

FireWire Port

Serial Port

Parallel Port

Figure 2.2   Various ports for connection external devices.

Once you have decided on a desktop computer, the next decision involves choosing the operating system. The operating system is the very crucial portion of the system software that enables communications between the application or end-user software and the hardware. The two choices are Macintosh and Windows. When making this decision, consider the following:

• Which type of platform is more predominant at your school site? It helps to stay consistent with other users at your school.
• Is the application software you want to use Macintosh, Windows, or both? There must be a match between software and hardware. It is actually better to select your software first and then match the hardware.
• Do you have a personal preference? Users tend to be more comfortable with the type of computer on which they learned.

Remember, applications purchased for one platform generally will not run on another system. It is possible, however, to buy additional hardware and/or software that will allow the Macintosh operating system to read software designed for the

Windows operating system. For example SoftWindows (Insignia) or Virtual PC (Connectix) will allow you to run Windows-based software on a Macintosh computer. However, these solutions tend to be slower than the original system. Another option is a Windows emulation card that fits inside a Macintosh computer. This provides you with a real PC with fewer problems and much faster speed. The disadvantage is that these cards are very expensive—almost as much as buying an additional computer.

Notebooks

Notebook computers (see Figure 2.3) weigh less than 10 pounds; sub-notebook computers weigh less than 3 pounds. Although the number and sometimes the variety of ports is limited compared to the desktop, and the screen is smaller, these computers are very mobile and are ideal for physical educators on the go. In addition, most notebook computers can be attached to a larger monitor when in the office.

When selecting a notebook computer you also must consider the type of operating system you desire. There are several Macintosh-based notebooks (PowerBooks, ibooks), and numerous PC-based notebooks that run the Windows operating system. Several other manufacturers are recognizing that students don't always need the full performance of a notebook

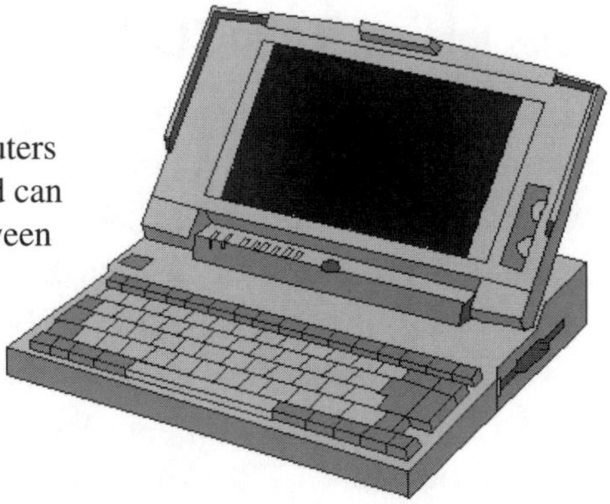

Figure 2.3   Notebook computers weigh less than 10 pounds and can be carried back and forth between home and school.

computer. Rather, they need durable, low-cost devices that can go anywhere.

Brother International Corporation has introduced the GeoBook Digital Notebook, which uses its own operating system and Perfect Solutions has developed three Digital Notebooks—two with monochrome monitors, and one with a color monitor which use a unique operating system. NTS Computer Systems has expanded its DreamWriter line to include a portable notebook for students called the DreamWriter IT, which operates using Windows CE (a "lite" version of Windows).

The PC Card (formerly PCMCIA) is a common expansion slot for a notebook computer. This slot can hold a wide variety of credit card-like devices. The most common are modems, Ethernet adapters, hard drives, and video input devices. There are three types of PC Cards, which are distinguished by thickness. Almost all notebooks have two Type II slots, stacked one on top of the other. These can hold all three types of PC Card (though there's only room for a single Type III). Sub-notebooks may only have a single slot. The Type 1 card is 3.3 mm thick and often contains applications for palmtops and Personal Digital Assistants (PDAs). The Type II card is 5 mm thick and is used for expanding memory, fax modems, and LAN adapters. The Type III is 10.5 mm thick and is typically used for hard disks.

Handheld and Palm PCs

Handheld PCs and palm PCs are smaller than a sub-notebook computer. These devices are battery operated, weigh less than two pounds, and fit in the hand or palm. For input, the handheld computers typically use a mini-keyboard and a stylus, while the palm computers typically use only a stylus for tapping on various buttons on the screen, tapping on a small keyboard image, or actually writing on the screen. The handheld/palm PCs can be kept in a pocket or fanny pack, and are convenient for on-the-field use. Some of the software for the handheld/ palm PCs—such as Learner Profile from Sunburst—requires that you interface (connect) with either a desktop or notebook computer, while other programs—such as GradePoint from Sunburst—allow you to be totally self-contained. In some cases, you can even print by connecting the handheld computer directly to a printer.

The Apple MessagePad (handheld computer), which uses the Newton operating system, has been very popular with physical educators because a number of grading programs (Learner Profile, GradePoint, and GradyProfile Companion from Aurbach & Associates) and fitness reporting software (Newton Fitness from Bonnie's Fitware) have been written specifically for the system. However, since Apple decided to discontinue support for the Newton operating system, the MessagePad 120, 130, 2000, and 2100 models are only viable options for those who already have the Apple MessagePad.

Although there are numerous operating systems for the hand/ palm PCs, the most popular one is the Palm Operating System, followed by Windows CE. The Palm OS only runs on palm-sized PCs, including the 3Com Palm III, Palm V, and Palm VII along with the Handspring Visor (see Figure 2.4) and Sony Clíe. It is intuitive, easy to operate, and comes with calendar, telephone book, and memo pad software.

Figure 2.4   Handspring Visor

There are literally thousands of application software that run on the Palm Operating System. These include database, spreadsheet, sport statistics, and grading programs. Much of this software is free.

The Windows CE Operating System runs on several handheld and palm-sized PCs, including those developed by Casio and Hewlett Packard. The palm version comes with word processing, spreadsheet, calendar, and address book software; the handheld version also comes with presentation software. Most of the handheld/palm PCs have some Internet capabilities, including e-mail and Web browsing.

Processor

The computer processor performs the data processing functions directed by the program, and it controls the transfer of instructions and data within the computer system. Processors differ in the speed at which they operate. Computers with quicker processors typically operate at a faster clock rate which is measured in megahertz (MHz) or millions of cycles (instructions) per second than do their slower counterparts. Computers with faster processors also typically are more expensive. However, be aware that CPU rating alone isn't the only measure of a computer's speed. Other factors include the size of the computer's cache as well as the design of the motherboard on which the CPU is installed.

Most computers offer two caches—a tiny one on the CPU and a second, larger cache on the logic board. This secondary or L2 (Level 2) cache is the one to inquire about. It should be 512 K or larger, and it should be fast. The idea behind cache is that once an instruction is completed, it takes less time to recall that instruction than to perform it from scratch since the computer continually stores completed instructions for reuse.

The best way to determine which machine meets your needs

is to perform a typical task on a variety of computers that operate at different speeds. The least expensive machine that meets your needs—the one that can run the software you want to use at a speed you are comfortable with—is the machine to purchase. However, your needs will change as you become more proficient with a computer, so you should plan for room to grow—both in terms of the computer's speed and the other variables identified in the following sections. I have never known anyone to be disappointed buying a more sophisticated machine when cost was not a factor.

Memory

There are two types of computer memory: read-only memory (ROM) and random-access memory (RAM). The information in ROM is placed there by the manufacturer, and it is permanent. It contains, among other things, information the computer needs to start up. RAM, on the other hand, is where programs and data are stored temporarily when the computer is in use. RAM also comes as Flash RAM, RAM cache, and virtual memory. When the power is turned off, the information in this area is erased. Each program requires a certain amount of RAM in order to load and run. The amount of memory that application software needs is shown on its packaging. You will probably want to load more than one program at a time, so you can move quickly from program to program. Therefore, your computer will need to have enough RAM to collectively hold all the programs you want available for use at one time.

Third Type of Memory

There is actually a third type of memory: the CMOS (complementary metal-oxide semiconductor) chip that is powered by its own battery. CMOS information may be modified to accommodate a new system configuration.

Memory is measured in bytes, kilobytes (KB), megabytes (MB), gigabytes (GB), and terabytes (TB). Each byte holds one character (single-digit number, letter, special symbol). A kilobyte is 1,024 bytes, a megabyte is about 1,000 kilobytes and a gigabyte is about 1,000 megabytes. As of 2001, computers come with a minimum of 64MB of RAM and typically have 128MB or more; however, this will double in 18 months. You can purchase and install additional RAM as you need additional memory. Currently, larger, more complicated programs are being developed that will require more and more memory.

Current operating systems support virtual memory and thus allow the allocation of additional (much slower) RAM on available hard drive space. By using extra space on the computer's hard drive, virtual memory tricks the computer into thinking there's more RAM available than there really is. The disadvantages, however, are that programs will run more slowly than with real RAM, and virtual memory uses hard drive space that would normally be available for storing data and application software. In addition, some programs won't work with virtual memory.

As you start to shop for a computer, you will notice that in addition to listing the speed of the computer, advertisers also list two numbers separated by a slash—256MB/20.0GB. These two numbers refer to the amount of RAM and the size of the hard drive. To better understand the differences between RAM and the hard drive, consider the analogy of a desk and a file

Minimum Recommendations for a Computer

CPU: at least 500MHz (500 million cycles per second)
L2 (secondary) cache: at least 512 (kilobytes)
RAM (memory): at least 128MB - expandable to 512MB
Hard Disk Space: at least 10GB
CD-ROM or DVD-ROM drive
Video Card: at least 4MB memory - expandable to 16MB

cabinet. The size of the desk is similar to the amount of RAM. The size of the file cabinet is similar to the size of the hard drive. When working in an office, you can only take so many folders out of the file cabinet to put on your desk at one time. This also is true in terms of the computer.

If you only have 64MB of RAM and you try to load three programs from your hard drive to memory, and each program requires 25MB of RAM, you won't be able to open the third program. There isn't enough RAM to hold 75MB of information. When selecting the size of your hard drive, remember that it should hold every program that you already own as well as the ones you plan to buy in the future. And, it should have additional space for files and unknown future software purchases.

Input

There are a number of options for communicating with the computer. These include keyboards, mice, joysticks, scanners, microphones, bar code readers, switches, digital cameras, digital camcorders, touch screens, storage, and modems.

Keyboard

Using a keyboard is much like using a typewriter, but with more options. Currently, the keyboard is the most common form of data input device. The computer recognizes the key that is pressed and displays that key's associated symbol on the monitor (unless the key has a special function). Variables to consider when selecting a keyboard include placement of F-keys (function keys) and the numerical keypad, whether the keyboard is angled or adjustable, and whether it requires a light or a heavy touch. Personal preference will guide your selection; however, an adjustable keyboard can alleviate wrist injuries. Finally, if you are going to purchase your keyboard from a third-party vendor, make sure it is compatible with your computer.

Alternative keyboards are available for use by those with physical disabilities. They also may be used by students who are too young to use a standard keyboard or who have developmental disabilities. Alternative keyboards are either condensed (mini) or expanded. The condensed keyboard is designed to help those with limited fields of motion but who possess fine motor skill. The keys are positioned closer together than on a standard keyboard so it requires less strength to depress each key. Examples include the Tash Mini Keyboard (Infogrip) and the Bat Personal Keyboard (Infogrip).

The expanded keyboard is a large, touch-sensitive table that can be programmed to accept overlays. An overlay might be a plastic sheet with an enlarged alphabet or a set of pictures. Overlays can be purchased or made by the user. There also are overlays that are designed to work with specific software applications. Examples include Key Largo (Don Johnston), Discover Board (Don Johnston), and IntelliKeys Keyboard and Overlay Maker (IntelliTools).

Mouse

Virtually all application software requires a mouse. The mouse is rolled across a flat surface or, with a trackball type, the ball is rolled around in its socket. The action of the mouse causes a pointer (cursor) on the screen to move. The computer monitors the location of the cursor and the status (clicked or not, right or left button) of the mouse. The mouse is used for pointing, selecting, and highlighting spots on the screen. Its more specific functions are determined by the software.

There also are wireless or cordless varieties. In this case, the mouse sends a signal through the air—using either radio waves or infrared technology—to a small receiving unit that relays the signal via a cord that plugs into the back of the computer. A radio-controlled cordless mouse usually costs more than an infrared cordless mouse, which must be within a direct line of sight. If your infrared cordless mouse begins to malfunction you have probably put something in front of its receiving unit. A wireless mouse is helpful when giving presentations. The teacher is free to move around and is not forced to stand by the computer.

Joystick

Joysticks are typically used in conjunction with computer games, including educational games. The joystick controls the cursor or some other screen motion with the back-and-forth and left-and-right movement of its handle. There are usually one or more buttons that initiate certain types of screen action. Look for more educational games involving sports to enter the market.

Scanners

The scanner (see Figure 2.5) works like a copy machine, except that the image (graphic or text) is copied into your computer and stored as digital data. When looking for a scanner, consider the resolution (the fineness of the image). The lower the resolution, the more grainy the image. Resolutions of 600x600 dots per inch or, even better, 1200x2400 dpi, are recommended along with 30- or 36-bit recognition. The bit recognition refers to the scanner's ability to capture brightness and extra colors. The extra bit depth also can be useful in eliminating electronic noise from a less than perfect scan.

Figure 2.5   A flatbed scanner transfers an entire page of information into a computer.

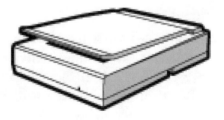

Scanners come in three basic types: flatbed, sheet-fed, and handheld. The flatbed is the most popular and produces the sharpest image. A sheet-fed scanner, which resembles a printer, remains stationary while the paper is rolled across it. This means that sheet-fed models can be smaller, but the images generally are not as sharp as those of flatbeds since the paper is moving. Handheld scanners are even smaller and are best used when scanning text instead of graphics. Scanners are great for teachers and students who are interested in developing their own multimedia projects, since scanned images can be inserted easily into most programs.

Speech Input

The use of the spoken language to enter commands and text into the computer is known as speech input. Originally used exclusively by individuals with physical, visual, or other disabilities, speech recognition systems now are available for the general public. NaturallySpeaking for Windows (Dragon Systems), Dragon PowerSecretary for the Macintosh (Dragon Systems), and ViaVoice for Windows and Macintosh (IBM) are examples of software solutions that incorporate the latest advances in speech recognition. Speech input provides for more rapid data input and provides the non-typist with an easy interface method. It is a good idea to use an external microphone when using speech input so the computer can more clearly interpret the sound of your voice.

Switches

Switches can be used by individuals who are unable to use other types of input devices. An activated switch, used with special software, can signal the student's choice or selection. A "scanning array" of options is displayed on the monitor and a cursor moves through a series of alternatives. The user activates the switch when the option he or she wants is highlighted.

Touch Screens

A touch screen is a device that is attached to a computer monitor or an external display system (i.e., Smart Board). The computer monitors the location of the touch on the screen and responds to it in a manner similar to a mouse movement. Touch screens are very popular in kiosks (stand-alone computers found at museums, shopping centers, and government buildings). They are useful in physical education when demonstrating software on a large external screen to a group of students.

Storage

Backing up critical data is one of the most important administrative tasks associated with using a computer. Backing up means making a duplicate copy of important data and program files. Then, if anything should happen to the original, you will have a copy. Historically, data and software were stored on tape and then on floppy disks. Today, the size of programs dictates the need for storage devices that can hold greater and greater quantities of information. As a result, a variety of storage device options are now available. They include floppy disks, hard drives, CD-ROMs and other optical disc formats, and tape.

Floppy Disk. Currently, many computers still come with a floppy disk drive. This is likely to change in the near future, however. In the past, all software was distributed on floppy disk (see Figure 2.6). Today, more and more application software—including educational programs—are distributed on CD-ROM. Floppy disks used to come in two sizes—5-1/4-inch and 3-1/2-inch. (Because the 3-1/2-inch disks are firmer than the 5-1/4-

Figure 2.6   The 3-1/2-inch floppy disk.

Icons

Graphic interfaces (like the Macintosh and Windows operating systems) allow you to interact and control the computer by pointing at small pictures on the screen with your cursor (an object on the screen, usually in the shape of an arrow, that you control with the mouse) and clicking on them. These small pictures are called icons, and they represent computer hardware, software, and software concepts, so that you do not have to memorize commands. There are icons representing hard disk drives, floppy drives, folders, data files, and software, to name a few.

---

inch disks, many beginners mistakenly think they are hard disks.) The size of the disk you use depends on the size of the disk drive installed in or connected to your computer. The 5-1/4-inch disk is virtually obsolete.

A 3-1/2-inch disk can hold from 720K to 1.44MB (approximately 320 pages of text), depending on the density of the disk and how it is formatted. Double-density (DD) disks can store from 720K to 800K of data, while high-density (HD) disks have from 1.2 to 1.3MB storage capacity. Double-density disks are all but obsolete today. The 3-1/2-inch disk is protected by a rigid plastic casting that makes it difficult to destroy. The computer writes information to the soft plastic circle through the read/write hole on the disk by moving back the sliding shutter that protects the data from external elements. It is write protected by sliding the tile on the lower left side of the disk so it closes the hole.

Floppy disk drives come in internal and external versions. Internal drives generally come as part of your computer system and are located inside the computer. External drives are attached to your computer by a cable. Windows and Macintosh operating systems portray a floppy disk by using an icon of a disk; Windows operating systems also refer to the floppy disk by using the letter "A".

To insert a 3-1/2-inch disk in the drive, simply insert the disk into the slot, metal end first and label side up, and gently push until the disk pops into the drive. The one rule when working with disk drives is to always make sure the red "reading" light on the drive is off before taking a disk out of the drive. If a disk is taken out of the drive when the red light is on, some of the information on the disk can be damaged or destroyed. Some computers eject 3-1/2-inch disks by keyboard command. For example, on Macintosh computers, the disk is ejected when the disk icon is dragged to the trash can icon. Other computers have an eject button next to the drive.

Hard Drive. The hard drive is a device that uses a magnetic medium to store large amounts of data. Hard drives are more reliable than floppy disks, because they are closed systems that do not allow dirt to enter and harm the read/write mechanism (the mechanism that allows you to read, add, or delete information). Hard drives are represented by an icon when using Windows or the Macintosh operating systems; Windows operating systems also refer to the hard drive using the letter "C".

Hard drives come in various sizes (measured in gigabytes) and speeds. The smallest hard drive you should consider buying is a 10GB; however, you can be confident in purchasing larger drives, knowing that programs are continuing to grow in size. Hard drives provide faster access than floppy disks, since they are constantly spinning. Be aware that the data on hard drives are never permanent. All hard drives will crash (fail) eventually due to disk failure, static electricity, or other ambient factors. Therefore, as with all storage devices, it is very important to back up your data.

When saving information, especially on larger capacity storage devices, it is important to think about how to organize your files. Remember, computer storage can be compared to a file cabinet

Figure 2.7   The compact disc-read only
memory (CD-ROM) provides 650MB of
information, but it doesn't allow you to store
information on it..

containing many folders. You may want to consider organizing
your data files by class period or by the type of activity (e.g.,
volleyball, badminton) you are teaching, for example.

Other types of magnetic medium are the zip and jaz drives. The
Iomega Zip (100MB or 250MB) and Jaz (2GB) drives allow
the user to record over and over again, and have become
increasingly popular with educators. Zip and Jaz drives are very
easy to use.

Optical Discs.   Another storage device is the optical disc, which
stores and retrieves data using laser technology. Optical discs
can hold hundreds of megabytes of data. The most common
optical disc is the CD-ROM (compact disc-read only memory).

CD-ROMs (see Figure 2.7) are manufactured with data already
on them; they can be read but not changed. One CD-ROM
holds 650MB of information, which is the equivalent of
270,000 pages of text. This makes it a great medium for
distributing encyclopedias, dictionaries, and graphics
libraries. The CD-ROM player includes an audio chip set
that allows you not only to play CD-ROMs, but also to listen
to music. The CD-ROM player can be hooked up to an
external amplifier and speaker for better sound. The CD or
CD-ROM, label side up, is either slipped into the CD-ROM
drive or placed into a sliding tray that pops in and out of the
CD-ROM drive.

Other types of compact discs include: CD-R and CD-RW. CD-
R discs let the user record information on the compact disc;
however, once recorded it can't be erased. CD-RW discs let the
user record over and over again on the compact disc.

The latest storage device is the DVD (short for Digital Versatile Disc or Digital Videodisc), which has the potential to do a variety of things. DVDs look like standard CDs, but they store 4.7GB (single-sided disc), 8.5 (single-sided disc with two layers), or 17.0GB (double sided disc) of data. The high-density drives have the potential to revolutionize storage media, since they also can read regular CDs.

DVD-RAMs also are arriving on the scene, providing users with a reusable disk format that allows information to be recorded and erased again and again. The DVD-RAM discs hold 2.6GB on a single-sided disc or 5.2GB per double-sided disc. They appear on the desktop, like a floppy disk, so transferring items is as simple as dragging and dropping them onto the disc icon.

Tape Cartridge. Tape cartridges—which have been around for a long time—are slow, and they require a tape drive. However, as hard drives have gotten larger, and backing up data on floppy disks has become more cumbersome, backing up data on tape cartridges has become more popular. If you find you have a large amount of data to back up, tape cartridges are a good

DVD Disc Format Application

DVD-Video	Interactive or linear video programs. This "read-only" format is typically used to hold full-length movies.
DVD-ROM	Multimedia programs or data storage of any type; requires a computer.
DVD-R	Record-once format used in developing DVD-Video or DVD-ROM programs.
DVD-RAM	Re-recordable format, used as a computer peripheral to store files.
DVD-Audio	Audio-only format; specifications still in development.

choice for backup purposes. A tape drive can be built into a computer or connected to a computer by a cable. Typically, an external tape drive is more expensive than an internal tape drive. Tape backup cartridges should be stored in a cool, dry place, away from electrical equipment. If cartridges are stored for a long time, they should be rotated regularly to prevent the tape from stretching or sagging.

Modem

A modem is another important component of any computer system. There are internal, external, and PC-card modems. When selecting a modem, be sure that it has 56K bps capability (bps is the speed of transfer). Popular modems include U.S. Robotics (3Com) and Global Village. More information about modems is provided in Chapters 7 and 8.

Output

Output refers to the information the processor generates and communicates to the user. In addition to storage devices and modems (which are input and output), monitors, speakers, and printers are considered output devices.

Monitor

Size is the most obvious characteristic of a monitor. The measurement of a monitor is taken diagonally from one corner of the screen to the other. Actual monitor area is roughly proportional to the square of the diagonal length, so a 20-inch monitor is more than four times as large as a 9-inch monitor. Most manufacturers cheat on their monitor sizes by measuring from one corner of the screen (or even the case) to the other, rather than from one edge of the visible display to the other. Then they round up to the nearest inch with the result that most "14-inch monitors" are closer to 12 1/2 inches when measured truthfully. The larger the monitor, the more expensive it is, and typically the easier it is on your eyes.

Resolution is measured in number of pixels or dots that can be displayed both horizontally and vertically. The more pixels, the finer the detail. Resolution defines how much information can be squeezed onto the screen. However, everything will appear smaller at the larger resolution, since the monitor has to fit more pixels into the same space. The clearest resolution for a monitor is whatever comes closest to fitting 72 pixels (or dots) into each inch.

The number of colors and pixels that you seen on the screen actually has little or nothing to do with the monitor. A typical monitor is just a big dumb tube that does what the computer tells it to do. The part of the computer that's in charge of pixels and colors is the video board. The primary measurement of a video board is the amount of VRAM that it provides. Most boards include 4MB to 8MB of VRAM. More VRAM means more color at higher resolutions. A 2MB board provides 16 million colors up to 800x600 pixels, whereas a 4MB board lets you display 16 million colors at resolutions up to 1152x864 pixels. Most boards top out at 8MB of VRAM, which permits 16 million colors at resolutions as high as 1600x1200.

Dot pitch defines how well you can see the image on the screen. (Larger dot pitches look fuzzier.) Most monitors have dot pitches of .39mm, .28mm, or .25mm. Refresh rate also affects how clear the picture appears—72Hz is the standard refresh rate for Macintosh monitors. That means the screen is repainted 72 times a second, more than twice as fast as your television screen. However, several PC monitors have refresh rates of 60Hz or even less. This begins to approach the level that contributes to eyestrain. Worse yet, these monitors are interlaced, which means that only half of the screen is redrawn on each pass. Interlaced monitors have a visible flicker effect, and should be avoided at all costs. Look for a monitor that's noninterlaced, with a dot pitch no greater than 0.28mm.

Alternatives to traditional monitors include projection systems. Projection systems connect to desktop or notebook computers and can project screen images as large as a wall. Video output cards convert the digital signal from the computer to an analog video signal, so the projection system can display the image. Many of the new projection systems actually have the built-in capability to convert digital video to analog video. This allows the physical educator to demonstrate software to an entire class or to make an electronic presentation.

Speakers

The sound coming out of your computer can beep and squawk through its own speakers, but if you want to listen to other sounds you will want to get a set of stereo speakers—one for each side of the monitor. The speakers must be self-powered and they must be shielded; the magnets inside normal stereo speakers are enough to distort the image on your monitor and destroy data on a floppy disk. You also can use a cable to plug your computer into your existing sound system.

Some students may have difficulty seeing standard, text-based software. For those students, it may be necessary to use speech synthesis, which converts written text into speech. OutSpoken (ALVA Access Group) offers software solutions for both the Macintosh and PC platforms.

Printers

A printer creates a paper copy of the information you develop on your computer. Printers are typically connected to computers through a parallel interface, a USB interface, or a serial interface; the interface determines how information is transmitted from the processor to the printer. Be sure to choose a printer with an interface that is compatible with your computer. If the interface is not compatible you can buy a converter, but that will add to your expense. Remember to turn the printer off when you're not printing, since printers can use up to 1,000 watts of electricity per hour. Today, educators typically choose between ink jet and laser printers.

Ink Jet. An ink jet printer is like a dot matrix printer—it prints characters in the form of tiny dots clustered together. However, a dot matrix prints either 9 or 24 dots per character whereas an ink jet sprays hundreds of dots per inch. An ink cartridge replaces an ink ribbon, and there is virtually no sound because there is no impact of metal against paper. The quality of the printing isn't quite laser-crisp, and the printed image can smear if it gets the least bit damp. Therefore, special coated paper is recommended, and it is more expensive than the paper used with laser printers.

Because it is relatively inexpensive, educators typically choose an ink jet printer for their first color printer. Colors are usually better from CMYK models (the color cartridge includes black) than from CMY models that blend cyan (C), magenta (M), and yellow (Y) inks to make black (K). The CMY models also require cartridge switching from plain text (black ink) to color printing and back. The resolution for ink jet printing is typically 600 dots per inch (dpi). The primary disadvantage of ink jet printers is their speed (only 5 to 17 pages per minute).

Laser Printers. Laser printers (see Figure 2.7) create photocopy-quality documents. The images are electronically created on a light-sensitive drum, usually with a scanning laser. Powdered toner sticks to areas where light has touched the drum and is then transferred to a sheet of paper that is briefly heated to permanently fuse the toner. Laser printers can print any text, in any style, at any size, and at any angle—and everything looks terrific. PostScript laser printers also can print phenomenal-looking graphics. They're quick (10 to 50 pages per minute), quiet, and hassle-free; most can print envelopes, mailing labels, and paper up to legal size. The more expensive the laser printer,

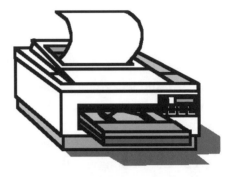

Figure 2.7   Laser printers
provide higher quality text
and graphics.

the better its quality and the larger its memory. The resolution
for laser printers is typically between 600 dpi and 1200 dpi.
Laser printers are the preferred printers, but they also are the
most expensive.

Power Supply

It is important to protect your investment in a computer. So,
invest in an Uninterruptible Power Supply (UPS) and surge
protector. The UPS provides power to the computer when the
main electrical system fails. It detects the power failure and
switches to battery power within a fraction of a second. This
allows you to finish tasks and safely shut down. The surge
protector provides protection to the computer from a fluctuation
in power that can damage your equipment. Many uninterruptible
power supplies have built-in surge protection.

Acquiring Your Computer

In many schools and districts, the type of computer you use
is governed by what the school or district already owns. This
is true whether you are going to an office or lab or are
purchasing the machine for your department. Some districts
adopt a certain type of operating system for all schools, or a
particular type of computer by grade level—for example,
elementary schools use Macintosh, intermediate schools use

Printing from Windows

1. Start up the computer.
2. Open the Printer folder.
3. Open the Add Printer icon.
4. Click the Next button twice.
5. Describe your printer's make and model by clicking on the printer's manufacturer and model number.
6. Click the Next button.
7. Pick the printer port from the list.
8. Click the Next button twice.
9. Click Finish.
   Note: If your printer isn't listed, you'll need to use the special installation disk that came with the printer.

Printing from the Mac

1. Select Chooser from the Apple Menu.
2. Click on the type of printer.
3. Select Active for AppleTalk if you are on a network.
   Note: If your printer isn't listed, you'll need the special piece of software (driver) that came with the printer. Drag the software to the system folder and restart the computer.

Common Commands

Copy-to make a duplicate of the information and store it on the clipboard.

Paste-to place the information from the clipboard at the insertion point.

Cut-to remove the information and store it on the clipboard.

Delete or clear-to remove the information.

Move-to remove the information and place it in a new location.

Windows, and high schools use Windows NT. Even if a school doesn't have a policy, departments should stay consistent with the rest of the school when possible.

Computers can be acquired through general funds, grants (e.g., from Apple Computers, IBM Corporation, federal funds, state funds, federal block grants, and private foundations), technology funds, and other financial avenues. Physical education departments should begin by acquiring one computer for each office. Ideally, each physical education teacher should be equipped with his or her own computer and have access to a presentation workstation. At minimum, each teacher's system should include a computer, monitor, input devices (keyboard and mouse), storage devices (floppy disks, hard drive, CD-ROM), modem, and printer. Presentation stations should include a projection system. Once each teacher is equipped, you can begin to secure computers for student use. When purchasing, compare special educational prices (i.e., Apple school discount), computer advertisements, and mail order catalogs. When you purchase by mail order you can save hundreds of dollars by avoiding sales tax, and you tend to get a pretty good price. Good sources for mail order include MacWarehouse and MicroWarehouse.

Getting Started

You ordered the equipment, and it has arrived—in a variety of boxes. Now the only question is, "How does it all go together?" Fortunately, the ports (sockets where cables connect) on the rear of most computers are marked with icons that symbolize the type of equipment that should be attached to them. For example, there is an icon of a mouse where the mouse plugs in, and one of a keyboard where the keyboard plugs in.

Once you have hooked the computer up to the peripherals,

46

it's time to turn it on. The computer itself can perform only a few functions written into its hardware (ROM). So, each time it is turned on, it needs "system software"—a set of instructions that tell the processor how to create type styles, set up the first screen on the monitor, and communicate with the storage devices, input devices, and printer. System software (i.e., Macintosh operating system, Windows operating system) should already be on the hard drive when you purchase the computer.

Different operating systems use different methods for starting programs and naming files, and they offer various levels of sophistication with graphic interfaces. (Graphic interfaces provide a more user-friendly environment.) Be sure to complete all tutorials that accompany your computer so you can take full advantage of its operating system. Finally, put all documentation and software (drivers, etc.) in one place where you can find it when you may need it. Attach tags to all the connecting power lines, printer cables, phone connection, etc., so that when, and if, you need to bring your system in for repair it will be easy to put it all back together.

Summary

Many decisions related to the purchase of a computer and peripherals are individual ones. However, it is important to purchase the best computer you can afford. That will allow you to stay up-to-date as long as possible before having to trade in your computer for a bigger and better one to meet your ever-increasing needs. Use the guidelines and recommendations from this chapter to guide your decisions. Also, refer to the many computer magazines on the market (see Appendix C) and the various companies' Internet sites for specific recommendations.

Reflection Questions

1. Which platform would you select when purchasing a new computer? Explain your reasoning.

2. Which of the peripherals (input/output devices) would you purchase? What would you intend to accomplish with each device?

Projects

1. Make a list of all the software you would like open at one time, determine the RAM requirements of each program, and then calculated your total RAM needs before purchasing a new computer.

2. Create a list of all the features you need in your next computer. Then, thumb through a computer catalog (i.e., MacWarehouse, MicroWarehouse) and locate all the computers that meet your criteria. Next, go on the Internet and find reviews of these computers. Then, you can make your final selection.

Chapter 3

Using Audio and Visual Technology in Physical Education

Today you start a new unit in physical education, a game called "Takraw". Many students have never heard of this activity, and they wonder why they should learn to play it. Some wonder why they should play anything except basketball. You play Oriam Sport's colorful "Takraw" video, set to popular music. Immediately, the students are drawn into the video and the game. After viewing the video, the students are eager to begin the new activity. The first skill to learn is the kick, and you use a video clip to demonstrate it. With the remote control, you access the starting frame for the segment on kicking and a model demonstration of the skill appears. In 10 minutes you have successfully introduced your new sport unit.

Human brains are programmed to learn through a combination of motion and sound. Seventy percent of the information reaching our brains comes through the eyes. Studies (Kulik, 1994; Kromhout & Butzin, 1993) show that significantly greater learning results when audiovisual media are integrated into traditional teaching programs. The use of sound and motion increases understanding by 30 percent over other presentation methods, and interest, motivation, and retention remain 33 percent higher for up to one year after viewing.

In addition, most students enjoy learning and participating in an activity more once they are somewhat familiar with it. Several technologies are available for familiarizing your students with new activities. Visual, audio, and video presentations can teach rules, illustrate game concepts, and demonstrate different offensive and defensive strategies. Showing model demonstrations in slow and fast motion can enhance explanations of motor skills and allow students to focus on specific aspects of skills and plays. Watching video clips at the beginning of class can generate interest in the new activity. Students can relate the activity to their own lives.

This chapter will introduce you to static visuals, audio and video technologies, and audio and video cables and plugs. It will help you identify appropriate hardware and software, and it will suggest specific ways to use these technologies in physical education classes.

Static Visuals

Static visuals include pictures, graphics, and three-dimensional models. Pictures attract attention, provide realistic images of objects, document events, and speak to those who are hearing-impaired, non-English speaking, or unable to read. Graphics contain pictures and words, but are distinguished by their use of symbols. They come in many forms: maps, diagrams, charts, tables, graphs, posters, and cartoons. They are designed to communicate information clearly, precisely, and efficiently.

Three-dimensional models are representations of real-life events. They include boards that depict playing fields and toy people that portray players who can be positioned on the board to demonstrate offensive and defensive strategies along with rule situations. When selecting static visuals, look for presentation style, text, technical quality, and effectiveness. Most static visuals can be held up, posted on bulletin boards, drawn on chalkboards or markerboards, and attached to walls or cones.

Three especially effective static visual applications are textbooks, worksheets, and task cards.

Textbooks

Textbooks are fairly new to physical education, but they are excellent resources for students, especially those who are visual learners. However, we do need to be careful how we use them in physical education, since using limited instructional time to have students read a chapter in a book is not consistent with physical education goals. Ideally, you will have access to one class set of textbooks for every class you teach, plus one extra class set. This will allow you to assign reading as homework. The extra class set of textbooks can be used in a number of different ways: Students who are excused from an activity can do a reading and writing assignment. Reading station(s) can be established as part of a circuit that includes more traditional physical activities (skill practice, exercises).

If, like many physical educators, you have limited equipment/ facilities for practice, the reading station can serve those students who might otherwise be waiting to practice a skill. During inclement weather, shortened instructional periods, and other special situations, you may assign a reading activity—reading and answering questions, researching a specific topic, or participating in a jigsaw activity (each student in a group of four is assigned one reading assignment, which he or she reads and learns in order to share with teammates). For teachers on more limited textbook budgets, one class set can be purchased and reading can be done in a circuit approach or on special occasions. Finally, teachers who can only secure several books will still be able to assign reading in a circuit approach or as resource material for students working on projects.

When selecting textbooks you will need to note the "reading level" of the textbook. Some publishers advertise the reading level at which the book was written; others do not. The highlight box on this page provides you with a formula for estimating the reading level of any textbook from a short passage. For a more accurate estimate, examine text content and style. Watch for profound thoughts expressed in simple terms, ambiguities, figures of speech, and complex grammatical constructions.

There are basically three types of texts on the market: sport activity textbooks, fitness-specific textbooks, and conceptually based textbooks. Australian Physical Education, Book 1 (Blackall 1986) and Australian Physical Education, Book 2 (Blackall & Davis 1987) are examples of sport activity textbooks. Designed for grades five through eight, they contain information on a variety of traditional activities (e.g., basketball, volleyball). Each chapter contains a description of one activity and its rules, skills, and safety issues. Short-answer questions, word searches, and crossword puzzles can be found at the end of each chapter. A similar book for the high school level is Physical Activity and Sport for the Secondary School Student (Dougherty, 1993). It also is organized by activity, with sections on skills and techniques, safety, scoring, rules, etiquette, strategies, equipment, and related terminology.

Estimating Reading Level
$$RGL=0.4(wps+\%hw)$$

• RGL is the grade level of students who, on the average, should have no difficulty reading and understanding the text.

• wps is the total number of words in a selected passage (at least 100 words) divided by the number of sentences in that passage.

• %hw is 100 times the number of hard words divided by the total number of words in the passage. Hard words are those with three or more syllables, excluding: (a) proper nouns; (b) combinations of short, easy words such as "forevermore"; and (c) verbs made into three syllables by the addition of a suffix (e.g., "studying").

Fitness books have become increasingly popular at the secondary level. Fitness for Life (Corbin & Lindsey 1997) is in its fourth edition. The package includes a student textbook, annotated teacher's edition, and teacher's resource book. Support materials include: a series of 10 videos entitled Teaching Lifetime Fitness, a Fit Fun Audio CD which contains music and timed sounds for activities, Fitness for Life Presentation Program (CD-ROM) which includes electronic presentations on each chapter, and Fitness for Life Fitness Profile Software (Macintosh and Windows) which allows students to enter fitness self-assessment scores and then print a complete personalized fitness profile. Fitness for Life provides a conceptual approach to fitness, covering both health-related and skill-related topics.

The textbook includes fitness activities that help students relate concepts to their personal fitness. Specific information on principles of fitness, cardiovascular fitness, strength, muscular endurance, flexibility, body composition, warm-ups, nutrition, stress, consumer issues, and planning and evaluating exercise programs is included. The teacher's resource book provides transparency masters, information sheets which include answers for the worksheets and tests, fitness focus instruction sheets, student questionnaires, self-assessment and activity record sheets, application worksheets, reinforcement worksheets, activity cards, and chapter tests. The annotated teacher's edition of the textbook includes background notes, teaching strategies, safety concerns, research data, professional articles, flexible management schedules, vocabulary lists, and suggestions for individualizing instruction. Written at an eighth grade reading level, it's best used at the eighth or ninth grade level.

Lifetime Personal Fitness (Stokes, Schultz, & Polansky, 1997) is another book in the fitness category. This book covers an introduction to fitness, fitness evaluation, principles of training, flexibility, cardiovascular fitness, muscular strength and endurance, nutrition, weight control, stress, exercising safely, planning an exercise program, and consumer awareness. The laboratory activities are especially effective for reinforcing the information in the textbook. These are hands-on activities, most of which involve actual physical activity. The teacher's edition provides motivational ideas and tips, a sample course outline, suggested student projects, games and activities for fitness, performance standards, suggested supplemental materials (films, videos, equipment, records, tapes, books, software), answers to chapter review questions, sample blackline masters (for overheads), and chapter tests. These books are best used at the ninth or tenth grade level.

Personal Fitness: Looking Good/Feeling Good (Williams, Harageones, Johnson, & Smith, 1998) also falls into the fitness category. The student text covers an introduction to fitness, components of fitness, goal setting, guidelines for exercise, principles of training, flexibility, cardiovascular fitness, muscular fitness, nutrition, body composition and weight control, stress, consumer issues, evaluation of activities, and designing a fitness program for high school students. The student text is accompanied by a hands-on student activity handbook that includes 51 different activities to reinforce and apply the fitness concepts.

The annotated teacher's edition includes a guide that addresses the following: features of the program; implementing the program; planning the program; fitness assessment; helping students set goals and develop exercise prescriptions; students with special needs; grading procedures; health, environmental, and safety considerations; and planning for emergencies. Annotations include teacher objectives, teaching notes and strategies, and answers to study questions. The teacher's resource book includes the following for each chapter: bulletin board ideas, transparency blackline masters, learning activities to reinforce fitness concepts, and chapter tests and answers. Also available are videos on fitness, a floppy disk (Mac or Windows) containing MicroTest for test development, and a CD-ROM containing materials for presentations, posters, and handouts. This book best serves the needs of tenth, eleventh, and twelfth grade students.

Foundations of Personal Fitness (Rainey & Murray, 1997) rounds out the fitness category with another textbook geared for high school students. Covering much of the same information as the previous textbooks, this textbook highlights the idea that "any body can be fit." The teacher's wraparound edition is an especially strong component with lesson plans, strategies for working with special populations, ideas for student evaluation, and tips for fitness testing. The teacher resource package also contains vocabulary worksheets, reteaching worksheets, transparency masters, color transparencies of key figures, chapter tests, and additional handouts. There is a video series entitled Foundations of Personal Fitness that addresses and reinforces many of the different topics covered in the book, such as muscular strength and endurance, weight training, aerobics, etc. On the software side, an informational nutrition laser disc/CD-ROM, diet analysis program, and computerized test bank complete the package.

Kendall/Hunt's Essentials of Physical Education series is in the conceptually-based category of books. The high school textbook (Spindt, Monti, & Hennessy, 1991) and middle school textbook series (Spindt, Monti, Hennessy, Holyoak, & Weinberg, 1992) comprise the first comprehensive textbook series for students in physical education. The sixth grade book is entitled Moving with Confidence, the seventh grade book is Moving with Skill, the eighth grade book is Moving as a Team, and the high school book is Moving for Life. This series covers motor skills, fitness, social skills, self-esteem concepts, pursuing lifelong movement activities, and promoting individual excellence. The teacher's edition for each level includes margin notes that direct teacher actions. The student portfolio for each grade level contains classroom, laboratory, and field activities for students to complete in and outside of class. There also are teacher resource books.

Physical Education: Theory and Practice (Davis, Kimmet, &

Auty, 1986) is another conceptually-based textbook for students. Designed for high school students, it is divided into six parts and covers each of the subdisciplines of physical education— anatomy and physiology, exercise physiology, biomechanics, motor learning, history, and sociology. Each chapter contains information, worksheets, and laboratories.

A recent edition to the conceptually-based textbook category is Senior Physical Education: An Integrated Approach (Kirk, Burgess-Limerick, Kiss, Lahey, & Penney, 1999). Written for juniors and seniors in high school, it is divided into three parts: Learning Physical Activity, Physiological Dimensions of Physical Activity, and Sociocultural Dimensions of Physical Activity. Test-yourself questions are found at the end of each chapter; answers are located in the back of the book. Focus activities and extension activities are located throughout the book to help reinforce concepts.

In order to determine the textbook that best meets your needs and those of your students, contact the publishers listed in the appendix. The publishers will either send you a complimentary copy or a review copy to keep for an established length of time. Either way, read through the book, have your students try several of the activities, and then approach the individual on your campus in charge of textbook purchases with your purchase request.

Worksheets

Worksheets (see Figure 3.1) provide students with directions for a physical or cognitive activity and a set format for written responses. Worksheets can be created by the teacher on a word processing program (see Chapter 6) or purchased in workbook form or as part of a textbook package. Cognitive worksheets can include steps for calculating personal target heart rate range, identifying muscles worked during different exercises, and matching biomechanic principles with their motor skill applications. Physical worksheets, sometimes referred to as data

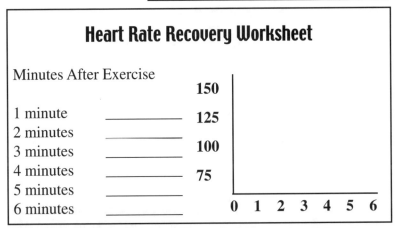

Figure 3.1   Sample worksheet where a student records and then charts his or her heart rate 1 minute, 2 minutes, 3 minutes, 4 minutes, 5 minutes, and 6 minutes after completing an exercise period.

collection sheets, include recording sheets for fitness tests as well as checklists for motor skill performance, heart rate data collection during different situations, and distance, time, and accuracy data collected while performing motor skills. Many teachers have found that worksheets help keep students on-task. Even though the teacher may not necessarily need or want the data collected, the worksheet holds the student accountable for performing the instructional task.

Task Cards

Task cards (see Figure 3.2) typically are used in circuit teaching. Each task card includes a series of directions for students to follow. Teachers can either purchase preprinted cards (from Sportime or Bonnie's Fitware) or create their own using a word processing or desktop publishing program (see Chapter 6). Print each task on a separate card and post one card at each station in the circuit. Then, instruct students, working in groups of four, to follow the directions on the task cards as they rotate through the stations in the circuit.

57

Practice Backhand Grip

___ Shake hands with base of racket.
___ Form "v" with thumb and index finger.
___ Rotate racket so "v" is on top.
___ Spread fingers slightly.

©2000 Bonnie's Fitware

Figure 3.2   Sample task card with critical features for the backhand grip.

To make your task cards do double duty, incorporate peer feedback: List the critical elements for each skill on the card so students can check one another's performance. When making your own task cards, be sure to include color and graphics, and laminate them so they will withstand the harsh physical education environment.

Audio

Watching a movie with no sound will help you understand the importance of sound in multimedia tutorials and presentations. Effective uses for sound include providing a speech synthesis of the text for visually impaired students, a language translation of the text for bilingual settings, directions that explain specific concepts for auditory learners, and music for rhythms, tumbling, dance, exercising, and other appropriate activities. Audio should be clear, engaging, accurate, and accented with special effects and music when appropriate. And, it is important to have a good sound system.

Sound systems are made up of audio components from a single manufacturer that are grouped together to offer optimum value and performance. You can be assured that the matched components will work well together and that little wiring will

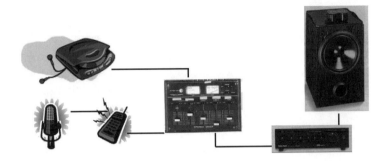

Figure 3.3   The wireless microphone sends a signal to the receiver that is connected to the mixer. The CD player sends a signal to the mixer. The mixer sends both signals to the amplifier and on to the speakers.

be required. In the past few years, mini- and microsystems have surpassed full-size systems in popularity. Many of these small systems reproduce sound faithfully, with output comparable to that of the bigger systems. It is important to have at least the following components in your system: amplifier, mixer, microphone, speakers, headphones, cassette player, and CD player.

The amplifier increases the sound so that it can be heard clearly. It also allows you to adjust the volume. The power output is stated in wattage. Fifty watts per channel is a minimum for classroom needs, while gymnasiums/outdoor areas require higher wattage (100 watts or more per channel). Keep in mind that most professional amplifiers do not have tone controls (bass and treble), since the mixer controls the tone in most professional workstations. So, if you don't plan to use a mixer, look for an amplifier that has tone controls.

Mixers are an important feature if you are going to combine sounds (i.e., voice and music). They give you the capability to adjust the microphone and the music independently of each other. A good mixer will help you compensate for old or damaged cassette tapes, poor room acoustics, and feedback. Purchase a mixer with independent tone controls (bass, treble, and mid frequency adjustments) for each channel.

A microphone is essential for teachers who must project their voices in a noisy gymnasium or over music. The signal strength of a teacher's voice is reduced by six decibels every time you double the distance from the teacher to the students. A wireless headband microphone is lightweight and durable. Most have a flexible gooseneck design that allows you to adjust the position of the mike. The microphone is attached to a small wireless transmitter. The teacher's voice is fed to the receiver, mixer, and amplifier, and then projected out into the gymnasium through the speaker.

Wireless microphone systems transmit sound using VHF (very high frequency) or UHF (ultra high frequency) radio and television frequencies. The VHF band of frequencies is more crowded and therefore makes VHF wireless microphone systems more susceptible to interference. The UHF wireless microphone systems, although slightly more expensive, will give you more reliable performance.

When it come to speakers, the first consideration is the quality of sound reproduction. Some speaker systems contain one full-range speaker cone designed to handle the entire frequency spectrum, while others contain two or three drivers for each channel. While a two-way system is almost always better than a single full-range speaker, a three-way system isn't necessarily better than a two-way system. The most important specification is frequency response. This indicates the highest and lowest frequencies of sound that a speaker is physically capable of reproducing. The ideal range is 20Hz to 20Khz, the range of an average ear. Other useful features include a separate volume and tone control for each speaker.

Headphones are a must if individual students will be listening to audio. Full base response with accurate tonal definition and balance from the mid-range frequencies up to the highest frequencies is best. The headphone must be lightweight and comfortable. Circumaural phones—headphones that cover the entire outer ear—block out all external sound and provide the best base sound.

The most popular audio products today are analog audiocassettes and digital CDs; therefore, it is a good idea to have both a tape deck player and CD player. The best tape decks use three separate audio heads—one each for erasing, recording, and playback. Most decks, however, have only two heads—one for erasing the tape and one combined record/playback head. Any tape deck with record input jacks will allow you to record sound, but purchase at least a medium-quality cassette recorder so the quality of the sound will be adequate. You also may wish to purchase a second budget-price deck for copying tapes. DAT, a new tape, records digitally using a system nearly identical to the CD system. DAT is to the analog cassette what CD is to the analog LP record. When reproducing DAT, there is no breakdown in quality.

Compact Discs (CDs) have revolutionized sound reproduction, producing the first commercially accepted digital sound format. CDs store sound as a string of numbers by sampling the sound thousands of times each second and assigning each sample a numeric value based on a binary code of zero or one. The CD stores its digital information as a series of microscopic pits arranged in a continuous spiral pattern below the disc's clear plastic surface. The CD player reads the reflection of a laser beam that tracks these pits. Nothing but the beam of light touches the CD while it plays, so there is no wear and tear on the disc. CDs usually surpass the sound quality of LPs and analog tapes because there is virtually no distortion. A programmable CD player can play specific tracks in ascending sequence or randomly, while many players also let you program the order in which the tracks will be heard.

Due to the rapid expansion of the Internet, MP3 audio programs are positioned to be the next "popular" audio product. MP3 is a method of compressing audio files into one-tenth of their normal size while still keeping near CD-quality sound. These files can be downloaded from the Internet on a song-by-song basis and stored on a computer or separate MP3 player. These players currently take the form of "walkmen" components and watches, but you will see them integrated into home and car stereo systems in the near future.

Two-Way Communication

Two-way radio communication has become increasingly popular with new small, lightweight, easy-to-carry radios. These radios are especially beneficial in the physical education environment where physical educators and their classes are often thousands of yards away from other people. In an emergency situation, the radio can be used to call for medical or security assistance. The qualities to look for when purchasing two-way radios include: rechargeable batteries, several frequency channel, and a maximum range equivalent to the campus size.

Video

Dynamic images (hereafter referred to as video) are the rapid showing of still images—typically shown at 30 frames (60 fields) per second. Students often concentrate better with video because the moving images hold their attention. Presenting information through video technology can speed up learning.

There are two types of video: analog and digital. Analog video refers to video stored as motion ("television" language). Digital video refers to video stored in a series of zeros and ones ("computer" language). Currently, television, cable, and videotapes are distributed as analog video. However, the trend is toward digital video in the form of satellite dish systems, digital cable boxes, CD-ROMs, and DVDs (digital versatile discs). Digital video has the advantages of image quality and ease of manipulation. Digital video can be cut, copied, and pasted just like text and graphics.

Fair Use Guidelines

Material	Copy for Teacher	Copies for Class
Books	1 chapter	1,000 words (10 %)
Encyclopedias	1 story	2,500 words (1 story)
Poems	1 poem	250 words (1 poem)
Periodicals	1 article	2,500 words (1 article)
Charts	1 per book	1 per book
Lectures	1 per book	1 per book

Note: Videotapes of TV (noneducational) programs may be shown twice to students within 10 days of broadcast and retained for a maximum of 45 days for evaluation purposes. Educational television may be recorded and used for educational purposes for a maximum of 7 days.

Source: Kenneth T. Murray, "Copyright and the Educator," Phi Delta Kappan, March 1994, p. 555.

Regardless of the source, video images require a display system. At the high (and expensive) end, there are presentation systems that can display images on a screen of any size. The images are bright (and getting brighter with each new generation) and have high resolution. At the low end is the basic monitor or television set. When going this route, be sure to purchase a 25-inch screen, and perhaps more than one, depending on the size of your class or group. Also, make sure the monitor can accept connections from your sources (see cables and plugs later in this chapter). Other output devices include:

- Flat-panel displays that offer lower voltage and fewer emissions than monitors of the same size (these can fit in smaller spaces and are generally much lighter).
- High-density television (HDTV) that provides greater visual detail (higher resolution) and wider screens; HDTV also requires special broadcasts.

Now, let's take a closer look at the various sources of video, including broadcasts, videocassettes, and DVD.

Broadcast Video

Broadcasts include televised, cable, and satellite-delivered video. Televised broadcasts are distributed via air waves. Instructional television began in the mid-1950s, when many school districts bought television equipment and produced their own programs. PBS has distributed instructional videos on a large scale. Many of the PBS programs are accompanied by study guides that summarize content, provide questions, make suggestions for preparatory and follow-up activities, and list supplementary readings.

Cable television systems tend to use fiber optic and coaxial cable to distribute video materials, whereas satellites, parked in orbits about 22,300 miles above the equator, function as aerial relay stations. As few as three satellites are needed to provide telecommunication services around the globe. A transmission is set up (uplinked) from a ground-based television station, received by the satellite, and then retransmitted (downlinked) back to earth, where it is received by a satellite dish. The signal from the satellite can be received by any dish in the satellite's coverage area that is pointed at that satellite and turned to the appropriate channel (transponder).

Instructional broadcasts for physical education have included Slim Goodbody Presents All Fit (Human Kinetics), PE-TV (PE-TV), and Leaps and Bounds (Agency for Instructional Technology). A current Cable in the Classroom offering is ESPN SportsFigures. This show is presented weekly throughout the school year on ESPN2. It uses sports and professional athletes to demonstrate math and physics concepts to high school students. Each lesson includes background, discussion, step-by-step explanations of equations, activities, answers, and suggestions for extending the lesson in the classroom. ESPN recently launched a companion web site http:// sportsfigures.espn.go.com/. The site is designed for teachers, students, and parents. It contains interactive components such as educational games and contests, chats and trivia, as well as audio and video clips and curriculum information.

Physical educators also use broadcasts such as professional sports, college/university sports, and the Olympics to illustrate excellence in sports. In addition, programs like The Wonder Years, Boston Public, Once and Again, and after-school specials focus on social and self-esteem issues related to physical activity.

Videocassettes

Videotape is still the number one source for video in schools. Videocassette players play back video, whereas videocassette recorders can play and record. When you shop for a videocassette recorder, consider durability, ease of operation, reliability and quality, ease of repair and maintenance, and cost. Critical features include:

- Three-prong UL safety plug.
- Front loading.
- Front panel AV inputs (for easy plug-in of other video components).
- Real time readout in hours, minutes, and seconds.
- Slow motion (including frame-by-frame action) using jog-shuttle dial.
- Freeze-frame.
- Fast forward viewing.
- Reverse viewing.
- Automatic tracking control.

The ability to operate these features by remote control is important in a class setting. A combination videocassette recorder and television is convenient for avoiding excess cable connections; however, the combination will cost the same as if the items were purchased separately, and combination sets often lack a variety of features.

Videocassette recorders come with two, four, or six heads. The actual recording and playback of information to and from tape occurs at the location of the heads. Two heads are standard, and they work fine for off-air recording and playback. In a physical education instructional setting, however, it is better to use four heads, with two for speed and two for slow motion. Six-head VCRs use the two extra heads for a high-fidelity (hi fi) audio track, which improves the sound quality.

If you are interested in making recordings from live broadcasts, you should purchase a machine you can program in advance. The ease of programming the machine, including either on-screen prompts or VCR Plus (which uses a short numeric code for programming), also should be considered. Try experimenting with the programming features before you make your purchase.

If you will be analyzing sports skills, a VCR that can encode the video will provide quicker access to different video segments. The encoder places a time code on the videotape, so that individual frames can be called up by number. This is more precise than the counter feature available on most videocassette recorders. Other access options include:

- Repeat playback, which designates a recorded tape segment for automatic replay.
- Index search, which places an electronic marker at selected locations.
- Real time search, which lets the user enter the length of tape that is to be skipped in minutes.
- Search and skip, which advances the tape in 30-second increments.

The counter is the least effective, the search and skip button is a little more effective, and the time encoder is the most effective. Cost corresponds to effectiveness; the encoder is the most expensive.

It is important to consider the grade of videotape you purchase. Premium and high grades are more expensive, but they tend to

Tape Storage

Store tapes upright.
Store tapes fully wound.
Store tapes at room temperature.
Store tapes in cases.
Store tapes away from any magnetic field.
Transfer your footage every seven years.

stand up to repeated use and have better quality color and sound. However, there are no industry standards for the grades. So, also consider using shorter tapes. Longer tapes tend to be thinner and thus stretch and sag more. Also, consider the tape's coercivity and retentivity ratings. A higher coercivity rating means greater detail and a higher retentivity rating means longer lasting.

Video copies made from the master (original tape) will look almost as good as the master. These are referred to as first-generation copies. A copy made from a first-generation copy is referred to as a second-generation copy, and the quality of the image is greatly reduced. By the third generation, the image is unacceptable. When videos are copied, horizontal lines, called noise, may be recorded onto the new tape. The tracking control on the videocassette recorder has two adjust buttons that can be manipulated to eliminate much of this noise distortion.

Each videocassette tape is equipped with a safety tab on its edge. By breaking off the tab you can protect a cassette from accidentally being erased. Once the tab is removed you will not be able to record onto the tape again unless you cover (i.e., place masking tape over) the hole.

DVD

Digital versatile discs (DVDs) are positioned to replace videotapes, CD-ROMs, and CDs. These CD-sized storage devices hold up to nine hours (17GB) of audio and video. Like audio CD players, only a beam of laser light ever touches the playing surface, so it is virtually indestructible. Its higher resolution means that DVD picture quality is very clean. DVD audio is noise free at digital quality. Key features include: multiple aspect ratios, slow motion (1/2, 1/8, and 1/16 regular speed), eight audio tracks (i.e., eight languages), and 32 subtitles. Interactive menus provide the user with random access to any scene on the disc, along with pan and scan options. Currently, popular movies are being distributed on DVD and it may be awhile before we see a large number of educational products distributed using this format.

Audio and Video Cables and Plugs

Cables connect one piece of equipment to another. Just as there are different types and sizes of light bulbs, there are different types of cables and plugs. Read the manual that comes with your equipment to find out which ones you need. Then, go to an electronics store (i.e., Radio Shack) and ask for that cable and/or plug.

The most common types of audio plugs are XLR, 1/4-inch connectors (called stereo mini plugs), extended mini plugs, and

| Mini Stereo | RCA | XLR |

Figure 3.4   Sample audio connectors.

| BNC | F-connector | S-video |

Figure 3.5   Sample video connectors.

Suggested Videos

Juggling Star (Human Kinetics)
Jump Rope Primer (Human Kinetics)
USTA Backboard Tennis (Human Kinetics)
Step by Step (Human Kinetics)
World of Volleyball (Human Kinetics)
Science and Myths of Tennis (Human Kinetics)
Golf with Al Geiberger (SyberVision)
SportsFigures (ESPN)

Video Reviews: http://clearinghouse.k12.ca.us

RCA connectors (see Figure 3.4). The XLR provides for the best quality of sound. The XLR cable has two inner conductors to carry the signal and a third which serves as the ground. It is typically used with high-quality microphones, mixers, and other audio equipment. The stereo mini plugs are typically used for musical instruments and stereo headphones. The extended mini plugs, which are slightly longer and found on voice-quality microphones, work only in your computer's sound input port. RCA connectors are used with consumer electronic equipment—typically to connect the audio from the videocassette recorder/player to the television or monitor. The ports and plugs are color coded—red is for the right port, black or white is for the left port, and yellow is for video.

The four most common types of video plugs are the F-connector, BNC connector, S-video, and RCA connector (see Figure 3.5). The cable that brings cable television into your home is probably a coaxial cable with F-connectors. Coaxial cables are commonly used with video to shield the signal from airwave interference. Most professional equipment and some equipment used by school districts now employs twist-locking BNC connectors for video. The S-video (compatible with both 7-pin and 4-pin S video plugs) connector is a round plug with several small metal pins. It is required for Super VHS. However, RCA connectors are still the most popular for composite video as well as audio.

Using Video in Physical Education

Broadcasts, video cassettes, and in the future DVDs have many uses in physical education. But they also can be misused—for example, showing videos that you have not previewed, showing videos for an entire instructional period, or providing no interaction with students regarding the video. We will turn our attention to several appropriate uses of video, including its use in providing anticipatory set, demonstrating a concept, modeling a skill, leading a routine, demonstrating strategies, illustrating movement patterns, setting up scenarios, analyzing movement, providing stimuli for mental imaging, assessing student learning, and providing raw material for student projects.

Providing an Anticipatory Set

In exemplary lessons, the teacher begins with an anticipatory set. This serves to motivate students and makes a connection

National Standards for Physical Education

1. Demonstrates competency in many movement forms and proficiency in a few movements forms.
2. Applies movement concepts and principles to the learning and development of motor skills.
3. Exhibits a physically active lifestyle.
4. Achieves and maintains a health-enhancing level of physical fitness.
5. Demonstrates responsible personal and social behavior in physical activity settings.
6. Demonstrates understanding and respect for differences among people in physical activity settings.
7. Understands that physical activity provides opportunities for enjoyment, challenge, self-expression, and social interaction.

between prior instruction and the new learning that is about to take place. The use of video is very appropriate for this task, as the example of the "Takraw" video from the vignette at the beginning of this chapter demonstrates—using the video on "Takraw" serves as a quick and effective way to jump start students' curiosity about the activity.

Demonstrating Concepts

Video has long been used to demonstrate concepts. As you review videos for use in your physical education program, consider how well each video addresses the National Standards for Physical Education. For example, PE-TV, available via instructional television and regular television, provides middle and high school students with fitness concepts related to National Standards 3 and 4 in a visually engaging format. Each segment is 12 minutes long; and there are more than 50 episodes.

The additional modality of visual images helps students understand the concepts and is especially valuable for visual learners. One segment of PE-TV can be shown each week throughout the year, or one segment can be shown each day during a fitness unit. For the elementary level, All Fit (Human Kinetics) provides a nice introduction to fitness areas and concepts.

National Standard 7 includes the subdiscipline of aesthetics. When teaching to this standard, video can be used to show professionals in dance, figure skating, tumbling, skiing, etc. Students who view the tapes can identify aesthetic features and note the elements they find especially meaningful. Videos can be shown in fast and slow motion so students have the opportunity to study each movement.

Two aspects of National Standard 2 deal with student understanding of biomechanic and motor learning concepts. Vic Braden has produced two videos that address these areas at a user friendly level. The first is The Science and Myths of Tennis

Using Video Successfully

1. Preview every program to ensure that the pace, language, and presentation are appropriate. Previewing allows you to identify, in advance, places where the program can be paused for student reflection, discussion, writing, or questions.
2. Have the videotape ready to start at the appropriate spot. Having to spend time searching through the videotape for the correct counter number will cause students to lose interest.
3. Show only the section of a videotape that adds to what is being taught. A well-focused 3-minute segment will have far more impact than a rambling 15-minute segment.
4. Video can be shown to large groups, or to small groups at one station in a circuit.
5. When you show a video to a large class, use a video projector and a large screen.
6. Do not turn out the lights. Students can see the video image clearly with the lights on, and they will be less likely to drift off, get restless, or fall asleep.
7. If you want to use more than one section on a tape, use the tape counter to assign a number to each section so you can fast forward when necessary.
8. Use the pause button when you need time to explain a term or concept.
9. Show some segments twice.
10. Lead a pre-video and post-video discussion.

(Human Kinetics). This video poses 20 commonly asked questions about tennis and then analyzes the answers using statistics, timed experiments, and slow motion graphics. The second video is Motor Learning: Secrets To Learning New Sports Skills (Human Kinetics). This video addresses the science of learning new motor skills in tennis. Both videos target the recreational and amateur player and are very appropriate for middle and high school students.

The historical perspective related to sports is addressed in National Standard 6. There are numerous videos on the Olympics—including highlights and historical events. There also are videos on the history of specific sports such as baseball, and athletes such as Michael Jordan, Wilma Rudolph, Jackie Robinson, and Roberto Clemente. Students learn not only the who, what, where, and when; they also learn the how and the why related to the event.

Showing Model Performances

Model demonstrations can improve learning, especially for those students who are visual learners or who have limited English proficiency. (Such demonstrations can help students develop and demonstrate competency and proficiency addressed in National Standard 1.) It is difficult for teachers to be proficient in all motor skills; a few minutes of video can demonstrate the technique students are to learn. The image not only serves as a substitute for teacher demonstration, but it lets students view the skill in both fast motion and slow motion as many times as they wish. And, you can pause at various points to comment on the critical features of the skill. This is especially important in less traditional activities such as karate, in-line skating, gymnastics, hockey, and mountain biking.

Leading Dance and Aerobic Routines

There are a number of videos on the market that lead students through dance and aerobic routines. Although it is tempting to simply turn these videos on and let the on-screen instructor do the work, it is important to preview the video and select the pieces for each lesson. It also is important to pause when students are having difficulty with a step, or in order to emphasize a particular step or concept. Physical educators also should be alert for contraindicated exercises, especially during aerobic routines. If these exercises are on the video, you will need to pause, explain the problem, and then proceed.

Demonstrating Game Strategies

Video clips of game situations can demonstrate offensive and defensive strategies. By showing a volleyball game in slow motion you can point out how effectively the offensive team fakes a spike or chooses to dink, depending on the defensive setup. There also are special video pens (such as those that come with the Smart Board) with a writing pad that hooks up to a videocassette recorder and monitor. You can write on the pad and superimpose diagrams of plays and formations over a video image. This is especially effective for sports such as football and basketball.

Identifying Movement Patterns

National Standard 2 addresses student understanding of various movement patterns, including foot patterns, pivot patterns, turning patterns, kicking patterns, throwing patterns, and absorption of force. Students must learn to identify movements and categorize them into appropriate patterns. Teachers can use video technology to show teams playing a game, pausing to point out different movement patterns. As the students become more familiar with the patterns, they can watch the game and categorize the movements for themselves. This activity allows students to construct their own meaning from movement and see that learning a new sport is easy, since they have executed the same movement patterns in other sports. This activity also can be used to assess student understanding.

Using Scenarios

In specialty classes such as sports medicine and athletic injuries, videos can be used to demonstrate athletic taping methods and injury analysis. Once students begin to understand injury analysis they can be shown a variety of injuries on video and asked to assess the situation and determine the appropriate action steps to take. Showing the initial accident scene from television shows such as 911 and asking students to assess the situation before showing them the actions of the paramedic can be an effective way to teach problem-solving skills and to assess student understanding.

Analyzing Movement

Viewing video performances can take on a new dimension when the goal is to learn about the science of movement. Analysis of movement requires that motor skills be viewed in slow motion or through the more scientific method of recording displacement. (Displacement is the amount of change in movement from one frame to the next.) Converting displacement to real world units by having an object of known length in the picture allows the viewer to determine the acceleration, velocity, etc., of any object or body part. This provides the viewer with the data necessary to analyze performances and to determine the critical features and biomechanic principles that make certain performances more successful than others. Students can use this method to analyze their own movement and compare it to the model to determine where they need to improve. Chapters 4 and 9 go into more detail on this strategy.

Providing Stimuli for Mental Imagery

The use of mental imagery (visualization) can help improve motor skills. Your mind doesn't know the difference between vividly imaged pictures and reality—it sends one-third of a neuromuscular contraction with either image. Students can observe an expert golfer's perfect form again and again as he or she hits a drive. The students then close their eyes and visualize themselves performing the skill before actually going out to practice it.

Companies such as SyberVision produce videos that demonstrate a model execution of a skill again and again at various speeds and from various angles for just this purpose. Initially, SyberVision focused on tennis and golf, but it has expanded its offerings to include racquetball, bowling, soccer, basketball, riding, baseball, softball, windsurfing, water aerobics, sailing, swimming, aerobics, and bench-stepping.

Administering Tests and Quizzes

You can use video clips during testing periods. Play a sequence of a motor skill and ask students to identify the critical features, errors, and/or biomechanic principles. If a computer is placed near the VCR/monitor, students can rotate in groups of three or four to the testing station and register their responses on the computer.

Creating a Medium for Student Projects

Students can use video clips to create their own projects. By selecting appropriate clips, they communicate their understanding of the critical features or biomechanic principles. For example, a group of students preparing a report on the biomechanical principles of stability can search through a videocassette to find examples from a variety of physical activities. They can develop a presentation for the rest of the class, accessing the appropriate frames to emphasize certain points. Students also can develop presentations using video images they have filmed themselves (see Chapter 4) or secured off the Internet (see Chapters 7 and 8). These images also can be used in multimedia projects (see Chapter 10).

Summary

Although technology is often thought of only as computers, it also includes visuals, audio, and video. Used appropriately, these technologies can add much to the learning process. In addition, they often are more readily available to the physical educator. Remember, the bottom line is the learning process, not the use of technology in and of itself.

Reflection Questions

1. Which of the uses for videotape presented in this chapter would you like to try? Why did you select this method?
2. Think about the last time you showed a videotape in your class, which National Standard for Physical Education were you targeting? How did you prepare your students for the video showing? What kind of follow-up activity did you schedule?

Projects

1. Investigate the sound systems currently available in your school and determine the additional parts required to use one of these systems in your teaching.
2. Contact the publishers of physical education textbooks for review copies. Read, compare, and select one textbook for use with your classes. Provide a rationale for the book selected.

Chapter 4

Capturing Audio and Video Images for Use in Physical Education

Before class, John Washington sets up 10 learning stations that will help his students learn the correct technique for bowling. When class begins, John divides the students into groups of four and has them move from one learning station to the next. In addition to the 6 skill-practice stations, 1 cognitive activity station, and 1 computer station, there also is a station where the students can videotape one another performing the bowling approach and release, and a station where students can review their performance using a videocassette player and monitor. This last station allows the students to immediately see and analyze their performance.

You will find many applications for capturing visual images for use in physical education—the scope is limited only by the limitations of the machine you choose. Digital cameras and video cameras allow you to capture visual images. Camcorders (self-contained video cameras) are especially good instructional aids. They provide students with the opportunity to see themselves in a physical activity, compare their performances to model performances, and create their own video projects. As schools continue their restructuring efforts and place increasing emphasis on process learning, student projects will play an even greater role and visual images will be a key element in these efforts.

This chapter will help you decide which digital camera and camcorder is right for you. I will describe the different types, basic features, and optional features (for those with additional funds). I also will suggest ways to use the images captured with these devices in your physical education class and will offer tips for successful shooting, taping, and reproducing the videos. The integration of video and computers will be addressed in Chapter 10.

Selecting a Digital Camera

Digital cameras differ from traditional cameras in that they don't record images on film. Instead, the images are stored in files of computer data, called pixels. The advantages of a digital camera are that you will never have to purchase film again, pictures are immediately available for use, and the images can be manipulated by your computer. The disadvantages include a reduction in the clarity of the photograph—most digital cameras take pictures from 300,000 pixels to 3.34 megapixels, whereas a 35mm camera takes pictures with 20 million pixels—and a delay after each shot (2.2 to 5.4 seconds) while the camera records and compresses the image.

Storage

Some digital cameras have built-in storage to hold the images. Others use tiny removable memory cards (i.e., SmartMedia, CompactFlash) or regular floppy disks and CD-R for image storage. Built-in storage requires the transfer of images from the camera to the computer—typically via a cable and special

Kid-Proof Camera

Kodak DC5000 comes with 2 megapixel resolution and a 2x optical zoom. It is an all-weather camera that can survive a three-foot drop!

Figure 4.1   You will need a card reader to transfer images from the memory card to your computer.

software on your computer. This can be inconvenient and slow down the process. In addition, if you are away from your computer you are limited in the number of images you can capture.

A floppy disk is very convenient as an image storage device. The floppy disk is removed from the camera and inserted directly into the computer. However, floppy disks are limited to 1.4 MB of storage space, or approximately 20 pictures. To provide greater storage, Sony developed the Mavica MVC-CD1000 which stores images to a 3-inch CD-R.

Most digital cameras today use either the SmartMedia or CompactFlash memory card (see Figure 4.1). The CompactFlash card is the thicker of the two and holds 192-300MB of data. The SmartMedia card is thinner, more vulnerable to damage (don't touch the memory element), and only holds 64MB. Both cards require either a card reader or an adapter (i.e. PC card adapter) in order to transfer the images to the computer.

Viewfinders

You will have a choice of viewfinders when you purchase a digital camera. Some cameras have small glass viewfinders, while others have a color Liquid Crystal Display (LCD) screen that shows you exactly what the lens sees. The LCD screen also lets you review your pictures while in the field—if you don't like the picture you can immediately erase it. This is a definite advantage for physical educators.

Lens

Many digital cameras have a zoom lens. A zoom lens allows you to change the focal length to see larger areas or close ups. A zoom level from 4.4-8.8mm is a good range for general purpose pictures. Optimal zoom uses a higher magnification to enlarge the focal length and enlarge the image. But a digital zoom uses part of the CCD to capture a section and enlarge it as would a magnifying glass. So, be aware that digital zoom sacrifices the resolution of the image in order to zoom in on one part of the image. Also be aware that the focal length of a digital camera is not the same as the focal length of a standard

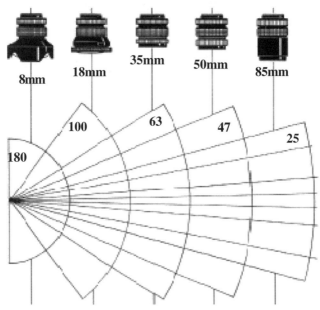

Figure 4.2   You can capture a larger area with a wider lens, but a telephoto lens works best for close ups.

35mm camera. For example, the Canon PowerShot 350 has a 6mm lens, which is the equivalent of a 42mm lens on a standard 35mm camera.

Batteries

Nickel metal hydride (NiMH) or lithium ion (LiOn) batteries are the best for choices for a digital camera. They can be charged at anytime and will last longer. If you use your camera infrequently, then a better choice is alkaline batteries. However, be sure to use an AC adapter when transferring images to your computer.

Digital Imaging Software

Digital imaging software (i.e., Adobe Photoshop Lite) is frequently bundled with the digital camera. Imaging software can greatly improve digital photos by changing colors, increasing sharpness, and replacing unwanted items in a photo. A few keystrokes can crop a photo, remove the red flash spots from someone's eyes, change the brightness, or switch a picture from left to right. The imaging software also can reduce the resolution and color depth for smaller images when posting to the web.

Selecting a Camcorder

As with videocassette recorders, the criteria for purchasing camcorders (see Figure 4.3) include cost, durability, ease of operation, reliability and quality, ease of repair and maintenance, and compatibility between camcorder and videocassette player. Camcorders fall into four major categories: VHS, VHS-C (compact form), 8mm, and digital. VHS camcorders are usually larger (bulkier and heavier), and record onto VHS-formatted videocassettes that are played on a VHS videocassette recorder (VCR). The VHS-C model is a compact version of the VHS format. Both the camcorder and the tape are smaller (about a third the size of regular VHS) and lighter than the VHS, but

Figure 4.3   A camcorder is
ideal for physical education.

there is some loss of quality. In addition, tape length is 40 minutes in standard play (SP) speed, and two hours at lower quality extended play (EP) speed. The VHS-C tape fits into a special adapter for playback on a VHS player. Generally, 8mm camcorders are much lighter (many models weigh less than 1.5 pounds), more compact, easier to use while traveling, and can record 150 minutes in standard play (SP) speed. The cassette is the size of an audio cassette, although it is slightly thicker. The quality of the 8mm picture is almost as good as VHS, and the audio is superior, except for VHS hi-fi models. However, the 8mm cassette cannot play on a VHS videocassette recorder, and therefore most be connected to the VCR via a cable or played in a special 8mm videocassette player.

The VHS, VHS-C, and 8mm recorders are available in a superior quality (S-VHS, S-VHS-C, and Hi8) format that enhances picture sharpness—especially in slow motion—and reduces false color effects and the wavy edges often seen on regular VHS recordings. The super VHS (S-VHS) uses a specially formulated, more expensive tape and superior electronics. The tape records up to 400 lines of resolution, compared to the 240 lines of resolution on the conventional VHS tape. Hi8 (Hi-Band 8mm) offers the same resolution as S-VHS, but Hi8 records with slightly less color noise (unwanted electrical signal that interferes with sound or image), making the picture quality better than the S-VHS. Hi 8 camcorders, like the S-VHS, include S-video jacks for maximum signal transfer quality to a television or an S-VHS VCR. However, most of the Hi8 advantages can be realized through ordinary cables.

Digital camcorders offer superior audio and video quality

compared to their analog counterparts. Using cassettes (digital video cassettes) that are slightly larger than a matchbox, these camcorders record and process information in much the same way as a digital camera. This means there is no film and virtually no loss of picture quality when you transfer the images to your computer. A digital video (DV) cassette tape holds up to 60 minutes of video and audio. Besides high-quality recording, most digital camcorders come with an IEEE1394 (i.link/ FireWire) connection that can send a digital signal directly to your computer.

Parts and Features

The features to consider when purchasing camcorders include weight, good picture quality, good viewfinder placement, power zoom lens, automatic focus, automatic white balance, flying erase head, low-light use, wireless microphone, shutter speed, rechargeable battery, counter, and tripod. There also are optional features to consider, depending on your budget and needs. Once you have selected the features that are important to you, the purchasing department in your school district can provide you with assistance on selecting the specific camcorder.

Weight and picture quality. Determine the acceptable weight and picture quality by experimenting with several camcorders in the store. The camera that feels light enough to carry around for a class period and whose picture looks good enough for the price is the one to buy. Be sure, however, to purchase a camcorder with an electronic image stabilization feature. It keeps track of the image, so it doesn't move—even if the camera does. The dual gyro digital image stabilization adjusts for both up-and-down and side-to-side movement. Be aware that image stabilization works best for distant subjects, and won't compensate for really wild gyrations.

Viewfinder. The viewfinder is the part of the camcorder that you look through when videotaping. It is a tiny television screen that also allows for instant review. A viewfinder that is adjustable for different angles, and that gives users a choice between using the left eye or the right eye is preferred. However, the three- or four-inch viewfinders are ideal for physical education, since students can replay the video in the camera and still see the images clearly. Some of these viewfinders are built-in, while other models have pivoting attachments that allow the monitor to swivel out for viewing.

Zoom lens. The lens should have a motorized, variable-speed zoom feature that moves in and out smoothly. The variable speed allows the user to press hard for a quick zoom in or out, and to reduce the zoom speed to a third by using less pressure. Focus only on the optical zoom ratio (i.e., 12:1) and not the digital zoom. Digital zoom electronically enlarges the central portion of the image by increasing the pixelization, which results in a loss of clarity, so you'll seldom use the digital zoom feature. A wide-angle lens is used for distance shots and a telephoto lens for close-up details (see Figure 4.2). This combination will allow you to capture a full-body shot of an individual performing a skill like a golf swing and then focus in on only the hands.

Automatic focus. The automatic focus feature helps to ensure great photography. However, there are times when the automatic focus may not function properly and should not be used—for example, when you are shooting through dirty glass, the subject has a shiny surface, part of the subject is near and another part is farther away, the subject has distinct horizontal stripes, you are shooting flat subjects such as white walls, no part of the subject is within the focusing zone frame, you are using the macro close-up function, you are shooting fast-moving action, or the lighting is poor. Under these conditions, you will want to switch to manual focus. Look for a camera that has small thumb wheels or rotating lens barrels that let you make subtle adjustments. Some models offer only tiny push buttons that are difficult to tweak accurately.

Automatic white balance. Picture quality and color are controlled by the white balance, which helps to keep colors true under different lighting conditions. An inaccurate white balance can produce a picture that is too pink or too blue. True white will differ, depending on whether you are shooting under regular (incandescent) bulbs, fluorescent light fixtures, outdoors in bright sun, or in some combination of these lighting conditions. White balance can be set automatically (shoot at something white and press "white balance") for easy and accurate use under varying light conditions. However, in certain circumstances the white balance should be set manually for indoor or outdoor use. These include situations where there are different illuminations on the subject and the camera, the subject or camera is in the shade, it is sunrise or sunset, or you are using the macro lens to videotape images at very close range.

Flying erase head. A flying erase head erases the video a split second before new information is recorded, reducing the jerkiness often seen when a new video sequence begins. The flying erase head is standard on most camcorders today.

Low-light use. The amount of light received by the camera is measured in lux (one lux is equal to approximately 10 footcandles), and is determined by a combination of shutter speed and aperture opening. A camcorder with a lux rating of 3-5 (the average indoor room provides 20-40 lux) provides adequate illumination in all but the worst situations. The auto-iris feature, which is found on almost all video cameras, automatically adjusts the lens aperture to optimize the exposure, even when you move from bright to dim areas. Built-in video lights are typically more than adequate to enhance colors and lift shadows in dim areas. Some video lights are programmed to turn on automatically if the available light isn't adequate, making it even more convenient for the user. More lighting can be added by attaching an external light to the camera's hot shoe extension, holding a portable light, or positioning "free standing" lights. If the sun is behind your object, be sure to use the backlight control, which can improve exposure when dark subjects are shot against brighter backgrounds.

Wireless microphone. Wireless camcorder microphone systems allow for cable-free audio recording at distances of up to 200 feet. There are three parts to the microphone system: receiver, transmitter, and microphone. The receiver is mounted on the camcorder's accessory shoe and plugged into the microphone input jack. An earphone or headphone jack on the receiver lets the user monitor the input. A single directional lapel microphone, headset microphone, or handheld microphone is attached to the transmitter and used by the person who is being videotaped. An in use indicator light tells the user when the transmitter and receiver are turned on and ready to go. Without the additional microphone, it is often difficult to hear what is being said through the built-in omnidirectional camcorder microphone. This is especially true in gymnasiums and indoor swimming areas where there are echoes.

Shutter Speed. The normal shutter speed on a camcorder is 30 frames (60 fields) per second; however, cameras can be purchased with variable shutter speeds. High-speed shutters from 2,000 to 10,000 frames per second are great for shooting sporting events and analyzing motor skills, since even small changes in movement can be captured. Be sure you have extra light when using high-speed shutters, as exposure times are very small.

Be aware that some camcorders are described as "high-speed cameras"; however, they are referring to the exposure time (e.g., 1/500th of a second) and not the number of frames per second. Capturing a field in 1/500 of a second ensures that moving objects do not move much as the image is being captured, so there is little or no blurring. But this does not make the camera "high-speed".

Batteries. Portable microphones and cameras use large amounts of electricity (especially if you are using the built-in light), so it is wise to have several rechargeable batteries on hand. NiCd batteries are the most expensive, but they can be recharged many more times, have a greater capacity per charge, and give constant voltage, unlike the less expensive lead-acid batteries. The camera will have some type of low-battery indicator that alerts you when batteries should be changed or an AC adapter used. Some cameras allow for the simultaneous use of the AC adapter while batteries are being charged.

Counter. The counter keeps track of the location of the tape. It can be either a regular number counter, which advances about 4,000 counter units per 30 minutes, or a time-lapse counter, which shows the amount of time (in minutes and seconds) that has elapsed. The reset button sets the counter to 0000, and then any forward movement of the tape increases the number, while any reversal of the tape decreases the number. Both regular and time-lapse counters allow the user to find a particular location on the tape, but the time-lapse counter is more accurate.

Tripod. A tripod is important because it provides a stable base of support for the camera. Several adjustments on the tripod control the movement: Pan control allows the camera to be rotated in a 360-degree circle; tilt control allows the camera to move up and down; and elevation controls allow the tripod's legs to be extended.

Optional Features. If your budget allows, you will want to purchase such additional features as a fade button and a character generator. A fade button allows for a gradual transition from one image to black, and then back to the next image. Character generators superimpose titles, times, and dates on the videotape. These are easy to attach and come with directions for composing titles and other character lines. Some camcorders offer "titlers" that have built-in titles ready to go. When selecting optional features, be sure you understand their purpose. Consider whether you will really use the feature before investing additional money in your purchase.

Successful Videotaping

Ideally, the background should be plain, uncluttered, and in contrast to the subject. Avoid shiny surfaces, which tend to create reflections. At the start of any shoot, assemble the tripod and set it to the correct height by adjusting the elevation controls. Then, connect the camera to the tripod and practice movements using the pan and tilt locks. Always place a blank label on the tape cassette before placing it in the camcorder and title it immediately after filming.

After you place the blank tape in the camcorder, press the play/ record button, and let the tape run for five seconds to ensure that you are past the lead and into the film. Set the standby switch on the camera to on, the white balance switch to automatic, and the focus to automatic. Zoom in on the subject. When you are ready to videotape, press the standby switch again to start the recording. The fast forward switch advances the tape forward quickly, the rewind switch moves the tape backward, the play switch shows what has been taped, and the stop switch literally stops the tape. When you are finished taping, film for an additional five seconds—the next time you videotape, the camera will rewind the tape slightly before recording, and you don't want to lose anything.

Holding the camera steady is vital to the success of filming, which is why a tripod is recommended. If you must hand hold the camera, you should lean against something, or even sit down. Use smooth and slow movements as you follow the action; for the best results, move your whole body. To make an object larger, move closer rather than zooming.

Video stills (such as videotaping a photograph) can make interesting additions to video projects. For example, students can videotape photographs that show the types of sports equipment used in different decades. When videotaping stills, use a box that has a place in the back to hold the photograph and an opening in the front for the camera lens. Put the video camera on a tripod and adjust the height so that the lens is even with the opening. Videotape the photograph for 10 seconds. Unneeded frames can always be cut later during editing.

Reproducing Videos

To copy or edit a tape, connect the camcorder to a videocassette recorder or connect two videocassette recorders together. (At a more sophisticated level, two videocassette recorders can be connected and controlled by an editing controller or a computer.) To connect a camcorder to a videocassette recorder or a videocassette recorder to another videocassette recorder, use two lines of cable with appropriate plugs for your machines. Plug one end of the cable into the camcorder's video output and the other end of the same cable into the videocassette's video input. Then, plug one end of the other cable into the camcorder's audio output and the other end into the videocassette's audio input. Another cable can connect the videocassette recorder to a television or monitor, so that you can watch the video as you record or edit.

Copying Videos

Most videotapes that you purchase are copyrighted, and it is illegal to copy them. However, you may come across some that you may legally copy—such as a video produced by an association to promote a new sport, or a video developed with public funds. To make a copy, place a blank tape in the videocassette recorder and the original tape in the camcorder or the second videocassette recorder. Rewind both tapes to their beginning and set both tape counters to zero. Press the record and play buttons on the videocassette recorder simultaneously and allow it to run for five seconds before pressing the play button on the camcorder (or second videocassette recorder). Once the entire tape has been played and recorded onto the new tape, press the stop button on the camcorder (or second videocassette recorder) and then press the stop button on the videocassette recorder.

Editing Videos

In many cases you will want to edit a video presentation. The manual editing process, which is similar to the copying process, allows you to copy certain portions of the tape into a new sequence. Rewind the original tape to its beginning, and set the counter to zero. As you watch the original tape, record the starting and ending number of each scene you wish to copy, and write with a brief description. Then, note the sequence in which you want the scenes organized in the final tape.

Place a new tape in the videocassette recorder and press the play and record buttons simultaneously, letting the tape run five seconds before pressing the pause button. Advance the original tape to the first scene to be recorded and press the pause button. Pressing both pause buttons simultaneously starts the recording. The pause buttons—not the stop and record buttons—are used because pressing the stop button usually rewinds the tape a short distance. Pressing the pause button, on the other hand, holds the tape in front of the recording heads. A synchro cable can be used to connect the two machines and control the pause function on both machines. This cable eliminates the chance of inadvertently starting one machine before the other.

For some video projects, you may want to add music or change the original audio portion. This can be accomplished easily if your camcorder has an audio dubbing button. Advance the videotape to the location where the audio dubbing will begin and press the pause button. Connect your new audio source and press the audio dubbing button and play button simultaneously to record. Similarly, video dubbing records video without disturbing the existing soundtrack. It allows you to cleanly replace a segment of videotape with a new one, without any lines of distortion. If you plan to do a lot of editing, video and audio dubbing should be two of the most important items you look for when deciding which camcorder to purchase.

Editing machines—either computer-based or stand alone boxes—are available. These devices allow for more professional transitions (fades, wipes, dissolves) between scenes, special effects, and audio/video mixing (fading the sound with the picture or switching in separate audio and video sources). Many editing machines also are capable of placing characters on the screen for titles, dates, and descriptions—replacing machines whose only function is to generate characters. If these devices are available on your campus, they will typically be located in your audiovisual department. Availability of these devices for use in physical education will be determined by your interest in learning to use them, your educational goals for their use, and your rapport with the video instructor. (Chapter 10 goes into more detail on computer-based video editing.)

Camera Care

Cameras require protection from the elements—especially rain, dust, and condensation. Keep a lens cap on the camera when it is not in use, and set the zoom lens to telephoto to prevent the tube from burning out. In addition, never point the camcorder directly at the sun or anything shiny, because this will scar the tube (the part of the camcorder that converts light waves into electrical waves so the image can be recorded). Condensation can be avoided by not breathing on the lens and by keeping the camcorder in a constant temperature. When you are videotaping around a swimming pool, place the camcorder in a tightly closed plastic bag until it warms up. If the camcorder's indicator reads

DEW, it means that so much condensation has built up inside the VHS that it will shut itself off in minutes. The camcorder should not be used for at least an hour after this occurs.

Videotapes also require some special care. Store tapes by standing them on their spine. Never lay a videocassette down on its tape side, since the pull of gravity will cause the tape to stretch. Break off the erasure prevention tab to prevent anyone from inadvertently taping over a previously recorded tape. If you later decide to rerecord on that tape, cover the tab area with a piece of tape.

Uses in Physical Education

You and your students can use digital cameras and camcorders to improve the overall learning environment and process. Student use includes replay of performances, biomechanical analysis, special projects, and documentation of learning. Teacher use includes the development of instructional aids, assistance for substitute teachers, demonstrations of model lessons, and monitoring student behavior. These devices also can help you analyze instructional effectiveness and create professional portfolios, which are described in Chapter 11.

Replaying Performance

Video and still image replay has been shown to be most effective when used with students of at least an advanced beginner skill level. Students need some knowledge of the skill and some viable mental image of it in order to use the information these images provide. Video and still images are especially effective when replayed immediately after the performance, when the teacher provides verbal feedback and cues while replaying the images, and when the performance is shown from at least five different angles (front, back, top, left, and right) including close up shots that focus on specific aspects of a performance

(Rothstein, 1981; Ross, Bird, Doody, & Zoeller, 1985; Darden & Shimon, 2000; Christina & Corcos, 1998; Lee, Swinnen, & Serrien, 1994; Darden, 1999; Doering, 2000). For students with advanced skills, replay also is useful for strategy and tactics. Because advanced movement is so fast and sometimes difficult to analyze at normal speed, slow motion replay and freeze frame capabilities are essential.

After students have had an opportunity to view replays with the teacher, they can capture and review their performances by themselves. Students can use the images to guide changes in their own internal imagery and improve their performance. Be sure to provide task analysis sheets so students can evaluate their performances against a set of criteria. They should focus on one aspect of the skill and, after viewing their performance, spend more time practicing before videotaping themselves again.

To provide for student self-analysis, place the digital camera/ camcorder at one station on a learning circuit. Begin by modeling each phase of the skill while students work in pairs to identify critical features, patterns, and concepts associated with the skill. Students also might draw stick figures to illustrate the different phases of the skill. Then, students should rotate through the stations in groups of four. For example, in a tennis circuit, one group would begin at the digital camera/camcorder station. One person tosses the tennis balls, the second person executes a forehand stroke, the third person acts as the coach, and the fourth person films the skill performance. Each group member is shot executing several forehand strokes. The student-coach uses the first set of columns on the criteria sheet to provide specific feedback. On the rotation after shooting, the students review the images while the next team shags the tennis balls and gets set up for its turn.

The instant replay provides immediate feedback for the performer, who uses the second set of columns on the criteria sheet to assess his or her own performance. The team then moves to the next court, where students practice the forehand stroke while the images of themselves executing the skill are still fresh in their minds. (The images also can be used by the teacher at the end of class to assess student progress.) Self-analysis is even more beneficial to the student than visual replay, since he or she is actively involved in both the performance and feedback stages.

Analyzing Movement

When students capture images of themselves and others practicing a skill, they gain a better understanding of the "why" behind the correct technique. Students compare the performance displayed on a monitor to a model performance displayed on a second monitor in terms of a particular biomechanical principle. For example, while comparing performances on the shot put, students might compare the angle of release or speed of approach. Software programs are available that allow for more detailed biomechanical analysis (see Chapter 9 for more details).

Project-Based Learning

Students can plan, shoot, and edit their own videotapes. Such projects allow students to demonstrate what they have learned about a particular concept. For example, after a unit on movement patterns, assign students to work in groups of four to develop an in-depth video on one particular movement pattern (overhand throw, underhand throw, catch, kick, etc.) The students videotape a description and demonstration of the correct technique for the pattern, explain the reasons for the technique, and then videotape different examples of the pattern. They might go from physical education class to physical education class, videotaping different skills to demonstrate their particular movement pattern. Students filming the overhand movement pattern might film the overhand serve or spike in volleyball, the overhand clear in badminton, and the overhand throw in softball. The students then show their completed projects to the rest of the class.

Another video project involves having students demonstrate their understanding of biomechanical principles. Students select one motor skill and videotape each person in their group as he or she performs it. The students then review the video to determine what was correct or incorrect about their performances, using biomechanical principles to justify their findings. The students then create and record an audio script that summarizes their findings to accompany their video performances, and share their work with the rest of the class.

Other project ideas include videotaping fitness plans developed by students, games created by the students, or demonstrations of rule situations for established sports. For example, cut up the rule sheet for any sport and tape each rule, description, and violation or foul onto a three-by-five-inch card. Again, the students should work in groups of four. One person from each group draws a rule card from the teacher's hand. The instructions for the video project are given verbally as well as posted on a portable dry board for reference. These include:

1. Reenact the foul or violation (create it in a game-like situation).
2. Verbally explain the foul or violation.
3. Demonstrate the penalty for the foul or violation.
4. Verbally explain the penalty and its advantages.

Each group creates their scenario and prepares for the videotaping. The entire class watches each completed video and reviews all the rules.

In specialty classes dealing with such subjects as sports medicine and athletic injuries, students can be videotaped while reenacting situations that resulted in athletic injuries. Students work in groups of four to plan and perform their scenes. One student is the opponent, the second student is the athlete who is injured,

97

the third student is the trainer, and the fourth student videotapes the event. The entire class views the video, discussing the following items: injury procedure, cause of injury, location, signs, assessment questions, and care/taping.

In still another video project, students might design a rehabilitation program for an athletic injury in a sport of choice. After learning about the therapeutic modalities and the therapeutic process of sport rehabilitation, groups of four use the following criteria to design their rehabilitation program: one of the three injury phases (acute, subacute, or chronic), warm-up exercises, stretching exercises, cardiorespiratory activities, strength training, sport specific drills, and a cool down. Again, the students critique each group's video using a criteria sheet based on the elements listed above.

Documenting Learning

Videotape is a relatively permanent media on which to record data. Students can capture images of themselves performing selected skills at the beginning of an instructional unit, midway through the unit, and at the end of the unit. (Use a separate videotape for each student.) At the end of the unit, students can quickly observe their performance and growth. Instructors can ask the students to write a reflection piece about their progress. For instructors with access to a computer with audio/video capture capabilities, these video clips can be digitized and stored on a Zip disk, CD-recordable, or CD-rewritable (see Chapter 10 for more details).

Developing Instructional Materials

Many of the preceding examples used either visual images or video images to meet the learning objectives. In this example, still images are used exclusively to model performance for task cards or reciprocal feedback sheets. Use your students as models for these materials—using instructional materials that include images of their friends is a great motivator! These same images can be included in newsletters that are distributed throughout the community or sent home to parents.

Assisting Substitute Teachers

You can prepare videotaped lessons of yourself for use when you are absent. State your expectations for the class, give a lecture, provide students with motivation, and give specific directions. The substitute teacher plays the video, and there is little question what the lesson involves because you have given the directions yourself. (You might even provide your substitute teacher with a list of student names accompanied by photos.) You may, at times, also choose to use the video to explain a series of steps to the students when you are in the classroom. This protocol allows you to rotate from student to student to ensure that they are following the directions correctly.

Demonstrating Model Lessons

While you may be unable to leave your classes to view outstanding teachers demonstrating model lessons, you might persuade them to have their lessons videotaped by a student or another teacher. You can start and stop the video as needed, or replay particular portions to better understand how outstanding teachers handle certain situations.

Monitoring Student Behavior

Using videos to monitor student behavior allows teachers, parents, and students to see what actually occurred during class. This eliminates unnecessary discussion about what students did or did not do during the lesson. It is a good idea to get parental permission before using this particular

Parent Permission Form for Videotaping

Dear Mr. Garcia,

This year I am participating in the Orange County Physical Education Leadership Academy. This learning experienced is sponsored by the Orange County Department of Education and the California Technology Assistance Project. The goal of the project is to enhance the teaching of physical education through the use of technology.

As part of my professional portfolio, I will be preparing short videotapes of the lessons I teach in your child's class. Although the videotape will involve both myself and students, the primary focus is on my teaching. In the course of taping however, your child may be filmed. These videotapes will be shared with other physical educators, both within and outside the Orange County Physical Education Leadership Academy setting. If, for any reason, you do not wish your child to be involved, please let me know by October 15.

Sincerely,

Mrs. Washington
Physical Educator

Please sign and return this form to indicate your wishes regarding your child's participation in this project.

____ I give my permission for my child to be videotaped.

____ I do not wish to have my child videotaped.

Name of student_____

Signature of parent _____

Date: _____

strategy. In addition, be sure to secure written parental permission before showing a video of a student outside the class. A sample letter is provided for your use (see highlight box on page 100).

Summary

Digital cameras and camcorders are effective for both instruction and assessment. They provide feedback and allow for analysis of movement and documentation of student learning. Digital cameras allow teachers to create instructional materials, and camcorders can help improve teacher effectiveness. Teachers can view tapes of effective teachers, they can create videos to assist substitute teachers, and they can use videos to monitor student behavior. The quality of both still and video images will continue to improve during the next several years, and their availability on school campuses will continue to increase. As "technology money" funnels its way into schools, consider purchasing video technology as well as computer technology for use in your physical education program.

Reflection Questions

1. Envision the last time you used a digital camera or camcorder in your teaching. Which of the standards were you addressing? What was your strategy? What was the impact on your students?
2. Several ideas were presented on how to use video technology in physical education. What other ways can you think of to use video technology in your classes?

Projects

1. Make a list of the features you would like on your next digital video camcorder. Then, peruse a catalog for cameras that fit your criteria. Finally, go on the Internet and compare reviews of these cameras.

2. Design a video-based learning project for your students. Identify the standard(s) you are addressing, the instructional strategies you will utilize, and how you will assess your students.

Chapter 5

Devices

The physical education department at Montebello Intermediate School has developed a fitness/wellness lab in an effort to motivate its students to assume a physically active lifestyle. It contains a cardiorespiratory circuit (consisting of rowing machines, stairsteppers and climbers, ergometers, recumbent cycles, steps, trampolines, and a treadmill), a strength circuit, a table center (for reading, writing, and art projects), and a computer lab (six Macintosh computers). Staff members schedule the facility so that all classes can take advantage of it. During their time in the lab, students rotate from the cardiorespiratory circuit where they wear heart monitors, to the computer lab where they upload their heart monitor data and update their electronic portfolios, to the strength circuit where they work on muscular strength and endurance, to the table center where they work on creating week-long fitness plans.

In the subdisciplines of exercise physiology, motor learning, and biomechanics, several low-end models of sophisticated machinery have brought a new dimension to the K-12 setting. Aerobic equipment, timing devices, measuring devices, positioning devices, spirometers and peak flow meters, electronic blood pressure devices, body composition analyzers, and heart monitors provide students with hands-on learning opportunities. Although these devices aren't always as sophisticated or expensive as models used in university and research settings, they do help students learn about the relationship between bodily functions, movement patterns, exercise, and success in physical activities.

How To Grow a Fitness Lab
Contributed by Scott Bowman

Step 1: Answer these questions

Is the lab going to be portable or a permanent facility?
Is the lab going to be used daily, weekly, or monthly?
What fitness program(s) do you want to provide for your students?
How many phases will it take to build the lab?
What resources do you need?

Step 2: Secure funding

Contact local exercise clubs, tell them your goal, and ask for their support in the form of dumbbells, free weights, and exercise machine donations.
Contact local business groups that might be involved in fitness and ask for their support.
Put together a parent newsletter and tell parents of your goal and ask for their support.
Look for grants that are offered in any area that would fit with lifelong fitness, at-risk students, or technology.

Step 3: Choose equipment

Purchase equipment that can be used by a large number of students.
Purchase equipment that is sized for your students.
Develop your lab around a circuit program.
Purchase equipment with as few moving pieces as possible.
Save top-end items for your second or third phase.

Step 4: Implement your program

Develop a three-year plan that will allow you to grow slowly.
Do not let "No" bother you; it is just an invitation to try somewhere else.
Get your entire school population involved.
Ask for media coverage for your program.
Do not give up.

Aerobic Equipment

The range of aerobic equipment that is available to schools continues to expand. Today we see treadmills, stationary bicycles, ergometers, rowers, stair climbers, cross-country ski simulators, striders, treadwalls, and downhill skiers in secondary school settings. Treadmills require the highest rate of energy expenditure, followed by cross-country skiers, rowers, and stair steppers (Zeni, Hoffman, & Clifford, 1996). However, most physical education departments purchase a variety of devices in order to motivate students to participate in aerobic activity.

When purchasing equipment, look for durability and safety features. For example, the more gadgets there are on a piece of equipment, the greater the possibility for breakdowns. Flywheels should be enclosed to prevent harm to fingers or damage from pencils or other foreign objects.

Videos provide a sense of realism for some pieces of exercise equipment. For example, cross-country ski videos place the user right on the trail, gliding over the snow with the real motion of cross-country skiing. Hiking videos provide added realism for steppers and stair climbing machines. A pleasant ride in the country along with comments on the scenic route provide the stationary bike user with a feeling of being an active participant in a cross-country bicycling tour. Rowing videos "put" the user in the bow, with Olympic team members in the front seats. Country Technology carries a variety of this type of videos.

Exercise equipment with an RS 232 interface provides users with the option of connecting to a personal computer. UltraCoach, a popular Windows-based interface software for running, swimming, and bicycling, records all of the user's workout data in real time, including heart rate, time, speed, and grade changes. It generates a detailed report that includes three-dimensional graphs showing heart rate distribution curves. Using an analysis feature, the software can prescribe new workouts based on past performance.

For those users of equipment without the RS 232 interface, the Computer Athlete (Computer Athlete) provides an easy-to-use interface between various types of exercise equipment and a Windows-based computer. The Computer Athlete consists of software, a motion detector, and a cable that connects the motion detector to the PC. The motion detector is positioned to monitor foot movement for bicycling and treadmill performance. The faster the feet move, the faster the motion on the computer screen. Interactive games are available with the software to provide motivation for using the equipment.

Before selecting any equipment, develop a layout plan for your fitness center. Consider good ventilation for the machines, adequate on-off access space, pathways for rotation from one piece of equipment to another, and safety considerations. It also is a good idea to visit schools where fitness centers already exist. Find out which pieces of equipment and which brands hold up best with daily use by teenagers. Or, go online and research various types of equipment. Busy Body Online (see Appendix A) is especially helpful at assessing various levels of exercise equipment.

Aerobic exercise equipment can be used in several ways:

1. The equipment is set up in a circuit and students rotate from one apparatus to another, maintaining their target heart rate for a period of time.
2. Students select one piece of equipment and exercise exclusively on that apparatus while maintaining their target heart rates.
3. Several circuits (computer, aerobic equipment, strength equipment) are set up and students rotate through each circuit, maintaining their target heart rate while in the aerobic circuit.
4. Students collect heart rate data while exercising on different pieces of aerobic equipment and write a comparison essay for homework.

Now, let's take a look at some special requirements for each type of equipment.

Treadmills

A treadmill (see Figure 5.1) is a wide belt stretched over a flat bed and around two or more rollers. Some units are powered by the users, others are motor driven. Treadmills are specifically designed for walking, jogging, or running, so it is important to purchase the one best suited for the needs of your students. When selecting a treadmill for educational purposes, pick one that is simple and easy to use, with a solid carbon or steel frame and all steel rollers for easy rolling, less slippage, and fewer maintenance problems. If students will use the machine, be sure to select a treadmill with handrails for safety. For the preferred motor-driven treadmills, 1.75-2.0 horsepower, for a maximum speed of 11 miles per hour with a maximum elevation of 15 percent with five increments is recommended. When considering horsepower, check whether it is a peak horsepower rating or a continuous horsepower rating. Neither one is better, but they can't be compared. In other words, a 2.0 horsepower peak duty motor may or may not be better than 1.5 horsepower continuous duty motor. As a general rule, as you go up in price you will get a larger, more sturdy treadmill, a maintenance free deck, and more pre-programmed interactive features.

Most treadmills come with easy-to-reach control panels that display heart rate, speed, and distance covered. Optional display features include exercise time, aerobic points, incline controls, and a variety of exercise modes (i.e., warm up, cool down, endurance, interval, cardiovascular, fat burn) that cause the treadmill to automatically adjust its incline and speed. A flat bed with more cushioning will reduce the impact shock to bones, joints, and muscles. Treadmills that incorporate upper body workouts also are available, but most users find the arm motion to be uncomfortable.

Figure 5.1   Treadmill   Figure 5.2   Exercise bicycle

Treadwalls

Treadwalls are essentially vertical treadmills. They are rock climbing simulations, and there are no electrical motors or parts that will need to be replaced. Treadwalls typically feature a 20-foot climbing surface that moves by body weight alone. As climbers move "up," the wall moves down along a continuous track. When the climbers stop, the wall stops as well. The braking system ensures that climbers are always in control, keeping them no more than 2 1/2 feet off the floor. Movable hand and foot holds and incline-adjustable wall angles accommodate varied fitness levels. The climbometer displays pertinent workout data such as distance climbed, time elapsed, and calories burned.

Exercise Bicycles

Exercise bicycles (see Figure 5.2) come in a variety of models, including ergometer, recumbent, and gravity bikes. True ergometers are unique in that they accurately measure the true power in watts being produced by the user. Recumbent bikes place the user in a position to maximize cardiorespiratory benefits while preventing lower back pain; they are ideal for those recovering from injuries. Gravity bikes—also known as riders—provide both upper body and lower body aerobic workouts. To use a gravity bike, you push with both feet as you pull on the handlebars. Resistance is controlled by adjusting a shock absorber-like cylinder, adding weights, repositioning feet to higher foot pegs, or adjusting the height of the handlebars.

Special features to look for in exercise bicycles include comfortable, wide, and adjustable seats; galvanized steel construction to prevent rusting; and an LCD (liquid crystal display) readout display showing pulse, revolutions per minute (RPM), calories burned, time elapsed, speed, and distance. Some models come with a variety of programs that include flat paths, hill-climbing challenges, and assessments of users' Max VO2 and fitness levels. The ergometer automatically adjusts the pedal resistance depending on the incline of the path and the user's heart rate.

Rowing Machines

Rowing machines simulate the action of rowing, providing a workout for both the abdominals and the back. When selecting a rowing machine, look for a smooth gliding seat and a sturdy glide rail that adjusts to the length of the user's legs. Silent magnetic resistance adds to the cost but is worth it if you prefer a quieter workout environment.

Special options include monitors that display elapsed time, strokes, workload, distance, calories burned, heart rate, and a fitness score at the end of each workout. Preset programs are included in several models that adjust the resistance based on the user's heart rate and the course selected. Rowers equipped with an RS 232 interface can be connected to a personal computer to keep performance records or for racing. The Concept II Rower provides racing options for up to 128 rowers configured as singles, doubles, fours, or eights. The monitor displays the position of 10 different boats simultaneously. Races can be conducted over distance or time. The software detects false starts and displays average pace, current pace, and projected finish. Using an optional attachment, rowers also can be connected to the Internet for races across the country.

Steppers

Steppers are designed to simulate hiking. Resistance options include air, electromagnetic, and friction brake cable drive. Air resistance, which increases as the speed increases, makes the workout more efficient. However, electromagnetic resistance provide users with the option of selecting a preset program or designing their own programs. Pedal resistance can be adjusted to simulate various inclines or to keep the heart rate in the fat-burning zone.

Optional features include oversized pedals and an advanced display. The oversized pedals provide comfort and safer motion. The advanced display includes elapsed time with alarm, bar graph showing steps per minute, total calorie consumption, and a five-second scan feature.

Stair Climbers

Stair climbers go one step farther than steppers by providing for an upper body workout as well as a lower body workout. The best climbers keep your feet on an even plane with the floor at all times, maintaining a totally natural foot articulation. Some machines prevent extreme foot flexion without keeping their steps completely horizontal. When purchasing a climber, look for sturdy handrails to aid balance, electronic programs, and easy-to-use resistance settings.

Ski Machines

Ski machines offer all the benefits of cross-country skiing— the poling motion builds upper body strength, the leg motion builds leg and lower back strength, and the combined motions provide a cardiorespiratory workout. NordicTrack introduced the first ski simulators in the mid '70s, and now many other

110

Customized Data Cards

Designed to work with fitness equipment, a user inserts his or her personal data card into a machine and it instantly inputs a personal profile and desired workout.

companies also offer ski machines. There are basically two types of ski machines: independent leg motion and dependent leg motion. The former is harder to master but offers a better workout; dependent models typically cost more. Worthwhile features on ski machines include an easy-to-use LCD monitor that performs a number of functions, a variety incline feature to increase front thigh workout, and preset resistance settings. Most ski machines fold for easy storage, and some have wheels for easy movement.

Downhill Skiers

A relatively new piece of exercise equipment, the Skier's Edge simulates downhill skiing. It strengthens the exact muscles used when skiing and provides a cardiorespiratory workout. Burning 800 calories per hour while improving rhythm, timing, balance, stance, and edging for skiing as well as tennis, racquetball, running, cycling, basketball, football, soccer, hockey, golf, and water skiing makes this device attractive for many users. With 13 different resistance settings, it is designed to accommodate skiers of all ages and skill levels. In 20 minutes, the user can make 1,800 turns simulating 5 to 10 challenging downhill runs. Optional features include the Black Diamond™ one-foot carriage that provides an intense workout for one leg at a time and the Assistant Coach™, a bar to hold onto instead of ski poles.

Striders

Striders are an offshoot of the ski simulators that move legs in a scissors-like motion. This provides for a lower body workout but does little for the upper body, since the hands grasp a stationary rail. Nevertheless, striders do provide a zero-impact aerobic workout when used on a regular basis.

Timing/Speed Devices

Printout stopwatches that store times and numbers for 100 to 10,000 runners (depending on the model) are used by most cross-country coaches. They also can benefit the physical educator because they print out completion times and give split times, lap times, accumulated elapsed times, and split-lap numbers to 99 places. These types of data can be very motivational for students. Several models have computer interfaces so that lane, place, and time data can be transferred to a computer. Other models have a 10-lane feature that allows for simultaneous timing of up to 10 lanes.

Sports radar guns are affordable and portable speed measuring devices that can be used with individuals and manipulatives (balls, bats, racquets). The continuous-on or trigger activation lets you select the data you want to collect. A beeper sounds with every new speed measured, and a large digital readout clock shows you the speed in one-mile-per-hour increments. You and your students can use the sports radar gun in many ways, including the following:

1. Compare running speed to jumping distance as students participate in the running long jump.
2. Compare running speed to throwing distance as students participate in the softball throw.
3. Compare running speed to vertical jumping height.
4. Compare running speed to high jump score.
5. Compare throwing speed to upper body strength.

Multi-Task Monitor

Mini Mitter 2000 (Mini Mitter Co.) collects data on temperature, activity level, ambient light, and heart rate over several weeks. Plus, you can transfers data to a PC for long-term storage.

Activity Monitors

Elementary school children should accumulate at least 30-60 minutes of age appropriate physical activity on all, or most days of the week (COPEC, 1998). Accelerometers are electronic devices used to measure the quantity and intensity of movement. Several studies have shown accelerometers to be valid and reliable in a variety of lab and field settings with children and adults (Welk & Corbin, 1995; Epstein et al., 1996; Sallis et al., 1993; Janz, Witt & Mahoney, 1995; Simons-Morton, Taylor, & Wei Huang, 1994; Janz, 1994; Freeson, 1991; Trost, Ward & Burke, 1998; Eston et al., 1998). Ernst (2000) has concluded that "accelerometers are generally considered objective, valid, and reliable."

Accelerometers are typically attached at the waist of the user. They contain a motion sensor and a very small computer programmed to convert acceleration to activity counts or energy expenditure (kcal). Depending on its design, the sensor can measure acceleration in one plane or three-dimensionally.

The CalTrac is considered one of the more popular accelerometers and is used in the K-12 setting. Its reliability and validity have been reported in several studies (Meijer, Klass, Westerter, & Foppe, 1989; Simons-Morton, Taylor & Huang, 1994; Sallis, Buono, Carlson & Nelson, 1990; Pambianco, Wing

Figure 5.3   CalTrac

Companies Distributing Devices for Physical Education

Country Technology
Creative Health Products

& Robertson, 1990). The CalTrac fits on your waistband and calculates the number of calories that you expend throughout the day. You also can program it for basal metabolic rate and calorie input. Although the CalTrac is primarily designed for recording horizontal movement, it has a feature that allows the user to program it for a pedaling (bicycling) or a weight lifting mode. At the conclusion of a collection period, the user can access a visual display of information in a number of ways, including total calories expended, activity calories expended, and net calories.

The Computer Science and Applications, Inc. (CSA) accelerometer is another popular uniaxial (horizontal motion) accelerometer. The added feature of the CSA is time-sampling capability, allowing movement to be recorded at 5-, 10-, or 60-second intervals. This additional data provides a chronological record of frequency, duration, and intensity of movement. The CSA monitor has been validated for children performing activities including treadmill, walking, jogging, catching a ball, playing hopscotch, and sitting (Eston, Rowland & Ingledew, 1998; Dale, Corbin & Dale, 2000; Nichols, Morgan, Chabot, Sallis & Calfas 2000; Melanson & Freedson, 1994; Janz, 1994; Janz et al., 1995).

The TriTac (Welk & Corbin, 1995; Freedson, 1991) provides an example of an accelerometer that collects movement data in three planes instead of one. It calculates a composite score based on the movement from all three planes. This device also has the capability of storing movement information on a minute-by-minute basis.

114

Pedometers

The first pedometer was designed more than 500 years ago by Leonardo DaVinci (Montoye et al., 1996). Pedometers provide an objective indicator of step counts that can be converted into distance and calorie expenditure. They possess similar benefits and weaknesses to motion sensors but with less accuracy and precision. The Fitness Walker Pedometer, with an automatic stride adjustment and three button operation for pedometer, odometer, and stopwatch ,has been identified as one of the most accurate pedometers (Dale, Corbin & Dale, 2000).

When purchasing a pedometer, look for devices that accept height and weight data along with separate stride length distances for walking and running. They also should adjust automatically for walking or running. The average pedometer records and displays the number of steps and the distance covered. Above-average models also record time, speed, and calories expended. More sophisticated models accept resting heart rate and age data to determine heart rate target zone, and they monitor and display pulse rate. There are even models that interface with a personal computer via a serial cable to download data from the workout. The personal computer software then creates detailed reports and graphs showing distance, speed, calories expended, and pulse rate.

Cyclometers are similar to pedometers and are used in conjunction with bicycles to display current speed, average

Figure 5.4   Pedometers

Digital Training Assistant (Physical Genius)

Communicates with a host computer through a programming stand and cable that plugs into the computer's serial port. Users select from a database of over 2500 predefined exercises or create their own. The 4x3.5x1.25 device automatically trains and guides clients through the workout. The unit collects the results of each workout for easy tracking, graphing, and workout modification.

---

speed, maximum speed, time, and distance ridden. A liquid crystal display shows the information in an easily readable format. A sending unit mounted on one of the spokes of the wheel and wired to the mounting bracket on the handlebar keeps track of wheel rotations.

Activity monitors, pedometers, and cyclometers provide feedback and motivation to the students as they walk, run, or cycle. And, students can devise experiments to determine which activity (walking, running, cycling) uses more calories and which has a greater impact on heart rate. The data from these devices also can be used in students' portfolios to demonstrate their participation in physical activity.

Positioning Devices

Global Positioning Systems (GPSs) provide location accuracy up to one meter. A GPS receives transmissions from a group of navigational satellites that orbit the Earth. Each satellite transmits its precise location and the start time of its transmission. The GPS receives the signal and determines the distance between it and the satellite. Once it has computed the range for at least three satellites, its location on Earth can be determined. Several models are capable of downloading and uploading data to a personal computer. Some models also can approximate altitude as well as latitude and longitude. Special features include plotting, navigation, and bearing. Plotting gives

Figure 5.5   GPS

you a map of where you've been; navigation tells you the direction in which you're headed; and bearing tells you your current latitude, longitude, and altitude. GPSs are excellent devices for orienteering, camping, and hiking units.

Spirometers and Peak Flow Meters

Spirometers are instruments that measure forced vital capacity (FVC)—total amount of air an individual is capable of exhaling at one time. Peak Flow Meters (Country Technologies), on the other hand, measure peak expiratory flow (PEF)—the speed of expiration. Spirometers are used to help estimate an individual's cardiorespiratory fitness (some evidence suggests that endurance training may have an effect on altering lung structure, volume, and capacity). Peak flow meters are typically used by individuals with asthma to record respiratory changes over time. Decreases (below 80 percent of normal) in peak flow meter readings can alert both the student and the teacher to pending asthma attacks. Both devices use disposable paper or plastic mouthpieces. The plastic mouthpieces are recommended, since they can be cleaned with bleach and water for reuse and thus are more cost-efficient in the long run.

117

Figure 5.6   Spirometer

Electronic Blood Pressure Machines

Electronic blood pressure machines help students learn about blood pressure. They also can screen to identify students who may have blood pressure problems. Many models allow students to take one another's blood pressure with very little training. The machines run on batteries, and are quite affordable ($60 to $200, depending on the model). Some machines take readings on the index finger; the preferred models employ a cuff around the upper arm and come with either automatic inflation or a manual bulb inflator. The cuff is inflated until the screen displays a reading of 180. The machine then automatically deflates the cuff, reading systolic and diastolic blood pressure as well as pulse rate. The results are held in memory, with blood pressure and pulse readings displayed alternately. A quick release valve purges pressure after measurement for greater comfort.

In addition to the electronic blood pressure devices, there also are blood pressure cuffs that connect, via a serial port, to a personal computer (DOS, Windows, or Macintosh). DynaPulse (Pulse Metric) is an example of this type of system. Inflation occurs via a manual inflation bulb and deflation is via an adjustable valve. The device measures systolic and diastolic pressure and pulse rate in much the same way as the electronic blood pressure devices. The software can detect irregular

118

Figure 5.7   Electronic Blood Pressure Machine

heartbeats and generate unique reports/graphs—systolic pressure, diastolic pressure, pulse, mean arterial pressure, pressure contour of individual heartbeats, statistical analysis, plot distributions using histograms, expansion of a single heartbeat wave, and analysis of detailed cardiorespiratory information.

Body Composition Analyzers

Body composition analyzers allow students to determine their percent body fat. Simply weighing themselves on a scale won't tell them their body composition—for instance, many athletes are heavy because they tend to be muscular, and muscle weighs more than fat, even though their percent body fat is within an acceptable range. There are a variety of devices available that measure body composition—underwater weighing, skinfold, automatic skinfold, infrared technology, and bioelectrical impedance.

The most accurate method of body composition is underwater weighing. Individuals are placed on a scale, asked to exhale to expel the air in their lungs, and submerge. All other methods compare their validity to this standard. However, underwater

119

weighing requires that participants fast for two hours, disrobe, refrain from exercising prior to the measurement, and void within 30 minutes of the test.

Skinfold calipers are the next best method for determining body composition. For people in the 15 to 45 percent body fat range, skinfold calipers are actually as accurate as underwater weighing. For people with less than 15 percent body fat, skinfold measurements are more accurate. Skinfold calipers require no fasting and can be used after exercise. However, taking skinfold measurements requires training and practice on the part of the examiner, and participants may need to disrobe, depending on the measurement sites. When selecting skinfold calipers, consider ease of use, durability, and cost. The Slim Guide, a relatively inexpensive, easy to use, durable, plastic pistol grip and trigger device for the K-12 environment, produces results that are almost as accurate as those of more expensive professional models such as the Lange caliper. The primary disadvantage is that the Slim Guide does not look professional, high tech, or sophisticated.

Automatic skinfold calipers have built-in computers that calculate percent body fat, so you don't have to add up the skinfold measurements and do the calculations. Skinfold caliper computers are preprogrammed, using one of the popular conversion formulas, to automatically display percent body fat after taking a few skinfold readings. The Skyndex™ System I is an excellent example of this type of device.

Infrared technology for determining body composition has demonstrated its accuracy (+-2 percent compared to hydrostatic weighing) in determining percent body fat (Cassady, Nielsen, Janz, Wu, Cook, & Hansen, 1993). Infrared devices do not require fasting or disrobing, and they can be used immediately following an exercise period. The Futrex 5000A Body Composition Analyzer is an example of an infrared technology device. It requests the student's age, gender, current weight, body frame, height, and exercise level. Its wand is placed on the biceps where it beams a harmless infrared light into the arm. An optical sensor measures the amount absorbed. After two measurements, the built-in microcomputer converts the absorption measurement into percent body fat and shows it on the LCD display. Using a built-in printer, the Futrex prints out the student's percent body fat and percent lean body weight. The printout compares the student's current data (percent body fat, age, height, weight, gender) to the National Institutes of Health reference data and generates diet and activity suggestions aimed at improving fitness and reducing health risks. Model 5000A/ZL is the model appropriate for students from age five and above and adults; Model 5000A/WL is for high school wrestlers, students age five and above, and adults; and Model 5000/XL is only for adults age 18 and older.

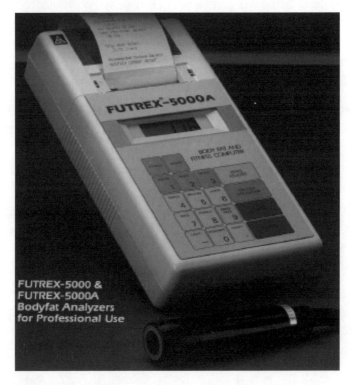

Figure 5.8   Futrex 5000 A

The final category of devices use the bioelectrical impedance method. Measurements are taken between the leg and arm, one foot and the other, and one hand and the other. These devices are based on the fact that lean tissue conducts electricity better than fat does. Leg to arm measurements have a .97 correlation with hydrostatic weighing. Burkett (1994) concluded that, "Bioelectrical impedance analyzers produced values for percent body fat that were acceptable for field testing subjects." Bioelectrical impedance devices require a four to six-hour fast, a two-hour wait after exercise, the removal of stockings, and voiding within 30 minutes of the test. Women cannot be measured prior to or during their menstrual period. Bioelectrical impedance should not be used on children under 10.

Adhesive sensors are applied to the student's hand, wrist, foot, and ankle, or to the wrist and ankle. The internal computer requests the student's gender, age, weight, and height, and then makes 256 measurements, calculates the average, and displays the results in 3-10 seconds. The data include percent body fat, lean weight, fat weight, basal metabolic rate, and total body water.

Tanita is the primary manufacturer of foot-to-foot bioelectrical impedance devices. Looking much like a scale, this battery-operated

Body Composition Analyzers

	Futrex	Bioimpedance
Fasting	No	Yes, 4-6 hrs
Disrobing	No	Yes, no stockings
Following Exercise	Yes	No, 2 hrs
Voiding	No	Yes, 30 minutes
Restrictions	No	Yes, menstrual cycle
Accuracy	Excellent	Excellent
Repeatability	Excellent	Excellent
Possible risks	None	Yes, defibrillator

device estimates body fat by sending a minute electric current up one leg, through the torso, and down the other leg, measuring differences in the body's electrical resistance and displaying the percent body fat. Users stand on the device in bare feet and enter their height, gender, and age. After sending the signal through the body, the built-in computer analyzes the signal, determines percent body fat, and displays the result on the digital readout.

Tanita makes several different models, both for home and institutional use. Some models are specifically for adults, while others are designed for children over the age of 10 and for athletes. The Tanita should not be used by anyone wearing a pacemaker, or by children under the age of 10. Since this is one of the newer devices on the market, more refinements and research are needed to confirm its viability in the educational setting. When compared to underwater weighing, the Tanita consistently has been inaccurate—readings have averaged three percentage points high for men and eight points high for women. However, in one study, the leg-to-leg bioelectrical device demonstrated an overall performance similar to the conventional arm-to-leg devices (Nunez, Gallagher, Visser, Pi-Sunyer, Wang, & Heymsfield, 1997).

Body Logic™ (Omron) is the primary manufacturer in the area of hand-to-hand bioelectrical impedance devices. These one-pound, battery operated devices estimate body fat by sending a minute electrical current up one arm, through the torso, and down the other arm, measuring differences in the body's electrical resistance. Users enter their height, weight, age, and gender. They then press start and hold onto the two handles. Within seven seconds, the built-in computer estimates and displays the percent body fat and body fat weight on its digital readout. Again, this is a newer device and more refinements and research are needed. However, for both the foot-to-foot impedance devices and the hand-to-hand impedance devices, the advantages are their ease of use and speed—two important considerations in the school setting.

Some type of body composition machine should be used during fitness testing at the beginning, middle, and end of the year. At the beginning of the year, students should set goals and develop plans for reducing, maintaining, or increasing their percent body fat. Throughout the school year, they should monitor their body composition, noting changes along with changes in eating and exercise behaviors. At the end of the year, students should be tested to determine whether they met their goal and to set goals for the summer.

Heart Rate Monitors

The goal of any cardiorespiratory workout is to maintain the heart rate in the target range. It is difficult, even for athletes, to count a heart rate that's up to 150 to 160 beats per minute. Pulse meters and heart monitors record heart rate, allowing students to concentrate on their workout while receiving constant updates on their pulse rates. Some monitors can be programmed to beep if the heart rate falls below or rises above the target range. All heart monitors record the heart rate while updating the display every eight seconds, allowing for the irregular rhythm of the human heart.

Heart rates are measured in beats per minute (bpm). Resting heart rate is measured when the student is sitting and relaxed, and it should be around 70 bpm—the lower the number the better. Ideally, the resting heart rate is measured when you first wake up in the morning, before getting out of bed. Maximum heart rate (Max HR) is the fastest your heart can beat for one minute. Maximum heart rate is used when calculating target heart rate. Target heart rate is the beats per minute your heart should be pumping when you are exercising. Historically, the following two calculations have been used to determine target heart rate ranges:

1. (220-age) * .70/.85

2. ((220-age) - resting heart rate) *.60/.80 + resting heart rate In these two calculations (220-age) is used to determine the maximum heart rate. However, there is evidence that maximum heart rate doesn't decrease with age if you exercise regularly. Therefore, some experts use the following formula: 210 - (1/2 age) - (1% body weight) + 4 [for males]

The preferred method of determining maximum heart rate is to participate in maximum heart rate assessment. Although this is usually not possible in a school setting, the "Maximum Heart Rate Assessment - Educational Setting Method" shows an example of one assessment that can be used in a school setting using heart rate monitors.

The .70, .85, .60, and .80 numbers in the calculations refer to percentages of maximum heart rate. Different percentages of maximum heart rate result in different benefits for the body. The "Heart Rate Zone Chart" shows the benefits at each of the various percentages (otherwise known as heart rate zones).

Maximum Heart Rate Assessment – Educational Setting Method

I. Select level of fitness
   Poor shape—has not exercised regularly during the last two months.
   Fair shape—pursues any aerobic activity for 20 minutes at least three times per week.
   Good shape—exercises regularly more than an hour a week, or walks or runs at least five miles a week.
II. Take the one-mile walk test
   The first three laps increase heart rate to a plateau.
   During the fourth lap hold the heart rate steady.
   Determine average heart rate for final lap.
III. Predict Maximum Heart Rate
   Poor shape— add 40 beats per minute.
   Fair shape— add 50 beats per minute.
   Good shape— add 60 beats per minute.

Heart Rate Zones Chart

50-60% of your individual Max HR—here you strengthen your heart and improve muscle mass while you reduce body fat, cholesterol, blood pressure, and your risk for degenerative disease. Your endurance or strength will not improve but it will increase your health. This also is the zone for warming up and cooling down before and after more vigorous zones.

60-70% of your individual Max HR—while still a relatively low level of effort, this zone starts training your body to increase the rate of fat released from the cells to the muscles for fuel. Up to 85 percent of the total calories burned in this zone is fat calories. To burn more total calories, you'll need to exercise for more time in this zone.

70-80% of your individual Max HR—the number and size of your blood vessels actually increase, you step up your lung capacity and respiratory rate, and your heart increases in size and strength so you can exercise longer before becoming fatigued. You're still metabolizing fats and carbohydrates at about a 50-50 rate.

80-90% of your individual Max HR—here you get faster and fitter, increasing your heart rate as you cross from aerobic to anaerobic training.

Now that you have an idea about maximum heart rate and target heart rate, we can explore the different types of devices that monitor beats per minute. There are three basic types of pulse meters or heart monitors, depending on the body site where the monitor attaches. The first type attaches to the hand, the second type to the index finger or earlobe, and the third type attaches to the chest. The first and second types—pulse meters—are inexpensive and use small infrared sensors to detect tiny changes due to the pulsing of the blood through the capillaries. However, head motion and changing light conditions can cause errors in readings, and they are uncomfortable and sometimes interfere with movement.

Even though it is more expensive and requires a little more time to adjust, the third type—the actual heart monitor—is the model of choice for both comfort and accuracy. A strap goes around the chest and holds the transmitter in place to pick up the heart beat (see Figure 5.3). The number of beats per minute is sent to the receiver, which is located in a watch worn on the wrist. The monitor reads the electrical impulses of the heart and provides a very accurate measurement for adults and children (Wajciechowski, Gayle, Andrews, & Dintiman, 1991; Macfarlane, Fogarty, & Hopkins, 1989; Durant et al., 1993; Treiber et al., 1989; Coleman, Saelens, Wiedrich-Smith, Finn & Epstein 1997; Freedson, 1991; Freedson, 1989; DuRant et al., 1993; Janz, 1994; Janz et al., 1992).

Two new features, currently available in Polar's SmartEdge model, are Own Zone and Own Cal. Own Zone calculates the user's best target heart rate zone based on parameters (e.g., current physical condition) programmed into the watch and the characteristics of the heart during warm up, or on age-predicted maximum heart rate. Own Cal is a calorie calculator that bases its results both on the user's programmed data (weight and gender) and on heart rate. This makes it much more accurate than other calorie estimating devices.

Figure 5.9   Heart monitors provide visual feedback of students' heart rates during exercise periods.

Heartalker (New Life Technologies)

This is an EKG-type heart monitor with a strap that goes around the chest. However, instead of a digital readout on a watch unit, a wire goes from the strap to a pair of earphones and the heart rate is heard at regular intervals in the earphones. The unit also announces the elapsed time since the start of the exercise, at 10 minute intervals. Volume and heart rate announcement intervals are adjustable. This particular heart monitor is not susceptible to interference from other equipment or other heart monitors. It comes in two models, with the more expensive model capable of calculating most used target zones (fat burning, stronger heart), providing motivational feedback, and summarizing the workout (total workout time, total time in target zone, and average heart rate).

The long-life lithium batteries used in heart monitors will typically last a year or more. Chest straps should last three to four years with average use. All the sensors—ear lobe, finger, or chest transmitters—will deteriorate over time and will need to be replaced.

If you find you are getting erratic readings, follow these steps to diagnose the problem:

1. Check the hardware to make sure you are using the equipment properly.
2. Try tightening the belt. Friction from even the slightest movement can case erratic readings.
3. Check the environment. Airplanes, cars, some exercise equipment, and electromagnetic waves from computers, power poles, home security systems, and electric fences can cause interference.
4. Check interference from other heart monitors in the vicinity. (The new "coded transmission" available in the high-end Polar heart monitors helps to eliminate the cross-talk from other users of heart rate monitors in close proximity.)

I recommend either the bottom or the top of the heart monitor line (Polar or CardioSport), and in the case of Polar, the Accurex IIa as well. I find that the models in between don't seem to meet the needs of most physical educators . The heart rate monitors at the bottom of the line accurately display the student's heart rate and are relatively inexpensive. The Accurex IIa has the added advantage of providing students with a summary (percent of time above, in, and below heart rate) at the end of the exercise period.

The top-of-the-line models can store heart rate data and, with an interface, rapidly transfer data from the heart monitor to a personal computer. The user places the wrist receiver on the interface unit and launches the transfer of data. The software analyzes the data and can print tables, line graphs, plot graphs, or bar charts. The information can then be printed out and stored. The Polar Training Advisor software also generates training schedules and recommendations based upon the data.

Ideally, every student will wear a heart monitor during physical education class. However, many of us are not able to purchase 20 to 60 heart monitors per teacher—at least not in one year. The next best alternative is to have students share these devices so that they wear one at least once a month. For example, assume a physical education department with four teachers, an average class size of 40, and eight heart monitors. Each teacher would

Caring for Heart Monitor

Don't stretch the electrode strips of the belt, especially when storing.
Keep the elastic chest belt clean by rinsing with a mild soap and water solution.
Lubricate transmitter snaps with silicon lubricant spray to prevent corrosion from moisture and sweat.
Keep all the components of your monitor clean and wipe off any extra moisture. Never store monitor in a closed, non-ventilated container such as a plastic bag or damp workout bag where moisture and humid air can be trapped. Always store the unit in a warm, dry location.

have access to the monitors for one week out of the month. During that time, eight students per day in each class, or 40 students per week, could wear the device. (It is a good idea to purchase two chest straps for each heart monitor to allow cleaning time between each wearing.)

The procedure for using these devices during the instructional period usually follows this sequence:

1. Students are handed a chest strap (with transmitter) before they change. Some departments have students purchase their own chest straps. Chest straps can be washed or disinfected between uses.
2. Distribute a watch to each student and record the number on the watch (permanent marker and nail polish are good for marking receivers).
3. Instruct students to begin recording data.
4. At the end of the period, collect watches and straps or instruct the students to transfer the data to the personal computer on their way into the locker room and then return watches and straps to the physical education office.

Heart Monitors in Sports Medicine Class

At Bell Gardens High School, Polar Vantage Heart Monitors are used during the rehabilitation unit of my sports medicine class. My students become trainers after a semester of learning how to recognize, care for, and treat specific injuries. Groups of four students are assigned to one student in the adapted physical education class. The trainers get to know their physically challenged client's case, and they focus on rehabilitation. A heart monitor is used to assess the client's current cardiorespiratory condition. Students learn how to operate, set, clear and upload the heart monitor data. Clients perform a variety of activities while wearing the heart monitor. The printouts are analyzed by the trainers and discussed with the client. As trainers, their project is to design an appropriate conditioning program for their client.

Carolyn Thompson, 1994 National Secondary Teacher of the Year

Heart rate monitors are most commonly used to help students monitor their heart rate during aerobic activity to ensure that they stay within their target heart rate zone. However, there are many other uses. For example, students might:

1. Compare heart rates during two activities (e.g., football and jump rope), and write an essay stating which activity is more aerobic and why.
2. Analyze their recovery heart rates (how long it takes to return the heart rate to normal after a workout) in order to determine their fitness level.
3. Compare the heart rates of 10 adults, 5 of whom exercise and 5 of whom don't. Calculate over a one-year period how many more times the non-exercisers' hearts beat.
4. Analyze their own heart rate printout for the mile run. (Printout and analysis can then be placed in either a regular portfolio or an electronic portfolio.)
5. Participate in an aerobic circuit while maintaining the same heart rate, and write an essay describing the difference between pieces of exercise equipment.
6. Wear a heart rate monitor for 24 hours and then analyze the printout.
7. Monitor a parent's heart rate for 24 hours and then analyze the printout.
8. Attempt to stay in their heart rate zone without looking at the watch.
9. Participate in interval training. Run 100 yards and wait for heart rate to drop 40 beats, then run another 100 yards. Repeat the process five times. Compare the number of seconds it took for the heart rate to drop 40 beats.
10. Complete a fitness assessment circuit that includes the following stations: blood pressure, curl ups, body composition measurement, spirometer, timed walk for distance wearing pedometer, back saver sit

and reach, peak flow meter, jump rope while wearing heart monitors, heart monitor interface for downloading of data, and push ups. Write an essay describing the current fitness level based on results at each of these stations.

Heart rate printouts from students can benefit physical educators and the physical education program. They provide a visual demonstration of the fact that physical education is a part of the "high-tech" educational system of the 21st century. In addition, they document the structure of the physical education class time for students, teachers, parents, administrators, and school board members.

Comprehensive Systems

Several of the devices mentioned in the previous sections overlap. For example, there are pedometers that also are pulse meters, heart rate monitors with internal stopwatch features, and electronic blood pressure devices that also record pulse rate. There also are some very comprehensive systems on the market that include a variety of assessment tools, software programs, and exercise options. Health First's TriFit is one such program.

TriFit is a modular program, so buyers can purchase one or more pieces. The first category deals with biometrics assessment. Included in this package is the ability to solicit, store, and analyze medical history, height, weight, body mass index, skinfold, impedance, resting blood pressure, heart rate, blood chemistries (total cholesterol, HDL cholesterol, total cholesterol/HDL ratio, LDL, triglycerides, glucose), girth measurements, and hip-to-waist ratio. An IBM compatible 486 computer, Hewlett Packard Deskjet Printer, and Health First TriFit system software provide data on online-biceps strength, hand grip, field tests (pushup, curl up, modified sit and reach, shoulder and trunk rotation, one-mile walk, Cooper run/walk, step test), online-modified sit and reach, online-bike ergometer, and online-treadmill. Several risk factor inventories can be purchased. These include health risk, heart disease risk, cancer risk, diabetes risk, stress risk, depression risk , nutrition habits, safety issues, prevention issues, and general health habits. The software analyzes the data and the results are displayed in a graph format.

Once the assessment is complete, the software can develop a custom program based upon the student's needs, personal objectives, and level of experience. The program consists of templates for body composition and caloric intake goals, cardiovascular fitness, and weight training programs. All programs and exercise calendars can be modified to meet specific goals, and they are based on guidelines from the American College of Sports Medicine. The optional meal planner develops nutritionally sound menus that target composition and caloric goals along with personal preferences. All plans follow the guidelines of the American Dietetic and Diabetic Associations. Built-in meal plan templates include vegetarian, youths under 18, weight loss, and weight training. The program includes an Internet option and a Health First Encyclopedia for researching various topics related to fitness and nutrition.

The TriFit program includes group and statistical report options. This software prints aggregate and statistical results of fitness and health risk appraisal results for any given group. You can compare the aggregate results between two groups or track the progress of a particular group over time. You also can analyze how groups of individuals answered health risk appraisal questions.

A competitive system to consider is MicroFit (MicroFit), although it is more assessment oriented without the educational pieces. MicroFit includes reports for overall wellness, fitness, exercise planning, and nutritional analysis. Specific measurements include body weight, body fat, heart rate, blood pressure, flexibility, strength, cardiovascular endurance, and an additional area for 10 additional test items. It allows the user to conduct a wellness profile (lifestyle behavior analysis) and design a custom exercise program.

Summary

The number of fitness center/labs in middle and high school settings is increasing. This increase, coupled with the increased interest in teaching students basic motor learning, biomechanics, and exercise physiology concepts—as evidenced by the National Standards for Physical Education (NASPE, 1995) and the subsequent publication of Concepts of Physical Education (Mohnsen, 1998)—necessitates new teaching and learning methods. Exercise equipment, heart monitors, electronic blood pressure devices, spirometers, pedometers, and body composition analyzers are but a few of the devices that can help students learn these important concepts and develop and maintain a physically active lifestyle.

Reflection Questions

1. Do you believe that the benefits of the technology devices listed in this chapter justify their cost? Why or why not?
2. Do you think it would be more cost effective to purchase one of the comprehensive fitness systems or the individual pieces that you need for your program? Provide evidence for your answer.

Projects

1. Review the various devices that can supplement a physical fitness unit. Choose the one device that you would most like to have for your program. Write a one-page proposal for your principal, describing why you need this item.
2. Select one type of fitness equipment (i.e., rower, treadmill) that you would like to have for your program. Make a list of the features you would look for when purchasing this item. Go to the Internet, find specific models that meet your criteria, and make a selection.

Chapter 6

Physical Education Productivity Software

Bill Washington comes in from his third period class and sits down at his computer, ready to take full advantage of his conference period. He types in his lesson plans for the next two classes, makes several locker changes, enters grades from last night's homework assignment, and prints out the students' current grades. Then, he begins to prepare the monthly newsletter he sends out to keep parents informed about the activities that are taking place in physical education.

I t takes time to maintain your grades and locker system, and it takes time to do the other tasks that you must attend to each day—time that you could be using to develop new lessons and to work with students. This chapter looks at computer software—specifically, software designed to help you handle your paperwork more efficiently and professionally.

Securing Software

There are three basic types of software: commercial, shareware, and public domain. Commercial software is created and distributed by the company that holds the copyright. The company sells the software directly or through other commercial outlets such as stores or mail-order houses. These programs are copyrighted, so it is illegal to duplicate them and give them away.

Public domain software, on the other hand, is usually developed by someone who develops computer programs as a hobby or by someone who has received a grant. Then, either by choice or as a requirement of the grant, the programmer donates the software to the public. This means the software may legally be copied and shared with others, since the programs are not subject to any copyright restrictions. However, even though the software may not be sold, there is often a charge for the disk itself, the labor involved in copying the program, and the cost for shipping and handling.

Shareware falls somewhere between commercial and public domain software. Shareware is usually developed by part-time programmers who distribute the software freely, using a combination of copyright law and the honor system. You send a fee to the creator if you decide to keep the software. This fee usually entitles you to a copy of the manual or additional directions, and newer versions cost-free or at a reduced price. A couple of good shareware programs you should have are StuffIt Expander for Macintosh, Aladdin Expander for Windows, and GIFConverter (see Chapters 7 and 8).

One variation of shareware is postcardware. Programmers ask that you send them a postcard in lieu of payment, so they can track who is using their software. Another variation is donationware—instead of sending money to the software maker, you're asked to make a donation to a charity.

Two other terms that you may hear are vaporware and demoware. Vaporware is software that has been endlessly talked about and promoted, but never seems to become a reality. Demoware is commercial software you can test with some of its features disabled. This allows you to get a feel for the program, but you must pay to take full advantage of the application.

There is not as much commercial software for physical education as there is for other subject areas. In the late 1980s, the American Alliance for Health, Physical Education, Recreation, and Dance

(AAHPERD) published the "Directory of Computer Software with Application to Sport Science, Health, and Dance" (Baumgartner & Cicciarella, 1987). It listed 208 programs, including shareware and public domain programs written by 75 programmers. Today, you can find shareware and public domain programs on the Internet (see Chapters 7 and 8).

Purchasing/Installation

When purchasing software, you must know how much random access memory (RAM) you have in your computer, and you must know the type and size of your drives (floppy disk, CD-ROM, hard drive). You also need to make sure that you secure the following:

• Macintosh software for Macintosh computers, and Windows software for Windows-based computers. Many programs now come as bi-platform software, which means they will work with both Macintosh and Windows operating systems.

• Software that requires less RAM than your computer has available.

• 3 1/2-inch disks for a 3 1/2-inch floppy disk drive, or CD-ROMs for a CD-ROM drive.

• Software that is compatible with your system software. Some of the newer software will not run with an older operating system (e.g., Windows 3.1), and some older versions of software (designed for Macintosh System 7, for example) will not work with the newer operating system (Macintosh System 8). The system requirements are noted on the packaging.

The majority of software programs now come on CD-ROM with an installation program. The user simply inserts the CD-ROM in the drive, double-clicks on the Installer icon, and the software provides all necessary directions for installation. If an install program is not included, be sure to read the installation directions provided by the publisher.

Purchasing Options for Schools

Publishers frequently offer schools discounts in the form of lab packs, licenses, discounts, and bundles. Lab packs are good for schools interested in buying multiple copies of a program for use in a single computer lab or classroom. A lab pack generally consists of several (5-10) copies of the program and a single set of documentation. It costs considerably less for the entire lab pack than it would cost to purchase an equivalent number of individual software packages.

Another purchasing option is a site license. This is a cost-effective way to acquire programs that are to be used widely throughout a school or district. In granting a site license, a publisher generally gives the licensee the right to make an unlimited number of copies of the program for use within a specific site. The site might be an individual school building, a district, or any other unit that the two parties agree upon. Some companies charge a standard rate for a certain type of site license; others base the price on the number of potential users at the site.

The distribution of software via a local area network (LAN) also is a form of duplication, because the software is available at more than one workstation at a time. Therefore, most networkable versions of programs come with a network license that indicates how the software can be used on the network. Some licenses allow for unlimited use of the program on a single LAN. Others define the number of network users (or workstations) that can have access to the program at any one time. Such limits are enforced by the network management system, which alerts users who attempt to access certain programs when all available copies are in use. Pricing varies, but it tends to be more cost-effective than purchasing an equivalent number of individual copies.

In addition to lab packs and licenses, most educational software companies offer other discounts to organizations that make large purchases. Some companies deduct a percentage of the cost for each order above a certain size, others offer "district memberships" that provide price breaks for participants who order a number of products during a longer period of time. Some larger entities—occasionally including entire states—have been able to negotiate special price breaks from software companies by placing especially large orders, or even by helping with the development of new products. Although individual schools and districts do not have the same buying power as a state, a number have found ways of saving money by joining together to place bulk orders. Most educational software companies are receptive to proposals for affordable ways of making large purchases.

Many educational software companies also offer special discount pricing for bundles of software that include several related titles or a number of programs in a series. Increasingly, we are seeing partnerships between different companies (often including both hardware and software providers) to deliver cost-effective bundles that address specific needs (e.g., web browsing, web site development, middle school education).

Versions

Most software programs are identified by number, and there may be one or two decimal places at the end of the number. These numbers refer to the version of the software. The greater the numeric difference between one version and the next, the more significant the changes in the software. The differences between version 4.0 and 5.0 are tremendous, whereas the difference between 4.01 and 4.02 may only represent the elimination of an error or bug, for example.

Using Software in Physical Education

Software programs to assist physical educators can be grouped into three major categories:

- Integrated packages (word processing, data base, spreadsheet, and mail merge).
- General teacher productivity tools.
- Physical education productivity tools.

The first two subgroups of software are used by all teachers; the last one is used exclusively by physical education teachers. Software contains the directions that tell computers how to perform. Data files hold the information you input. Data files can be saved with special symbols embedded in the text that denote the format provided by the software, or they can be saved as ASCII, or "plain text" files, that eliminate the software-specific symbols and save the information as text only. These data files are easily transferred from one type of operating system to another.

Integrated Packages

Word processing, data base, and spreadsheet programs are sold either as individual applications or as one integrated program (sometimes referred to as a suite when additional software is included). Integrated packages tend to be less sophisticated, but they also are considerably less expensive and easier to use. Therefore, integrated packages are recommended as your first purchase. You can purchase more sophisticated programs as you develop a need for them. Most of the integrated packages are very similar, so the specific package that you buy (i.e., AppleWorks, MicroSoft Works, MicroSoft Office) should be based on cost and what others are using at your school.

Word processing allows the computer to replace the typewriter. Anything that you used to do on a typewriter can now be done on a computer. Similarly, data base programs replace Rolodexes and information files. You can use data base software to enter the information (telephone number, birth date, address, etc.) about a person that used to be placed on a Rolodex card, sort it in any number of ways, and print it out in a variety of formats.

Spreadsheets, in turn, replace ledgers and inventory sheets. Spreadsheets place data in rows and columns, so that calculations can be performed. As soon as a new entry is made, the spreadsheet updates itself and recalculates any parts affected by the change. Many integrated programs also include graphics, desktop publishing, drawing, and painting features. Let's look now at how each of these works in physical education.

Word Processing. Curriculum guides, lesson plans, homework assignments, rule sheets, agendas, contracts, evaluations, worksheets, task cards, letters to parents, minutes, and policies are commonly placed in word processing files (see Figure 6.1). Such information can be updated quickly when it is time to make revisions. No longer do you have to retype entire documents to make a few minor changes. You can now keep your rule sheets up-to-date and change lesson plans at the last minute. Many word processing programs also come with templates (predesigned letters, newsletter, certificates, etc.) that make your job even easier.

Word processing programs allow the user to set margins, spacing, justification, tabs, headers, footers, and character spacing for the entire document or to change the specifications for every word, line, or paragraph. You determine font size and style (e.g., underline, bold, italic), according to preference and what is available on your computer. If, after entering information, you decide that the last paragraph should be the first, you simply select the paragraph, choose "Cut" to place the information on the clipboard (a temporary holding location), reposition the cursor at the location where you want to move the paragraph, and choose "Paste" to complete the move.

Most word processing programs come with spell checkers and grammar tools. Some programs also come with a draw feature that allows you to insert and manipulate lines, polygons, and pictures. High-end features include automatic indexing, a table of contents generator, and a thesaurus. You also can get

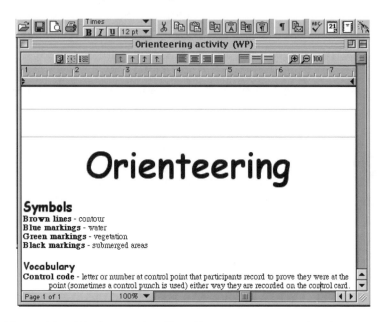

Figure 6.1   Word processing files allow you to create and update documents quickly.

programs, such as Power Translator (Globalink), that translate your word processing document into another language. There are three basic rules to remember when using word processing programs: don't press the return key at the end of each line, put only one space after a period, and don't use the "L" key to make the number 1.

Desktop publishing programs are essentially advanced word processing programs that allow for the more complex integration of text with graphic images. They can create columns, generate tables, create indexes, automatically number pages, flow text automatically from one page to the next, and assemble separate documents quickly. You can import graphics from programs that provide a variety of clip art images, or you can develop your own graphics using drawing or painting programs.

High-quality, royalty free clip art images covering a wide variety of subjects are now available. One exceptional program for

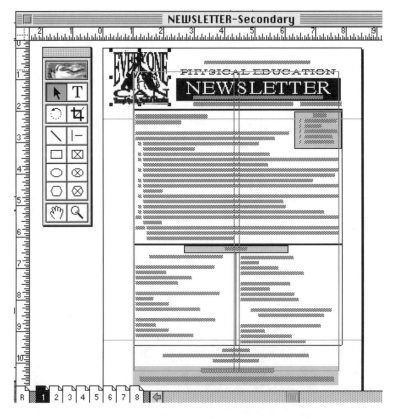

Figure 6.2   Spice up your newsletters with graphics, columns, and multiple typestyles and fonts by using desktop publishing programs.

physical educators is Super Anatomy Collection (TechPool Studio). It contains anatomical images of the human circulatory, skeletal, muscular, digestive, endocrine, reproductive, nervous, and urinary systems. Photographs also can be imported into desktop publishing programs. You can use this software to produce weekly or monthly newsletters (see Figure 6.2), event brochures, task cards, overheads, flyers, certificates, and material for bulletin boards.

Data Base Software.   Data base software is used to organize such information as event schedules, locker assignments, student records, facility schedules, equipment checkout forms, eligibility lists, accident reports, and anything else that would normally be maintained on file cards or in folders. The key benefits of a data base include: reducing data redundancy, saving time locating and updating information, and allowing for comparisons of information across files. Data bases also allow for the creation of a wide variety of reports. A relational data base is like a simple data base, but it can access data from several different data bases at one time. This is possible as long as the data bases are all related by one piece of identical information— such as a student name or number.

A data base consists of fields (spaces in which you insert information) and records (complete sets of fields). The consistency of fields across all records is what allows data bases to quickly arrange (sort) records by one or more field. The record selection feature permits you to specify which records are viewed

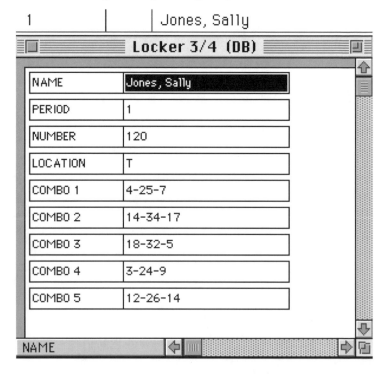

Figure 6.3   A data base view of one record with all of its fields.

NAME	PERIOD	NUMBER	LOCATION	COMBO 1	COMBO 2	COMBO 3	COMBO 4	COMBO 5
Jones, Sally	1	120	T	4-25-7	14-34-17	18-32-5	3-24-9	12-26-14
	2	121	M	8-35-9	9-14-4	15-31-11	12-15-11	18-25-34
	3	122	B	13-27-15	2-19-1	8-29-14	15-31-11	9-30-2
	4	123	T	19-34-7	17-28-9	11-32-8	8-29-14	15-31-11
	5	124	M	5-26-11	11-32-8	3-12-2	11-28-8	4-30-7
	6	125	B	14-28-16	16-38-19	11-39-14	11-39-12	6-26-11
	1	126	T	16-36-19	13-24-8	22-39-26	15-29-17	16-36-1
	2	127	M	11-39-12	7-16-14	10-39-11	20-34-24	25-7-14
	3	128	B	15-29-17	5-26-11	12-26-14	8-31-18	34-17-11
	4	129	T	5-31-11	2-36-9	3-24-9	13-20-9	9-14-8
	5	130	M	9-30-2	9-30-2	18-32-21	19-21-11	12-38-11

Figure 6.4   A data base in list form shows records and fields.

at one time. For example, in a grade 9-12 data base, you may opt to view only those records for grade 10 students. Many inexpensive data bases also have the ability to do some minor calculations. A data base can be viewed in different layouts (see Figures 6.3 and 6.4), and can be printed using a number of different report formats.

Data base software is especially effective in managing locker systems. The data base in Figures 6.3 and 6.4 is based on a system where the lock is built into the locker with five different combination settings that can be changed in sequence. Nine fields are labeled Locker Number, Combination 1, Combination 2, Combination 3, Combination 4, Combination 5, Student Name, Physical Education Period, and Location of Locker (top, middle, or bottom). The locker number, location, and five combinations are keyed in advance, and the locker numbers and current combinations are printed out on labels before the students arrive at school. Student names and periods are entered as the students are assigned their lockers and combinations.

Data bases also can be used to develop and monitor the scope and sequence of curriculum. When curriculum records are kept on a data base, you can access the curriculum information that you need from your own computer. Because the information is stored electronically, schools and districts can share information more easily. On the monitoring side, you can keep track of each student's mastery of standards and more efficiently determine future learning needs.

Mail Merge. The mail merge option, available with many word processing and integrated programs, adds a new dimension to letter writing. Using this feature, you can write one letter and personalize it for a number of recipients (see Figures 6.5a-6.5c). The individualized information is entered as fields in records, either in a data base or a second word processing document. Each record contains the individualized information for one letter. The letter is typed in a word processing program that uses special symbols to tell the computer where to insert the individualized information. By selecting the Print Merge command, you can print out a separate letter for each record in the data base.

Spreadsheets. Budgets, inventories, grades, and attendance records are examples of information that can be monitored using a spreadsheet program. Spreadsheets also are used for logging running mileage, planning progressive resistance training programs, designing interval workouts, and with any other application where the organization of numbers is useful. You can play "what if," using the spreadsheet to determine the implica-

Screen Capture

Macintosh
Press the command key, shift key and the number 3 simultaneously - listen for the click (Macintosh).
The image will save to your hard drive with the name PICTURE X (Macintosh).
    x = number

Windows
Press the Print Screen (PrtSc) button on the top of your keyboard (Windows).
The image saves to the clipboard. Use Edit->Paste in Paint to paste the image and save it (Windows).

File Edit Form Data Report Window
1
Josie Garcia
Rolodex5 (DB)
STUDENT
PARENT
ADDRESS
CITY
TARDIES
Josie Garcia
Juan Garcia
1883 Washington Blvd
Los Angeles, CA 90042
8

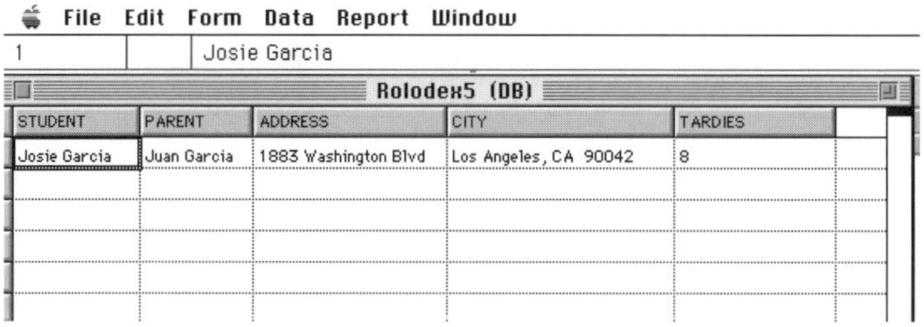

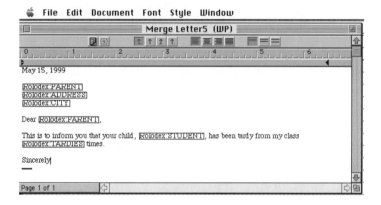

Figure 6.5a Enter selected information on each student into a single file.

File Edit Document Font Style Window
Merge Letter5 (WP)
May 15, 1999
Rolodex:PARENT
Rolodex:ADDRESS
Rolodex:CITY
Dear Rolodex:PARENT,
This is to inform you that your child, Rolodex:STUDENT, has been tardy from my class
Rolodex:TARDIES times.
Sincerely
Page 1 of 1

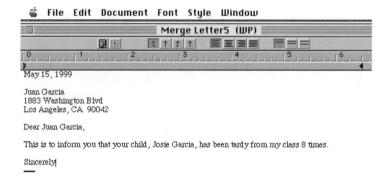

Figure 6.5b Set up your form letter by merging the field titles.

File Edit Document Font Style Window
Merge Letter5 (WP)
May 15, 1999
Juan Garcia
1883 Washington Blvd
Los Angeles, CA 90042
Dear Juan Garcia,
This is to inform you that your child, Josie Garcia, has been tardy from my class 8 times.
Sincerely

Figure 6.5c. Print the merge to save time and effort.

tions of certain changes. For example, with respect to budget, what if the supply account allocation increased, or what if teachers' salaries increased? How would these changes affect the entire physical education budget?

Users often are unsure when to use a spreadsheet and when to use a data base. In fact, as each of these programs matures, the lines do become blurred and sometimes one can replace the other. However, if the fields in a data base contain mostly numbers, then a spreadsheet will probably work better. If a spreadsheet contains more labels and text that requires sorting, a data base probably will be your best choice.

Electronic spreadsheets appear as grids with rows and columns. Each intersection is called a "cell" and is referred to by its column letter and row number. You can type words, numbers, or formulas into the cells. The formulas can include math operators (+, -, *, /) and special operators called "functions." These include Sum. In Cells F2 and F3, both formulas add the numbers in Columns B, C, D, and E. In cell F3, the ":" symbol refers to "through" (in a few spreadsheet programs this symbol is ".."), thus adding numbers in Columns B through E. Other popular functions include Average (which determines the mean for the cells specified), and Count (which determines the number of cells that contain numbers or letters). Functions are always preceded by either "=" or "@", depending on the software package.

Spreadsheets make especially effective electronic roll books. To create an attendance record, list student names in the first column and insert dates as column headings. Type either the number "1" or a letter in the cell (the intersection of student's name and the date) to record an absence. If you use the number 1, the Sum command will give you the total number of absences. If you use a letter, the Count command will give you the total number of absences.

Grades also can be manipulated easily using spreadsheet software. Again, list student names in the first column, with
148

	A	B	C	D	E	F
1	NAME	STANDARD 1	STANDARD 2	STANDARD 4	STANDARD 6	TOTAL
2	Adam, Rick	4	2	4	3	=B2+C2+D2+E2
3	Brown, Sue	3	3	3	2	=Sum(B3:E3)
4	Capps, John	2	2	2	3	=Sum(B4:E4)
5	Dowd, James	3	1	2	2	=Sum(B5:E5)
6	Fischer, Bill	1	3	1	1	=Sum(B6:E6)
7	Leed, Janet	3	2	2	2	=Sum(B7:E7)
8	Moore, Ann	2	3	2	3	=Sum(B8:E8)
9						

Figure 6.6a   A grading file developed using a spreadsheet program, showing students' names and their scores on four assignments or tests. The formula =sum(B2:E2) tells the spreadsheet to add together the scores in Cells B2, C2, D2, and E2 and put the result in F2.

	A	B	C	D	E	F
1	NAME	STANDARD 1	STANDARD 2	STANDARD 4	STANDARD 6	TOTAL
2	Adam, Rick	4	2	4	3	13
3	Brown, Sue	3	3	3	2	11
4	Capps, John	2	2	2	3	9
5	Dowd, James	3	1	2	2	8
6	Fischer, Bill	1	3	1	1	6
7	Leed, Janet	3	2	2	2	9
8	Moore, Ann	2	3	2	3	10
9						

Figure 6.6b   Results of these calculations.

	A	B	C	D	E
1	NAME	LAY UP	DRIBBLE – TIME	DRIBBLE – SCORE	STANDARD 1
2	Brown, Jim	3	15	=Lookup(C2,A8:E8,A9:E9)	=B2+D2
3	Jones, Sally	2	23	=Lookup(C3,A8:E8,A9:E9)	=B3+D3
4	Landon, Tom	2	21	=Lookup(C4,A8:E8,A9:E9)	=B4+D4
5	Smith, Betty	3	14	=Lookup(C5,A8:E8,A9:E9)	=B5+D5
6					
7	DRIBBLE				
8		5	15	20	24	0
9		0	1	2	3	4
10					

Figure 6.7   A more sophisticated grading file developed using a spreadsheet. The formula =Lookup(C2, A8:E8, A9:E9) tells the spreadsheet to look in Row 8 (A8:E8) for the number that is less than or equal to the number in Cell C2 and then return the number to the same column in Row 9 (A9:E9).

assignments and tests as column headings. The last column is the total column, where Sum totals the points. The spreadsheet in Figure 6.6a shows the formulas and the spreadsheet in Figure 6.6b shows the results of the calculations. If you have a more complicated grading system, subtotals (based on the type of grade) can be calculated, different grades can be weighted using multiply (*), or the Average function can be used.

Figure 6.7 shows a more sophisticated grading file that uses the Lookup function to calculate grades based on scores from norm-referenced tests. Set up your grading file as explained previously and establish a norm-referenced table somewhere in the spreadsheet. For example, set up a two-row table in Rows 8 and 9, listing the grades (0, 1, 2, 3, 4 represent F, D, C, B, A) in Row 9 and the corresponding times (in seconds) for a basketball dribble test in Row 8 (see Figure 6.7, Rows 8-9). Then, in the dribble score column (D), use Lookup to tell the spreadsheet to look in Row 8 for the number that is less than or equal to the student's dribble time (found in column C) and return the grade found in the same column in Row 9 (see Figure 6.7).

Inventories (see Figure 6.8) are another way to use spreadsheets in physical education. Label the first column "Equipment," and list storage rooms as other column headings. In the first cell of each row, enter the name of a type of equipment, and in the following cells of that row enter the amount of equipment in each storage room. Enter "Total" as the heading for the last column, and use Sum in each row to add together the amount of each type of equipment in the storage rooms.

A more sophisticated inventory file for equipment (see Figures 6.9a and 6.9b) will tell you when and what you need to reorder. To the inventory file I just described, add a "Number To Order" section. For example, in Rows 11 through 16 under column A, list the equipment that you need to reorder. In Rows 11 through 16 under Column B, use the "If" function to calculate how many pieces of equipment should be reordered. With basketballs, for example, you may want to always have 30 in storage; the If function will compare the number in storage to 30 and determine the difference. If it is less, the spreadsheet calculates and returns that number; otherwise it returns zero.

Many businesses use spreadsheets to maintain budgets, and physical education departments can do so as well. When developing a computerized budget system (see Figure 6.10), you must first determine what is to be monitored, how it is to be accomplished, and how results are to be used. For example, suppose a department chairperson is allocated $1,000 for equipment and $500 for supplies. Each amount is listed as income, and each requisition is listed as an expenditure. By maintaining a total of the expenditures and calculating the difference between the original allocation and the total expenditures, the department chairperson can immediately ascertain the amount still available to spend in each budget category. Since most spreadsheets have graphing capabilities (see Figure 6.11), he or she can depict the type of expenditures in graph form.

Drawing and Painting Software. Drawing and/or painting software often is part of an integrated program. Paint programs allow you to use a variety of tools (pencil, paint brush, paint can) to create images on the screen, pixel by pixel. Advanced painting programs allow the user to integrate all sorts of interesting effects (i.e., gradients, smudges). Drawing programs allow you to create images as objects that can be edited and manipulated. Using either program, you can create diagrams of fields or even simple stick figures that depict various motor skills.

General Teacher Productivity

General teacher productivity software can make any teacher's job, including a physical educator's easier. But, if you don't want to put extra money into the programs in this section,

151

File   Edit   Format   Options   Chart   Window

A1

Inventory 8 (SS)

	A	B	C	D	E	F
1		Storage	Room 1	Room 2	Room 3	Total
2	Basketballs	20	12	0	12	=Sum(B2:E2)
3	Bowling Balls	10	0	15	0	=Sum(B3:E3)
4	Footballs	6	0	0	15	=Sum(B4:E4)
5	Gloves	4	0	40	0	=Sum(B5:E5)
6	Softballs	19	0	30	0	=Sum(B6:E6)
7	Volleyballs	8	10	0	10	=Sum(B7:E7)
8						
9						

Figure 6.8   Inventory developed using a spreadsheet. The formula =Sum(B2:E2) tells the spreadsheet to add together the numbers in Cells B2, C2, D2, and E2.

File   Edit   Format   Options   Chart   Window

A1

Inventory 9 (SS)

	A	B	C	D	E	F
1		Storage	Room 1	Room 2	Room 3	Total
2	Basketballs	20	12	0	12	=Sum(B2:E2)
3	Bowling Balls	10	0	15	0	=Sum(B3:E3)
4	Footballs	6	0	0	15	=Sum(B4:E4)
5	Gloves	4	0	40	0	=Sum(B5:E5)
6	Softballs	19	0	30	0	=Sum(B6:E6)
7	Volleyballs	8	10	0	10	=Sum(B7:E7)
8						
9						
10		Number to Order				
11	Basketballs	=If(F2<30,30-F2,0)				
12	Bowling Balls	=If(F3<12,12-F3,0)				
13	Footballs	=If(F4<30,30-F4,0)				
14	Gloves	=If(F5<50,50-F5,0)				
15	Softballs	=If(F6<60,60-F6,0)				
16	Volleyballs	=If(F7<40,40-F7,0)				

Figure 6.9a.   The addition of the formula =If(F2<30,30-F2,0) tells the spreadsheet to compare the number in Cell F2 to 30 (F2<30) and, if the number in F2 is less than 30, return the difference between 30 and the number in F2 (30-F2). Otherwise, return 0.

Inventory 9 (SS)

	A	B	C	D	E	F
1		Storage	Room 1	Room 2	Room 3	Total
2	Basketballs	20	12	0	12	44
3	Bowling Balls	10	0	15	0	25
4	Footballs	6	0	0	15	21
5	Gloves	4	0	40	0	44
6	Softballs	19	0	30	0	49
7	Volleyballs	8	10	0	10	28
8						
9						
10		Number to Order				
11	Basketballs	0				
12	Bowling Balls	0				
13	Footballs	9				
14	Gloves	6				
15	Softballs	11				
16	Volleyballs	12				

Figure 6.9b   Results of these calculations.

D19

	A	B	C	D
				Budget (SS)
1	EQUIPMENT			1000
2	5/15/99	Gymnastics Mats	500	
3				
4				
5				
6	TOTAL SPENT			=Sum(C2:C5)
7	BALANCE - EQUIPMENT			=D1-D6
8				
9	SUPPLIES			500
10		Basketballs	84	
11		Stop Watches	96	
12				
13				
14				
15	TOTAL SPENT			=Sum(C10:C14)
16	BALANCE - SUPPLIES			=D9-D15
17				

Figure 6.10   This typical physical education budget, produced using a spreadsheet, shows beginning balances, expenses, and remaining balances for equipment and supplies.

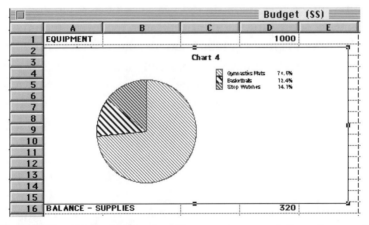

Figure 6.11   Spreadsheets also allow you to create informative graphics that can add perspective to facts and figures.

consider purchasing an integrated program like AppleWorks, which comes with numerous templates and assistants to help you design your own certificates, calendars, brochures, grading reports, lesson plan formats, statistics, banners, presentations, and posters using the tools already available in the program. You also will find several of these programs on the Internet where they can be used for free (see Chapters 7 and 8).

Organizational Programs

Organizational programs such as Inspiration (Inspiration), can help students and teachers organize their thinking. The software allows quick access to concept maps, webs, and other graphic organizers. The integrated outline view enables the user to quickly prioritize and rearrange ideas. Organizational programs are especially effective for brainstorming about future goals and objectives.

Banner and Poster Programs

Bulletin boards are an important element of the classroom and gymnasium environment. In the past, teachers without artistic skills were forced to either cut and paste magazine pictures or purchase commercial bulletin board displays. With a computer, anyone can easily produce professional looking bulletin boards. Several programs (including desktop publishing programs, described earlier in this chapter) can assist with this task; however, there also are specific banner and poster programs, such as Print Shop® (Mattel Interactive) and PrintMaster® (Mattel Interactive).

Certificate Makers

Award 2000 (Baudville) for the Mac and Windows environments makes creating your own certificates and awards a snap. The software contains a border library, pre-written text (or create your own), graphics, and award seals. It also comes with a variety of templates for various achievements. The physical educator selects the appropriate template and enters the appropriate information for each student.

Calendar Programs

Calendar programs can help you and your students create calendars and keep track of projects and activities. Depending on their size, you also can use these programs to keep track of lesson plans. Calendar programs to consider include single function programs such as Now Up To Date (PowerOn Software) or multi-task programs that also feature a calendar program, such as Lotus Notes (Lotus).

Puzzle Programs

Puzzle programs provide you with quick and easy ways to develop crossword puzzles, word searches, and other puzzles that can help students learn. For example, Crossword Magic (Mattel Interactive) is a popular, user-friendly program for making crossword puzzles of any size. The crossword puzzles can be viewed on screen or printed out. Other popular puzzle makers include Crossword Studio (Forest) and Wordsearch Studio (Forest). The word search program allows the user to create word puzzles in a variety of shapes and sizes. The teacher enters the words and/or definitions and the software creates the puzzles.

Testing

Your computer can help you construct written tests by storing and sorting your questions. You have the choice of using a word processing program, a data base program, or a packaged testing program that formats the test for you. Test Designer Supreme (Super School Software) and MicroTest (Chariot) are test generating programs that give you a choice of formats. These include multiple choice, matching, true/false, fill in the blank, puzzle questions (i.e., crossword puzzles and word searches), and short essay. After you have developed a battery of test items within one of these formats, the program will randomly select a desired number of questions based on topic, level of difficulty, and type of question.

FitSmart (Human Kinetics) is a 50-item, multiple-choice test designed to measure high school students' knowledge of basic fitness concepts. It is based on the National Youth Physical Fitness Knowledge Test. Students can take the test online or from a printed form. Either way, the computer can grade the test using a weighted system. It also can convert raw scores to standards scores and provide feedback to students about the test results.

IEP Assistants

IEP Assistant software can help special education teachers, including adapted physical educators, with their paperwork. These programs prompt users for required information and then print out the required forms. Three popular programs are IEP Works Pro (K-12 MicroMedia Publishing), IEP Pro (Chalkware Education Solutions), and IEP Writer Supreme (Super School Software).

IEP Works Pro can help teachers create an IEP in less than 15 minutes. With more than 1,300 goals and objectives, you can easily select those that are appropriate for your students and customize as necessary. IEP state-approved forms for Alabama, California, Connecticut, Florida, Indiana, Maryland, New Jersey, North Carolina, Oregon, Tennessee, Texas, Virginia, and Wisconsin are included.

Created for both the Macintosh and Windows environments, IEP Pro provides most, if not all, the forms needed for the IEP process. But, just in case you need another form, district forms also can be designed using the text formatting and spell check functions in this program. Included in the program is a goals and objectives library that can be searched using key words. These goals and objectives can be linked to the various IEP forms.

The IEP Writer Supreme is similar to IEP Works Pro, but it also includes special education program planning tools, inservice training materials for regular and special education teachers, and diagnostic checklists. Both programs allow data to be saved in a format that facilitates the writing of IEPs in subsequent years.

Electronic Gradebooks

Earlier in this chapter, I showed you how to set up grade files using spreadsheet programs. But you may prefer more user-friendly programs for recording grades. Grading programs prompt you for student names, test/assignment names, and grading practices. Then, you enter the grades and the program calculates the final grade for you. Grading programs also can create and print class lists and blank score sheets and produce progress reports.

There are a wide variety of grading programs on the market for teachers in all areas of the curriculum. Popular desktop grading programs for physical education include Making the Grade (Jay Klein Productions) and Grade Machine (Misty City Software). Popular handheld grading programs for physical education include GradePoint (Sunburst), LearnerProfile (Sunburst), and Palm Record Book (Bonnie's Fitware). Base your selection on the specific features and report formats you need. Just make sure the program you select can handle the number of students you have in each class and the total number of classes you teach.

Making the Grade (Jay Klein) accommodates multiple grading schemes, including points, letters, and symbols. Additional options include tracking attendance and behavior, weighting grades (up to 10 assignment categories), and arranging groups. The program has room for 80 students per class with 320 assignments and 250 days of attendance or behavioral data. All calculations are instantly and automatically updated on the screen. Data can be viewed in numerous formats, including a seating chart. A variety of reports can be generated in English or Spanish.

Grade Machine (Misty City Software), which is designed to

Comparison Criteria for Grading Programs

Customer support
Suitability for physical education
Documentation, tutorial, and online help
Cross-platform compatibility
Number of students per class
Number of assignments per class
Grading periods
Assignment categories
Overall grade summaries
Grading scales
Scoring options
Special scores
Easy score entry
Types of reports
Password protection
Importing and exporting features

look like a grade book, also accommodates multiple grading schemes defined by the teacher, including letter grades and points. Additional options include weighting grades, sorting students, using excused scores for long-term absences or late arrivals, and an automatic backup system. The program has room for 250 students, 250 assignments, 10 weighted categories, and 20 grading periods. Full-screen editing lets you scroll through students, assignments, or scores to enter and edit grades. Grade Machine generates progress reports for individuals, a certain category of students, or an entire class. This software program even allows you to post grades on the Web.

Grade Point (Sunburst), for the Newton Operating System, provides physical educators with a grading program at their fingertips. Similar to the desktop computer grading programs, Grade Point provides an excellent user interface that makes screen choices very intuitive. It lets you enter assignments, assign assignment categories, add grades, or take attendance by tapping or writing on the screen. Tardies are noted by the time

Additional Grading Programs

Teacher's Toolbox (Ablesoft) - provides report card generator, grading, scheduling, seating chart design, attendance monitoring, and student reporting.

GradeBook2 (Excelsior Software) - grade creation wizards allow teachers to establish description and weighting process with predefined templates.

GradeQuick (Jackson Software) - complete grading and attendance options with seating charts.

that the student arrives in class. Both absences and tardies can be marked excused or deleted on screen if there is an error. Student summaries can be viewed on screen and on hard copy in one of four reports: assignment statistics, class averages, missing assignments, and end-of-term report. Grade Point also produces six other hard copy reports: class roster, class grade sheet, notes, student progression reports, assignment statistics, and class average. Final grades are determined either by calculating averages using total points or weighted categories.

Learner Profile (Sunburst), for the Palm Operating System and the Newton Operating System, is an assessment program that allows the user to collect student data. Learner Profile is loaded onto a desktop computer (Macintosh or Windows), and plans for conducting observations are created. You select the standards (observables) and the rubrics (qualifiers). The information is then downloaded to the palm computer (Palm Operating System) or Apple MessagePad, which you use to collect and organize data by tapping the handheld unit's touchscreen. Handwritten notes for unplanned observations can be recorded as well. Data, including attendance and level of competency, are collected simultaneously with learning (embedded assessment) during the instructional period. At the end of the day, the data are uploaded to the desktop computer, where they become part of Learner Profile's data base.

Fifty different reports—including daily attendance, comment list, observation frequency, observation list, observation summary, daily summary, qualifiers by student, and qualifiers by observables—can be printed. This information is used to design appropriate follow-up lessons, identify students who need remediation or enrichment activities, and track student progress.

GradeMaker (Sunburst) for the Macintosh is a companion piece to Learner Profile. Grade Maker allows you to turn Learner Profile observational data into grades by assigning numerical values to Learner Profile qualifiers (for example: Developing = 75, Mastered = 85, Integrating = 95). Grade Maker also can create a wide variety of grade reports organized by students, observables, or date.

Recently on the scene is Palm Record Book (Bonnie's Fitware) which allows for the collection of attendance, behavior, and grading information using the Palm Operating System. The program allows you to enter assignments, categorize assignments according to the standard assessed, weight assignments and standards, record grades, note absences and tardies along with behavior issues, and transfer the data to the computer where it is analyzed. Once analyzed a number of different reports are available for print out.

Physical Education Productivity

Physical education productivity software is specifically designed to simplify many tasks involved in teaching physical education—such as calculating the nutritional values of foods and monitoring fitness scores. Since students typically enter their own eating habits into the computer, nutritional software will be examined in Chapter 9. However, we will look at fitness monitoring software in this section.

Fitness Reports

Fitness reporting programs comprise one of the earliest uses of computers in physical education. These programs analyze raw fitness scores, print summaries, and store data for pre-/post-test comparisons. Fitness reporting programs can follow a student from kindergarten through 12th grade, providing year-to-year comparisons. Raw scores can be analyzed quickly to provide information on student improvement. In addition, class averages for each test item allow you to ascertain if the instructional program is producing the intended learning outcomes. You can easily print a variety of reports, and you can send them home to keep parents up-to-date on their children's progress. Keep in mind, however, that entering data can be very time consuming unless you use some type of scanner or similar input device.

Since the 1980s, a variety of software programs have been developed to monitor physical fitness data. Some of the more popular ones include Fitnessgram (Human Kinetics), Fitness Report (Bonnie's Fitware), and Fitness Reporter (Fitness Reporter). Each program offers unique features. Choose the one that fits your needs, your computer, and the test items to be administered.

Fitnessgram (Human Kinetics). Fitnessgram focuses on health-related fitness, providing users with the option of pacer walk/target heart rate or one-mile run for cardiorespiratory endurance; push ups, pull ups, modified pull ups, or flexed arm hang for upper body strength and endurance; curl ups for abdominal strength and endurance; trunk lifts for lower back strength and flexibility; back saver sit and reach or shoulder stretch for flexibility; and body mass index (calculated from height and weight data) or skinfold measurements (triceps and medial calf) for body composition. Data can be entered by keyboard or scanner, or it can be imported. The program outputs results onto a preprinted student report card with a graph showing which test scores were above or below the criterion level, the actual test score, an individualized exercise prescription for where the student's scores were low, a total fitness index, and a cumulative record of test results.

The program allows for one pre- and one post-test, with both scores written on the second fitnessgram. The back side of the fitness card has space for the student to record out-of-school activity levels. Reports include a class summary by student with test score. Statistics include number of students, mean score, standard deviation, highest score, lowest score, and percentage of students achieving the minimum standard for each test item. The disadvantages of this program are the costs for the cards, even though they are quite attractive, and the complexity of working with the master data base, which requires several steps to locate the class and students whose data you are entering.

Fitness Report (Bonnie's Fitware). Fitness Report (Macintosh or Windows) also focuses on health-related fitness, providing users with the option of pacer, walk/target heart rate, or one-mile run for cardiorespiratory endurance; push ups, pull ups, modified pull ups, or flexed arm hang for upper body strength and endurance; curl ups for abdominal strength and endurance; trunk lift for lower back strength and flexibility; back saver sit and reach or shoulder stretch for flexibility; and body mass index (calculated from height and weight data) or skinfold measurements (triceps and medial calves) for body composition.

Input is by keyboard or through the palm computer (Palm Operating System (see Figure 6.12) or Apple MessagePad (handheld computer). The fitness pre-test printout (see Figure 6.13) shows the pre-test score, minimum standards, whether the student met the minimum standards, and the recommended improvement. It provides space for students to write their own goals for improvement. The fitness post-test printout includes the pre- and post- fitness scores, pre- and post- met or not met,

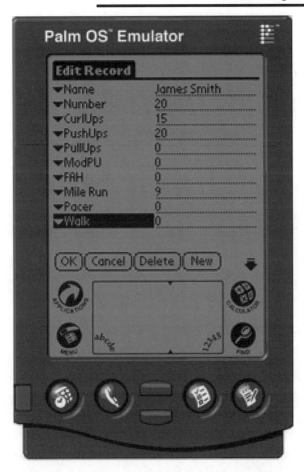

Figure 6.12   Bonnie's Fitware offers the option of collecting fitness scores while still on the field using the palm computer (palm operating system).

and the minimum competency scores. The statistics program includes averages for each test item and the number of students meeting minimum standards on 6 out of 6, 5 out of 6, 4 out of 6, 3 out of 6, 2 out of 6, 1 out of 6, and 0 out of 6 test items. Reports that list class summary by students and scores also are available.

Fitness Reporter (Fitness Reporter). Fitness Reporter focuses on health-related fitness, providing users with test items from both the Fitnessgram and the President's Challenge (President's

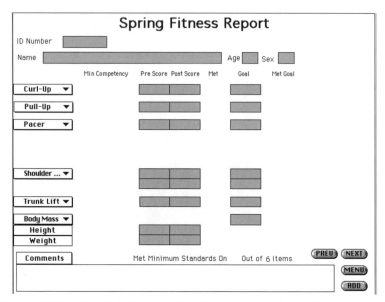

Figure 6.13   Bonnie's Fitware offers fitness reports for goal setting at the start of the school year (see above) and reports that include pre-test and post-test scores for the end of the school year.

Council on Physical Fitness). Input is via a keyboard, using data collected on the field and preprinted data entry forms. Fitness Reporter generates both fall and spring fitness reports that analyze the data using minimum competencies or percentiles for normative data. The reports denote areas needing improvement. The fall report provides for goal setting, and the spring report compares fall and spring scores. Automatic continuation from year to year is possible by adding new students and removing transfers and graduates. One unique feature of this program is a locks module that keeps track of lockers, locks, and the students who use them.

Evaluating Software

The important points to consider when selecting software are user friendliness, anticipation of user errors, error free programming, texts and graphics that are easy to read, accuracy of content, and documentation. User friendly means the program is easy to use. Just as important as user friendliness is the software's ability to anticipate user errors. Programs that crash when the user makes an entry error are not as desirable as programs that let users know they have made an error and give them an opportunity to correct it.

It also is important that the program is sound—that it does what it is supposed to do. Programs with bugs, or programming errors, are very frustrating, especially to beginning users. Readability of the text and precision of the graphics also should be considerations when evaluating software. And—while this point is sometimes missed in the hype of the technology—it is important that the content in the software is accurate. You will find most documentation to be useful as long as you are willing to take the time to read it or use it when a problem occurs.

Summary

There are a number of software programs that can assist the physical educator with daily chores. These include word processing, data base, spreadsheet, grading, and fitness programs. Such programs can help you become more efficient—but only if you know how to take advantage of their many features. Why not take a course this year, or buy a book that includes a tutorial so you can take full advantage of the software you already own!

Reflection Questions

1. Considering that there are many free software programs available to educator—including Web based, shareware, and public domain, why would an educator purchase a software program such as Crossword Magic?
2. How might the use of fitness reports help students to improve their fitness scores?

3. What are your strongest computer skills? What computer skills do you need to improve?

Projects

1. Create a spreadsheet based on your grading system.
2. Create a newsletter that describes your physical education program.

Chapter 7

Using Telecommunication Applications in Physical Education

Tim Jones sits down at his computer between classes and calls up the messages left for him while he was teaching the previous hour. One message is from the district office, reminding him of an upcoming curriculum meeting. Another is from the main office at his school, requesting his quarter grades. Tim brings his grade report up on the screen, recalculates it to include this week's grades, and sends the grades to the main office. Tim then composes an e-mail message requesting information on a good videotape to introduce a unit on Frisbee and sends it to the NASPE listserv. He is confident that one of the many physical educators on the list will respond within a few hours.

Telecommunication refers to any type of data transfer between two points. Sending messages to others in your school system, requesting a calendar listing of conferences and workshops from an association, and collaborating with colleagues hundreds of miles away on new instructional strategies are examples of how you can use telecommunications to improve your effectiveness and save time. This chapter will introduce you to telecommunications hardware and software, describe various telecommunications applications, and provide you with ideas on how to use this technology.

Computer Connections

A network consists of individually controlled computers linked by a cable. The network can connect two individuals in a physical education office, or it can link a group of offices in a school. Most local area networks (LANs) use one powerful computer as a host and link many less powerful computers to it. The host machine stores network versions of software programs, and through it other computers on the network can legally access the software. Networks also allow computers to share hardware devices such as a laser printers, color printers, and scanners, and to exchange messages between computers. Today, organizations using wireless networks no longer need a "cable."

Those of you not on wireless systems or cabled to a network will need some type of modem (the name is an abbreviation for modulator/demodulator). "Modulate" means to change data into electronic pulses, and "demodulate" means to change pulses back into data. There are external, internal, and PC card modems. The PC cards plug into a PC card slot in the computer. See the Highlight Box on page 164 for a comparison of the various connection options.

You will need to connect the telephone wire or cable wire (cable modem) from the wall to the line port on the modem in order to use your modem. The software that controls the modem typically comes with the modem or when you register with an Internet Service Provider (see the section on the Internet). When you send information from a file on your disk to another computer, you are uploading. When you receive information from another computer and store it on your disk, you are downloading.

Networks allow schools and districts to submit data and allow different institutions and departments to access the information as needed. For example, fitness scores can be submitted electronically to the district office, which in turn will compile reports and submit them to the state department of education.

Major Connection Options

	Speed (sec..)	Cost	Note
Dial Up	56KB	$50 modem $19.95/mo	Slow access speed
Cable Modem	500 KB-10MB	$150 modem $30-50/mo	Not available in all areas
DSL	256KB-7MB	$200 modem $30-70/mo	Not available in all areas Uses regular phone lines
Satellite	400 KB	$200 for dish $29.95/mo	

Later, anyone on the education network can access those scores. This type of information is especially important when writing grants.

Internet

The Internet is a collection of smaller networks that provide a connection between computers located around the world. Each local network is connected to one or more other networks, usually via high-speed digital phone lines. There are more than 100,000 interconnected networks in more than 100 countries. These include commercial, academic, and government networks. The Internet also is referred to as the Information Super Highway or the World Wide Web, although the Web is actually a subset of the Internet.

Your first order of business, once you decide to connect to the Internet, is to select an Internet Service Provider (ISP), unless your school or district provides one for you. When selecting an ISP, talk to a technology expert in your area about local service providers. At a minimum, the provider should assign you an e-mail address, connect you to the Internet, allow you unlimited access to the WWW, feature a helpline, and provide local access numbers. If you have difficulty selecting a service provider,

Free ISP

http://www.bluelight.com
http://www.freeinternet.com
http://www.juno.com
http://www.lycos.com
http://www.netzeroc.om
http://www.FreeDSL.com

then I recommend AOL (America Online) for beginners and Earthlink for intermediate users. AOL is not only an Internet Service Provider, it also is a commercial online information service. This means that in addition to the information available on the WWW, you will have access to information on the AOL computers (including magazine subscriptions and software). There also are free Internet Service Providers that are supported through banner advertisements.

Telecommunication Applications

Once you are connected to the Internet, you will have access to a number of different telecommunication applications. These include electronic mail (e-mail), fax services, listservs, newsgroups, Web discussion groups, instant e-mail, chat sessions, audio conferencing, and video conferencing. Each of these applications can provide physical educators with a new way to reach out and communicate with colleagues. An additional telecommunication application, searching for information on the WWW, will be addressed in Chapter 8.

Electronic Mail

Having an Internet account is somewhat like having a post office box. Your friends and colleagues can send mail to your post office box. Then, when you have time, you go to the post office, open your post office box, and retrieve your mail. The process is the same for accessing electronic mail. However, instead of a physical post office box, you have a mail box with your ISP. Your friends and colleagues send electronic mail to your electronic mailbox located on the computer of your Internet Service Provider, and when you have time, you access (e.g., dial up) the ISP and retrieve your mail (see Figures 7.1 and 7.2).

In an electronic mail system, all users have a private mailbox address and a password to use when accessing that mailbox. Once you have an e-mail address, you can send and receive mail just like you do with snail mail (the Internet users' name for traditional mail service). If you would like to try sending a message, feel free to send me one at: bmohnsen@ pesoftware.com ("bmohnsen" is my mailbox number, and "pesoftware.com" is the network on which I have my mailbox). The main difference between e-mail and snail mail is that your message is delivered immediately and, if the receiver is available and wishes to do so, immediately answered.

You compose an e-mail message on your computer and send it to your ISP's computer. That computer processes it and sends it to the address you designate. All electronic mail software provides you with a template (see Figure 7.3) for sending mail. The process is very similar to snail mail. You type in one or more addresses, write your message, and send the message (by clicking on the Send button). The recipient retrieves the message, opens it, reads it, and—if he or she wishes—sends a reply. The recipient also may "forward" the message to other individuals. All e-mail programs will have something that resembles an in

Email Etiquette Rules

Write subject lines that describe the main theme of your message and then stick to that theme.
Be careful with sarcasm and humor.
Don't use all capital letters - it means you are shouting.
Don't send a mass-mailing advertisement.

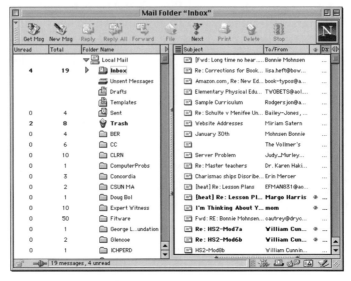

Figure 7.1   Netscape mail.

Figure 7.2   Outlook mail.

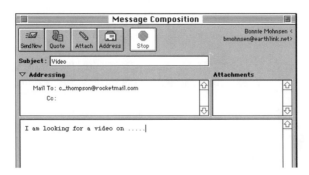

Figure 7.3   Message composition.

E-mail Abbreviations and Emoticons

IMHO	in my humble opinion
BTW	by the way
FYI	for your information
:-)	basic smiley or happy face
;-)	wink
:-(	frown

box, where incoming mail is stored until it can be read; an out box, where e-mail messages that have been sent are stored; and a wastebasket, where deleted messages are stored until you exit the program. You can even attach files to an e-mail message. If your e-mail supports MIME (Multipurpose Internet Mail Extensions), then simply click on the Attach button and point to the file; otherwise you will need to encode the file in a format such as Binhex or UUCP (Unix-to-Unix Copy Protocol). (See the section in Chapter 8 on plug-ins).

E-mail is especially helpful when you are trying to connect with colleagues to share information or get answers to questions. For example, in one school system, a college supervisor, master teacher, and student teacher were all linked by electronic mail. The student teacher wrote her lesson plans and submitted them simultaneously to the supervisor and the master teacher. The supervisor and master teacher read the lessons and sent suggestions back to the student teacher at their convenience, prior to the lessons.

Just like with telephone numbers and addresses, it easier to set

Finding People on the Net

Four 11 - http://www.Four11.com/
Search - http://www.yahoo.com/search/people/
Who Where? - http://www.whowhere.com/
Switchboard - http://www.switchboard.com

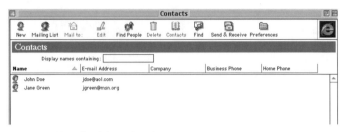

Figure 7.4   Email address book.

up an address book for electronic mail addresses than to remember them. Most e-mail software (Eudora, AOL, Netscape) have the capacity to store electronic mail addresses. The address book (see figure 7.4) typically accepts both the name of the individual and his or her address, so that when you are ready to send a message you simply click on the person's name and an electronic mail template (addressed to the recipient) is created. Most address books also allow you to group individuals so that you can send a message to a selected group. Figure 7.5 shows a group listing.

Fax Services

Fax services (i.e., efax.com) let you send and receive faxes for free. They provide you with an unique fax number that you can give to people who want to send you faxes. These faxes are then routed to your e-mail account. Most of these services require that you download some "free" software before you can use their service. Most also will provide you with an 800 fax number for a small monthly fee.

Listservs

A listserv is an extension of e-mail that works much like a mailing list. You send one message to the listserv distribution address and a copy of the message goes to everyone on the list. If you would like to join a physical education listserv, then follow the directions below for joining NASPE-L (National Association

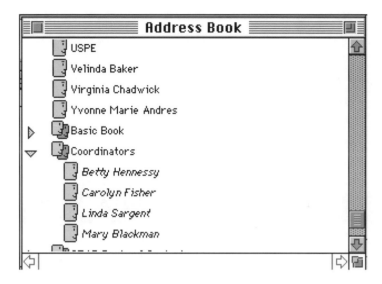

Figure 7.5   Email address book.

for Sport and Physical Education):

1. Send an email to the listserv address:
   listserv@listserv.vt.edu
2. Leave the subject line blank
3. In the body of the text indicate that you want to subscribe:
   Sub NASPE-L firstname lastname (see Figure 7.6)
4. You will receive a message regarding your acceptance to the list
5. You may now send a message to the list at NASPE-L@listserv.vt.edu

If you would like to remove yourself from the listserv, then follow the directions below for unsubscribing to NASPE:

1. Send an email to the listserv address:
   listserv@listserv.vt.edu
2. Leave the subject line blank
3. In the body of the text type:
   Unsubscribe NASPE-L
4. You will receive a message regarding your removal from the list

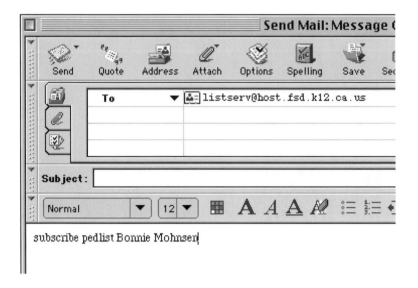

Figure 7.6   Signing up for a listserv.

Once you have joined a listserv, there are a number of commands you can use to request specific information. Refer to the highlight box above for these special commands.

Listservs are a great source of support for isolated physical educators. They provide you with the opportunity to connect with other physical educators. You can ask questions (i.e., what is a good video for teaching juggling, which instructional strategies are best for students with attention deficit disorder). Listservs also can be set up locally for your students, so that discussions can occur between your students and between you and your students. You can set up your own listserv at http://www.egroups.com/.

Newsgroups

Internet discussion groups, known as newsgroups, serve as forums on almost any topic imaginable. They are essentially bulletin boards where people can read and post messages about

Common Listserv Commands

Lists: get a description of all lists
Subscribe Listserv: subscribe to a list
Unsubscribe Listserv: unsubscribe to a list
Review Listserv: review a list
Index Listserv: order a list of listserv files
Get Listserv: order a file from listserv
Set Listserv nomail: suspends mailing of materials from the list
Set Listserv mail: resumes mailing of materials to your account
Set Listserv digest: all mail is collected on the server and sent out
daily in the form of a single message
Set Liserv nodigest: removes the digest option

Note: Listserv refers to the name of the listserv

topics of their choice. When you post a message to a newsgroup, everyone who visits that newsgroup can read your comments and respond if they wish. Newsgroups are accessed by using a "newsreader" software program or the built-in version included in Netscape Navigator and Internet Explorer. The messages are organized by topic, allowing the viewer to designate an entire conversational strand as already read if it is not relevant. A listing of all newsgroups can be found at http://www.deja.com/.

Some commercial services allow you to identify topics that are of particular interest. The information service searches for and retrieves the information from various newsgroups and produces daily, weekly, or monthly reports that include only those references that fit your areas of interest. This kind of service has tremendous potential for physical educators who do not have time to search through the many e-mail messages or newsgroups.

Web Discussion Groups

Web-based discussion groups provide an alternative to newsgroups. Individuals interested in a particular topic are given a URL (universal resource locator) address (see Chapter 8 for how to access a site) where they can read messages that have been left and leave messages of their own. Web discussion groups can be useful in many circumstances, although they currently lack many of the amenities provided by newsgroups. Most such groups do not provide an easy way to mark, hide, or delete previously read postings, or to mark an entire topic thread as read with a single keystroke. Web discussion groups can be used as online bulletin boards where you leave messages for your students and, they in turn, leave messages for you. You can create your own web discussion board at http://www2.eboard.com/.

Instant e-mail

This form of telecommunication is known as instant e-mail because it offers real-time conversation with another person in text form by way of a pop-up box on your computer screen. Most instant messaging programs let you set up a list of people with whom you'd like to converse, and when those people go online and are ready to accept messages, the software will notify you. The most popular example is AOL's Instant Messenger (http://www.aol.com), which is available to non-AOL members as well as AOl members.

Lists of Listservs

http://www.thelist.com
http://www.best.be/iap

Physical Education Listservs

Sportime
    pe-talk-digest-request@lists.sportime.com (listserv)
    pe-talk-digest@lists.sportime.com (list)
Pedlist
    listserv@host.fsd.k12.ca.us (listserv)
    pedlist@host.fsd.k12.ca.us (list)

You can use instant e-mail much like you use regular e-mail, except that the communication will be faster, since it is in real-time.

Chat Conferencing

Internet Relay Chat (IRC) is like an international CB system or conference call on your computer. You might think of it as a virtual area where people gather to use their computers and modems to "chat" in real time. The server is a central place where you join in discussions with other users who are connected to the same chat server.

In order to participate in chat conferencing, you must first obtain an IRC program called a client. Two of the most popular are mIRC (Windows) and MacIRC (Macintosh). After installing the client, it is easy to log onto a server where you can find the IRC's individual channels. Pick a "handle" (online name) and choose a public channel (topic) to connect to, ask to join a private one, or create a channel of your own. A "#" symbol in a channel name means the channel is available worldwide. An "&" symbol in a channel name means the channel is available only on the IRC server to which the user is connected.

Selecting a channel from the thousands that exist can be the most difficult part of IRC. You have a range of topics from which to choose—including everything from sports groups, to computers, to education. Once you join a channel, you can communicate with the other people there by simply typing what you want to say.

A browser-based IRC is now available through Web sites such as Talk City. Using Netscape Navigator or Internet Explorer you can access and communicate in various chat rooms (channels). Simply follow the directions:

1. Type in URL: http://www.talkcity.com/.

2. Click on Chat.

3. Choose a chat room.

4. Complete the log in.

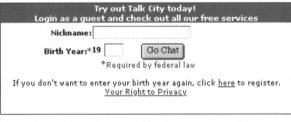

5. Type a message and click on send.

Again, this type of communication allows for instant conversation on a physical education-related topic. Except in the case of chat sessions, several individuals can participate. In my county, we use this form of communication monthly to share questions, concerns, and updates. Nationally, we use chats to help prepare individuals for National Board Certification (see Chapter 11).

Audio Conferencing

An audio conference uses telephone conference equipment Internet telephony (a combination of Internet and telephone using software such as net2phone), or the Internet to link geographically dispersed people for audio communication. When connecting via the Internet, users enter the IP address (computer number) of the computer they are trying to reach. Individuals who are connected via a network typically have a static or unchanging IP address. However, if you use a dial-up connection you will usually be given a dynamic IP address. This means that each time you connect, your computer will be assigned a temporary address for the duration of your call.

This technology is great for communicating with guest speakers, content experts, and colleagues across the United States and around the world. Several teachers and/or students at each site can communicate simultaneously, allowing for "real-time" interaction between participants. Students can interview athletes, medical doctors, nutritionists, professors, and other experts as part of a research project or report.

Desktop Video Conferencing

Desktop video conferencing uses telephone connections or the Internet to take advantage of text, audio, and video transmissions in real time. Full-motion video, which provides 30 new frames per second (fps), requires a very fast baud rate. Since many users are unable to connect at these speeds, compressed video (CODEC) analyzes each new frame and transmits only the pixels that have changed. This reduces the speed at which the pictures are transmitted. Because audio quality is far more important than video quality, users will forgive diminished video quality if your content is substantive.

Placing an audio/video call via the Internet is similar to placing an audio call—simply enter the IP address of the person you're calling. The receiver needs to be connected and have compatible conferencing software (i.e., CU-SeeMe, NetMeeting) running. Good practices to follow when using audio/video conferencing include reducing movement, speaking clearly, waiting for others to stop talking before speaking, wearing solid colored clothing (avoid bright red, yellow, or orange), and muting the microphone when not speaking.

Chat, Audio, and Video Software

mIRC: http://www.mirc.com
MacIRC: http://www.macirc.com
Net2Phone: http://www.net2phone.com
CU-SeeMe: http://www.rocketcharged.com

CU-SeeMe (Cornell) is a public domain video conferencing program for both the Macintosh and Windows environments. User requirements include an Internet connection, a video camera, and a video input card or device for the computer. Connections can be point-to-point (between two locations) or multipoint (multiple locations). A program called a reflector is necessary for multipoint locations.

Desktop video conferencing provides the same opportunities as instant messaging, chats, and audio conferencing—with the added bonus of being able to see the other individuals. This makes the conversation seem even more like a real, in-person conversation. However, if your Internet connection is slow it is better to bypass the video conferencing and stick with instant messaging, chats, or audio conferencing.

Telecommunication Projects

There are many worthwhile learning activities on the Internet that physical educators and their students can join. These include keypals, guest speakers, question-and-answer forums, information searches, data base creation, electronic publishing, electronic fieldtrips, pooled data analysis, parallel problem solving, sequential problem solving, telepresence problem solving, simulations, and social action projects (some of these are covered in Chapter 8). Students also can compete in Virtual Track Meets and make connections with Olympic athletes.

Key Pals for Students

Many of us had pen pals when we were students. Today, our students can have key pals. Key pals are students who connect with one another via electronic mail. They share ideas, concerns, physical education/activity experiences, information, written assignments, and research. And, they learn to accept individuals from other communities and cultures. If the key pal idea is of interest to you, go to the Physical Education Keypal Internet site (http://www.stan-co.k12.ca.us/calpe/keypals.html) to find pals for yourself, your students, or both.

Virtual Track Meet

Virtual Track Meet (http://www.ofcn.org) allows students from across the United States and abroad to compete in a number of different track events. Teachers post students' times on the Internet so comparisons can be made and winners determined. The students share information, via e-mail, about their schools, communities, interests, hobbies, and cultural differences. Students can access the Mapquest (http://www.mapquest.com) web site to locate one anothers' schools.

Connections with Famous People

Electronic mail also can provide access to an array of individuals with knowledge and expertise of interest to physical educators and their students. Olympic athletes, professional athletes,

E-mail from an Olympic athlete

In the next two weeks we will begin the difficult process of selection. Today there are about 20 athletes training here for the Olympics. Our coach has to pick the top 8 for the premier boat, then 4 for the next boat, and 2 for the last boat. Selection is often the hardest part of the year because it is the time when people's dreams are realized or their failures are faced. Everyone wants to be in the top boat, but there are only 8 seats available. And after the 4 and the 2-man boats are chosen there are some guys who won't get to go to the Olympics at all. You can imagine how hard it would be to train all these years and not make the team. The other hard part about selection is that we are all friends. We have established strong emotional ties over the years and it will be tough to see friends feel such disappointment. -Steven biomechanists, exercise physiologists, motor learning specialists, outstanding physical education teachers and leaders, and others are available to any one of us via electronic mail.

The Orange County Department of Education sponsors the Olympic Athlete Project. During the 1995-1996 school year, an Olympic rower was identified who was willing to share his trip to the Olympics with students. Steven Segaloff was a potential Olympic coxswain when he began communicating with students across the United States. He sent e-mail messages (see highlight box on page 184) every other week that dealt with his sport, his training program, the selection process, his relationship with the other rowers (teamwork), and his feelings about training and participating in the Olympics. During1999-2000, Mickisha Hurley, an Olympic volleyball athlete participated in the project.

Summary

Many physical educators feel isolated from their colleagues. They miss the interaction and sharing of instructional ideas, class management techniques, assessment tools, and resources. Telecommunications can help fill this void by providing them with the opportunity to communicate with other physical educators via e-mail, listservs, newsgroups, Web discussion groups, chat sessions, and audio/video communications.

Reflection Questions

1. Which of the telecommunication tools would best fit your communication style? Why?
2. Which of the telecommunication tools would work best for your students? Why?

Projects

1. Join one of the listservs noted in this chapter. Sit back for a

while and observe the conversations, then jump in with your own comments or questions.

2. Arrange a time to meet a friend or colleague at the TalkCity Web site to participate in a chat session.

Chapter 8

Accessing the World Wide Web

Carolyn Brown wonders whether there are any data to support her concern that students need daily physical education. So, during her conference period, she boots up her browser software and begins to visit sites she feels may have relevant information. They include the Centers for Disease Control and the Institute for Aerobic Research. Although she finds some information, Carolyn still thinks she needs additional information for the Board presentation she is planning. So, she visits the AltaVista search site and enters the following words: +"daily physical education" +benefits. Immediately, 1,000 hits are listed. Carolyn's next decision is whether to search all 1,000 sites or to refine her search. With only 30 minutes left in her conference period, she decides to refine her search. She clicks on "Refine," and by the end of her conference period has more than enough information to present to her Board of Education.

W hen the Internet was introduced in the late 1960s, the goal was to develop a global network of computers. Today, the Internet has met that goal. You can access journals, books, research papers, clip art, and news reports plus a variety of information on topics ranging from computers, to education, to sports. The World Wide Web, a subset of the Internet, provides access to information through a graphical user interface. Specifically, the World Wide Web (WWW) allows you to look at information stored on computers around the world by typing in an address or pointing the mouse at a link (typically text in a different color and underlined) and clicking. Different links access different pieces of information on different computers. The World Wide Web is the biggest thing driving computer sales today.

Web Browsers

A Web browser is software designed to facilitate viewing information on the World Wide Web. Browser programs support hypertext markup language (html), which allows you to see text, graphics, and pictures. Browsers also allow you to bookmark your favorite pages and save or print pages for viewing off-line. Plug ins can be added to make these programs even more powerful. The two most popular web browsers are Netscape Navigator (http://www.netscape.com) and MicroSoft Internet Explorer (http://www.microsoft.com/). Both can be downloaded for free.

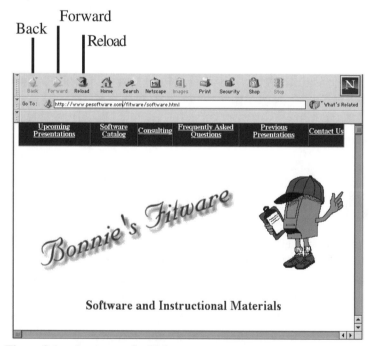

Figure 8.1   Anatomy of a Web page

Browser Commands

Open/Location Field - where you can enter an address. Type in the URL and you instantly bring the information from that site to your computer screen.

Back - clicking the Back button allows you to retrace your steps and return to sites you've already visited.

Forward - reverses the action of Back.

Reload/Refresh - reloads the page currently on display. This may be necessary if the page loads incorrectly or the content of the page changes frequently.

Stop - stops the loading of the current page.

Print - prints all the pages on the current screen without any prompts.

Home - brings the web page you have designated as your opening location back to the screen.

Plug ins

In order to access audio/video clips on the Internet, you will need special plug ins. Plug ins (and their cousins, helper applications) expand upon your browser's basic functions. With plug ins, you'll be able to hear live radio broadcasts and watch videos of sport skills without leaving your browser. Plug-ins are small utilities that give your browser the ability to display a wider variety of documents, images, and other online files.

The current sophistication of Netscape Navigator and Internet Explorer include code that can handle most of the files you're likely to encounter on the Internet. Additionally, both browsers include Apple's QuickTime plug in, which can play nearly any multimedia file you're likely to encounter. However, older browsers may require the installation of one or more plug-ins.

Most plug ins are free and are downloaded from the sites that use them. Web sites that use special plug ins will actually check your system and alert you to the need for a plug in. Adding plug ins is one of the easiest procedures on the Internet—your browser does most of the work. When you load a page that requires a plug in you haven't installed, Netscape Navigator notifies you and lets you see a list of suggested plug ins. If you use MicroSoft Internet Explorer and ActiveX, the browser automatically downloads and installs the necessary plug in. However, rather than waiting to install plug ins when you need them, you may want to gather and install several at once.

The plug ins listed in highlight box are the most important for your continual enjoyment of the Internet. When you download a plug in, pay attention to where it is saved on your hard drive. After you download a plug in, you will need to quit your browser and locate the downloaded file. Double click on it and follow the directions it gives for installation. You typically will be asked to register your name, workplace, address, e-mail, and other identifying information when you download the software. You also will be asked to read the terms of agreement for use and agree to those terms before the installation can be completed. Once the installation is complete, your new plug in will be active.

Helper Applications

Helper applications run or display files that aren't integrated into Web pages and don't display inside the browser's window. Three popular helper applications are Adobe Acrobat Reader, StuffIt Expander, and WinZip.

Securing Helper Applications and Plug ins

1. Go to the appropriate web site.
2. Register your name and address (not required at all sites).
3. Select the appropriate application for your computer platform and language.
4. Click on the "Download" button, then read the installation instructions.
5. Click on the geographically appropriate download link to download the plug in.
6. Wait for it to load (time depends on your modem, connection speed, etc.).
7. Follow the installation instructions.

Browser Plug ins

Quicktime VR: http ://www.apple.com
Flash: http://www.macromedia.com
ShockWave: http://www.macromedia.com
RealPlayer: http://www.real.com/products/player
Real Jukebox: http://www.digitaldivide.org/

Helper Applications

Adobe Acrobat Reader: http://www.adobe.com
StuffIt Expander: http://www.aladdinsys.com
WinZip: http://www.winzip.com

Portable Document Format (PDF) is a file format that enables the user to retain the typographical format (fonts, line breaks, graphics) of a document. Using Adobe Acrobat Reader, you can open, view, browse, search, and print PDF files on any of the major desktop computing platforms. You can tell that a file is in PDF format by the file name extension—.pdf. When properly configured on a computer, the browser launches Acrobat Reader whenever a PDF file is encountered. This is the easiest way to ensure that the document you receive resembles the original document.

StuffIt Expander and WinZip are applications that assist with the transfer of files from the Internet to the user's computer. Many times files are encoded and/or compressed prior to transfer (see the File Transfer section in this chapter). The encoding helps to retain the document's original format, and compression makes the file smaller so that it can transfer more quickly. The way in which a file has been translated and compressed is indicated by its suffix. Normally, a file will have a name something like filename.xxx.yyy (.xxx indicates how it was compressed and .yyy indicates how it was translated). Since the file has been modified twice (compressed and then translated), it must be translated and decompressed before it can be read. StuffIt Expander can handle files that have been binhexed (.hqx)—a common method of encoding on the Macintosh—and uuencoded (.uue)—a common method of encoding on the PC.

StuffIt Expander also can decompress files that have been compressed (or "stuffed") using the StuffIt program, and WinZip can do the same for files compressed using Zip. You also will find self-extracting archive files on the Internet. A self-extracting file (.sea) is an executable program, which when loaded, automatically translates and decompresses itself.

Locating a Web Page

Everywhere you look today, you see long strings of text that look something like this:
http://www.pesoftware.com/news.html.

These strings are referred to as universal resource locators (URLs). They begin with a protocol, like "http://" (HyperText Transfer Protocol) or "ftp" (File Transfer Protocol) followed by a variety of letters, numbers, and punctuation marks. URLs are to the World Wide Web what telephone numbers are to the phone system. They allow you to connect with the location you desire. Typically, the first section after "http://" contains www, indicating that the site is on the world wide web. However, you may also encounter www2, which is a separate group on the internet for educational resources. The next section is the name of the server or computer (pesoftware) that houses the

Changing Font Size

Internet Explorer - go to the View menu, point to Text Size, and then choose a larger or smaller font for the text on that page.
Netscape - go to Edit, then Preferences, then Category scroll list. Choose Fonts under Appearance, then choose a different size or type of font.

information. The computer's name often ends with a period, followed by a three-letter combination such as edu, com, gov, or org. Each suffix refers to a particular type of organization. For example:

com = commercial
edu = education
gov = government
org = organization

More recently, we have begun to see suffixes that refer to the physical location of the computer. For example, "ca.us" refers to a site from California, USA, and "gov.ab.ca" to a government organization in Alberta, Canada. The most common errors when typing in a URL include omitting one of the parts, using the wrong domain designator (edu, or com, or org), punctuation errors (~) or omissions, misspellings, using either upper or lower case when the other is called for, and using a space instead of an underscore.

All browsers have an Open button where you can enter an address (URL). By typing in the URL (http://physed.ocde.k12.ca.us), you can instantly bring the information from that site to your computer screen. This is often referred to as the home page or the first in a series of linked documents. You can think of the home page as the main menu or the table of contents in a book. In order to move from the home page to linked pages, you simply click on the hyperlink (special text embedded with a URL, often a different color and underlined) that brings the new document to your screen. By clicking the Back button you can retrace your steps and return to sites you've already visited. You also can go directly to these pages if you know the URL. For example, in the URL , http:/www.pesoftware.com/fitware/software.html, "software.html" is the name of the document or page, and it is located in a folder entitled "fitware" that is located on the computer named "www.pesoftware.com." When typing in the URL, you can omit the http://.

Physical Education Sites

AAHPERD: http://www.aahperd.org

Active Trainer: http://www.ActiveTrainer.com/

AlbertaLearn:http://ednet.edc.gov.ab.ca/physicaleducationonline/

Body Quest: http://library.advanced.org/10348

California Physical Education: http://www.stan-co.k12.ca.us/calpe/

Centers for Disease Control: http://www.cdc.gov/

Challenge Course: http://www.pa.org/low.html

Circus Skills: http://www.juggling.org/

Fitness Files: http://rcc.webpoint.com/

Folk Dances: http://www.folkdance.com/

Franklin Institute Museum: http://sln.fi.edu/

Global Schoolhouse Net: http://www.gsn.org

Golf: http://www.teachkidsgolf.com

Human Kinetics: http://www.hkusa.com/

Inner Body: http://www.InnerBody.com/

Kids Health: http://www.kidshealth.org/

Line Dance Fun: http://www.linedancefun.com/

Orienteering: http://www.uio.no/~kjetikj/compass/lesson1.html

PE Central: http://www.pecentral.com/

PE Links 4 U: http://www.pelinks4u.org/

Olympic Movement: http://www.olympic.org/

1 on 1 Basketball: http://voltec.springweb.com/main.shtml

Sports ID: http://www.sportsid.com/

Sports Illustrated for Kids: http://www.sikids.com/

Sports Media: http://www.sports_media.org/

Sport Science: http://www.exploratorium.edu/sport/

The Heart: http://sln.fi.edu/biosci/heart.html

The difficulty in going directly to sites such as these is remembering the long series of letters, numbers, and punctuation marks that make up the URL. Luckily, all browsers contain a "bookmark" or "favorites" feature that allows you to mark a page you may wish to revisit. Your bookmarks or favorites will become extremely important to you, so be sure to back up the files. The Highlight Box below provides directions. You also can save or back up your bookmarks online at sites such as http://www.hotlink.com/.

A bookmark is a valuable tool that can save you time by taking you to a previously explored Web page without having to go through multiple menus or hyperlinks. However, be aware that there are some situations (i.e., visiting a link from within a site with frames) in which you cannot bookmark a site.

Saving and Printing

As you visit various sites, you will no doubt run across information you either want to save or print. The browser allows you to do both easily. For example, using Netscape Navigator, go to the web page that is of interest to you. Select File from the menu bar, and then select Save to save the information from the web page to your hard drive. Or, select File from the menu bar, and then select Print to generate a hard copy of the information. Be careful when printing web sites with frames. You must first click the mouse on the information you wish to print, and then select File-Print.

Saving Bookmark/Favorite Files

In Navigator, open your Netscape folder (it's probably in your Program Files\Netscape\Navigator subfolder or System\Preferences\Netscape) and locate the bookmark.htm file. Copy it to a disk.

In Internet Explorer, go to Windows\Favorites subfolder and locate the Favorites file. Copy it to a disk.

However, when you print the information from the site you might get pages you do not need. To avoid this, go to Print Preview and determine how many pages you need. Now specify in the Print dialog box which pages you want to print. If your browser does not have Print Preview, arbitrarily set a fixed number of pages in the Print dialog box.

You also can save images from the Web onto your computer. Again, using Netscape Navigator, perform the steps in one of the following methods:

Method 1:
1. Macintosh: Click and hold the mouse over the image.
1. Windows: Right click and hold the mouse over the image.
2. When the pop-up menu appears, choose "Save this image as."
3. Type in a name for the image.
4. Select the location on your hard drive where you would like the image to be saved.

Method 2:
1. On Macintosh: Click and hold the mouse over the image.
1. Using Windows: Right click and hold the mouse over the image.
2. Choose the command, "Copy this image."
3. Using Macintosh: Go to the apple, drag down to scrapbook, and select Edit-Paste.
3. Using Windows: The image will automatically be placed on the clipboard.

Searching the Web

No doubt you have heard the term "surfing the net." It's much like window shopping— it means roaming around online until you find something of interest. This is actually the least efficient method of searching for information. In fact, it is only beneficial once you find a page that has numerous links to related information. Search engines, on the other hand, make it possible to find the information you need quickly.

There are several kinds of search tools (see highlight box on page 198), including search engines, Web directories, and metasearchers. A metasearcher, lets you build a single search and then apply it to multiple search sites simultaneously. However, these searches take much longer than a single search, and they are not as focused as a search engine.

Directories are organized collections of links to Web resources; somewhat like a book's table of contents. Links are usually added by human operators who solicit Internet users to submit links and actively search for new links to add themselves. You look for keywords in subdirectory headings titles and descriptions of links to Web sites.

Search engines consist of data bases containing the full or partial text of sites. Their data bases are built by automated tools called bots, crawlers, or spiders, that roam the Web exploring links and collecting the entire content or abstracts of the content found at different Web sites. When you use search engines, you search their entire data base.

The same query will get different results from each of these tools. There is no charge to use search tools, because they are supported by advertisers who post banners on the search result pages. There are dozens of search tools; two particularly popular ones are Yahoo (Web directory) and AltaVista (search engine). You access the search tool by typing in its Internet address.

Once at the Web site, you will see a rectangular area where you can type in a topic (i.e., volleyball, Medieval games). You then click on the word Search, and the software shows you a list of locations where related information is stored. When you click on one of those locations, the information from that site appears on your screen. Search engines list the best matches first—those pages that have the highest number of matching keywords or phrases on them.

No matter which tool you use, a focused search will produce

more exact results. You will need to be as specific as possible in order to conduct a successful search. It is not unusual to type in something general like "sports" and end up with more than one million sites. Therefore, it is better to perform many narrow searches that result in fewer matches than to make your search too broad and spend valuable time looking at information that doesn't interest you. A narrow search is performed by using limiting words such as AND (+), OR, or PHRASE. If you enter the words —Teaching adolescents volleyball—separated by spaces, some search engines will perform an OR search and return all the pages that have the word "Teaching" and all of the pages that have the word "adolescents" and all the pages that have the word "volleyball." This isn't exactly what you wanted.

Some engines require you to specify a phrase search, put your phrase in quotes, put the word AND between your search words, or use a plus sign in front of each word. Each search engine contains directions for using it on its search page.

Search engines do have their limitations, including out-of-date sites. The information associated with the link may have been moved or eliminated. In addition, not all search engines are created equal. You are usually better off with search engines that support phrase searches that allow you to input several words and narrow your results.

Search Tools

Directories:
http://www.yahoo.com
http://www.dmoz.org/

Meta Search Tools
http://www.search.com
http://www.isleuth.com
http://www.metacrawler.com

Search
http://www.altavista.com/
http://www.google.com
http://www.alltheweb.com/
http://www.looksmart.com/
http://www.go.com/
http://www.askjeeves.com/

File Transfer

File transfer protocol (FTP) is a procedure for defining how files are transferred from one computer to another. You can use FTP by going to a site (ftp://) on the World Wide Web and letting your browser handle the details, or you can use an FTP client (software) to access FTP sites. The most popular FTP clients are FETCH for the Macintosh and WS-FTP Pro (Ipswitch) for Windows. With FETCH you can send and receive files as long as you have permission from the site. You also can transfer files as attachments to electronic mail; however, be aware that not all e-mail systems support attachments.

Files can contain text, executable programs, graphics, or compressed data. Archive files are single files that contain many files in compressed form, making it faster and easier to transfer them by modem. Most files available by FTP have been compressed and encoded to allow them to more easily pass through different computers (see section on plug ins).

Web Activities

When you are searching the Web it is important to find high-quality sites that contain accurate information. Sites sponsored by professional organizations and journals are excellent places to begin your search. There also are portals (subscription-based or free) that provide gateways to the best information on the Web. You can follow the hyperlinks noted on these sites, since they usually have been reviewed prior to inclusion.

Physical educators can find a great deal of information on the Web to help in developing curriculum, planning lessons, and producing instructional materials (see highlight box on page 200). The Web also can be an extremely valuable instructional resource for students. They can use the Internet to engage in treasure hunts, complete WebQuests, conduct research,

Online Teacher Resources

A to Z: http://www.atozteacherstuff.com/

Assessment Tools: http://www.rubrics.com/

Brainium: http://www.brainium.com/

Certificate Creator: http://www.CertificateCreator.com/

Educate Now: http://www.educatenow.com/

Education World: http://www.educationworld.com/

Encyclopedias: http://responsiblekids.net/encyclopedias.htm

Explor Asource: http://www.explorasource.com/educator/

Fact Monster: http://www.factmonster.com/

4Teachers: http://www.4teachers.org/

Free Worksheets: http://www.freeworksheets.com/

FunBrain: http://www.funbrain.com

Gateway to Ed Materials: http://thegateway.org/

Grants: http://www.schoolgrants.com/

Great Online Tools: http://www.gotschool.com/

Language Translators: http://www.freetranslation.com/

Microsoft Lesson Connection: http://www.k12.msn.com/

Multiple Choice Tests: http://interactivetest.com/

PBS: http://www.pbs.org/teachersource/

Shareware Software: http://shareware.com/

Teacher Central: http://www.teachercentral.com/

Teacher Web: http://www.teacherweb.com/

Teach the Teachers: http://www.teachtheteachers.org/

Tools: http://school.discovery.com/teachingtools/teachingtools.html

Quiz Creator: http://eleaston.com/quizzes.html

Virtual Tours: http://www.virtualfreesites.com/tours.html

participate in electronic field trips, solve problems, complete tutorials, and perform simulations.

Treasure hunts. In treasure hunts, students are given questions about a specific topic along with specific Web sites where they can find the answers. Well-written questions can extend understanding beyond isolated facts and guide students to deeper thinker. Culminating with a "big idea" question allows students to synthesize what they have learned and apply it to real-life settings.

WebQuest. In WebQuests (http://edweb.sdsu.edu/webquest/webquest.html), students are given an authentic problem to solve along with Web resources on the topic. Then, they are asked to formulate a solution. Students typically work in collaborative groups or teams, Each student explores the linked sites related to a specific role on the team. Students then teach what they have learned to the other team members. Finally, higher-level questions guide students toward more challenging thinking and

Treasure Hunt– Multicultural Games
Germantown Academy

Sites:
http://www.germantownacademy.org/Academics/MS/6th/MCGAMES/
    Gamelink.htm
http://www.germantownacademy.org/Academics/MS/6th/MCGAMES/
    Directory.htm
http://www.germantownacademy.org/Academics/MS/6th/MCGAMES/
    Template.htm

Questions:
1. List countries where the game originated and where it is currently played.
2. Describe how your game is played. State the object of the game. Describe rules/boundaries. List equipment.
3. Recommend the type of athlete who would enjoy playing this game. What skills does the game demand? What are your impressions of this game? Did you enjoy playing it? Would you recommend it?

a deeper understanding of the topic being explored.

Here is an overview of a WebQuest on rope jumping (http://lincoln.midcoast.com/~wps/pewriting/introduction.htm):

> This WebQuest is an opportunity for children to explore the topic of rope jumping while at the same time allowing them to make strong connections within the curriculum areas of English and language arts, health, physical education, and technology. Your children will act as a jump rope enthusiast. Their job will be to research the benefits of rope jumping, finding specific information concerning the numerous benefits. Students will need to complete reading activities and exploring. A note taking sheet containing eight reasons why rope jumping can be beneficial will be completed. This

Personal Trainer WebQuest
http://www.itdc.sbcss.k12.ca.us/curricululm/
personaltrainer.html

Choose one of the people below and develop a menu and exercise program to improve their overall health. You must:
Find the appropriate goal weight for the person.
Develop a weekly exercise program.
Develop a one-week menu.
Provide helpful survival tips.
Give your client specific recommendations.

Sample Client:
Michelle is a 17-year-old high school junior. She stands 5' 6" tall and weighs 135 pounds. Michelle is involved in Key Club and sings in the school choir. Michelle spends her evening hours talking on the phone, watching TV and/or hanging out with her friends. Michelle 's family isn't big on family meals, so Michelle is responsible for preparing most of her own meals. Michelle doesn't eat breakfast, eats fast food a lot, and is on a first-name basis with the fine folks at Taco Bell. Michelle feels her body may still be growing but is concerned with the fact that some of her clothes are getting tight. She would like to drop a few pounds.

information will be helpful to the children as they create a pamphlet that will persuade others to participate in the sport of rope jumping. As a culmination, there will be an oral presentation to classmates. All facts included in the pamphlet need to be supported by the information that they have researched in this lesson.

A second example of a WebQuest, this one related to fitness concepts, can be found in the highlight box on page 202. The complete activity can be found online.

Research Projects. Students can use the Internet to research areas of interest. For example, they can investigate proper exercises, new motor skill techniques, or the history of a sport or dance. However, it is important that you prepare your students to use this research tool. Online encyclopedias are an excellent place to start, but other sites also contain excellent information. Students must learn to double check all references and to examine author credentials. It also is important that your students learn how to properly cite references (see Highlight Box on page 205) from the Internet.

Electronic Field Trips. Electronic field trips can be valuable Internet experiences. The high cost of field trips and the sheer size of the earth may make it impossible for students to physically explore the world outside their school district. However, students can explore the world through virtual fields trips. Your students can explore the materials from past trips or

---

What Makes a Good Web Resource?

Accurate	Author credentials	Free
Current	Fast load	Short pages
Reliable	Good information	Readability
Graphics	Links to other sites	Purpose
References	Reviewed	Searchable
Style	Updated	Well organized

join a trip in progress. There are opportunities to share ideas with the travelers as well as other students following the trip. Many virtual field trips provide daily updates with photographs, movies, sound clips, and journal entries.

Turner Educational Services (http://turnerlearning.com/efts/) has been one of the leaders in the area of electronic fieldtrips. They have sponsored field trips to the Indianapolis 500 and to baseball training camps. During their "Calculations on a Curve Ball: The Many Figures of Baseball" field trip, students learned to use mathematical equations to calculate the percentages of runs, hits, and errors of their favorite players. Using the sciences of physiology, physics, chemistry, and meteorology, students learned to improve motor skills related to the game of baseball. Through

Web Citations

Basic Citation:
Author's Last Name, First Name. [author's Internet address, if available]. "Title of Work" or "title line of message." In "Title of Complete Work" or title of list/site if appropriate. [Internet address]. Date.

Listserv Citation:
Sender's Name. [Sender's e-mail]. "Title of e-mail." In "Name of listserv." [listserv address]. Date.

E-mail Citation:
Sender's Name. [Sender's e-mail]. "Title of e-mail." Private e-mail message to name of receiver, [e-mail address of receiver]. Date.

Newspaper Online Citation:
Author. "Title." Newspaper name. Date: paging or indicator of length. [Type of medium]. Available: web site/path/file or supplier or database name. [access date].

Magazine Online Citation:
Author. "Article Title." Magazine name. Date: paging or indicator or length. [Type of medium]. Available: web site/path/file. [access date].

history and literature they explored the relationship between baseball and American culture. And, they applied economic principles to the business of baseball as they "became" the team owner and created a budget for a winning season.

Throughout the journey, the students met players, coaches, trainers, announcers, statisticians, and others related to the baseball environment. Information was sent via live interactive telecasts and received either by satellite or cable. There were live Internet chats and discussion groups as well as toll-free phone numbers to call with questions. Data disks and Web sites provided primary and secondary resources. Turner Educational Services continues to produce new electronic field trips during each school year. Online services such as America Online and CompuServe also sponsor free electronic field trips.

The Whitbread Race is a 32,000 nautical mile race around the world. It is held once every four years, and it takes nine months to complete. During the 1998 season, the entire trip was tracked on the World Wide Web. Students were able to access information about the event, current standings, and the weather. They could even view events on the boats via live video cameras and digitized images from a still camera. Students were able to interact with the athletes via e-mail, and they could even participate in a sailing simulation where they raced their own boat against the actual competitors.

Problem-based learning (PBL). PBL is learning organized around the investigation and resolution of an authentic, ill-structured problem. PBL includes three main characteristics (Torp & Sage, 1998):
-it engages students as stakeholders in a problem situation.
-it organizes curriculum around this holistic problem, enabling students to learn in relevant and connected ways.
-it creates a learning environment in which teachers coach student thinking and guide student inquiry, facilitating deeper levels of understanding.

Sailing the Whitbread Web Site
http://www.sailingworld.com/whitbred/whithub.htm

Update:
Official position reports and weather.

Chronicle:
Daily multimedia diary

Whitbread Race Office's Official Area:
Daily bulletins, scoring and rules information, and a history of the event.

Info:
Web site and race FAQs, TV schedules, and a calendar of events.

Teams:
Each of the nine teams has its own page on the site; team information, team member photos and biographies.

Gallery:
Each boat carries three video cameras and one still digital camera

E-mail:
Crews send e-mail to the web site describing daily living.

V Race:
Virtual Whitbread Race is an online sailing simulation that allows you to enter your own boats in the race, sailing against both the actual Whitbread racers and fellow virtual racers

The difference between project-based learning and problem-based learning, is that problems are messier. The teacher designs a problem that fits the current standards. Then, students collaborate with other students to solve the problem using a number of different resources to investigate and recommend a solution. The teacher's role includes: building the teaching/learning template, coaching students on critical learning events, and providing embedded assessment of student learning. The critical components of PBL include:

-prepare the learners

-introduce the problem

-identify what they need to know

206

-define the problem
-gather and share information
-generate possible solutions
-determine the "best" solution
-present solutions
-debrief the activity

Web tutorials are designed to teach a particular concept. Good tutorials address a specific objective and provide new information, including lots of examples. The tutorial should include an introduction, options for help, and opportunities for students to practice. Feedback also should be provided. An example of an outstanding tutorial is the Science of Cycling (http://www.exploratorium.edu/cycling/) which combines information on science and physical activity.

Virtual simulations help students apply their skills to "real life" situations by providing an environment in which they can manipulate variables, examine relationships, and make decisions. Simulations can help to prepare students for a field trip or a real experiment. While some simulations have a particular mission to accomplish, others are intended to help students explore a particular situation or environment. In most cases, simulations should be used as a culminating activity after students have basic skills in the concepts being addressed either on the Web site or in other classroom activities. The classic virtual simulation is the Virtual Frog Dissection Kit at http://george.lbl.gov/ITG.hm.pg.docs/dissect/dissect.html.

Some physical educators have actually combined the formats of virtual simulations and virtual field trips by having their students design community activities. An educator in Iowa had her students design a virtual canoe field trip. They were given x amount of fake money with which to buy equipment and arrange for transportation and lodging. They used MapQuest to plan their travels, online shopping to make purchases, and research tools to locate the "skill-appropriate" river/lake and to hone their canoeing skills.

Free Web Hosting

GeoCities: http://www.geocities.com/
Teacher Web: http://www.teacherweb.com/
Tripod: http://www.tripod.com/
One Stop: http://www.onestop.com/
My School Online: http://www.myschoolonline.com/

Working Offline

If you do not have access to the Internet at your teaching location, you can still provide your students with Internet learning opportunities. Programs such as Web Buddy allow teachers to collect pages and even entire sites from the Web for viewing offline. Many professional speakers use these programs so they can demonstrate the Internet without having to wait for the transfer of information or worry about a disconnection. Physical educators can do the same by downloading the Web pages and placing them on a local server or computer. Students can access the information as if they were actually on the World Wide Web.

Developing Web Pages

If you would like to add to the Internet information on physical education and sports you can set up your own Web page. Web authoring programs such as Claris HomePage, Adobe PageMill, or Netscape Composer make it very easy for you to do so. These programs function much like a word processing program; however, the output is in the form of a code known as html. Short for "hypertext markup language," html allows a variety of Internet users, regardless of their operating system, to view Web pages. Authoring programs also allow the user to embed links to other Web pages, as well as sounds, pictures, and video clips (see Chapter 10 for capturing video clips).

When designing a Web site, be sure to follow these steps:
1. Plan

Web Design Guidelines

1. Start small and have a plan.
2. Add material gradually.
3. Create one main folder for your entire site.
4. Create a separate folder inside the main folder for each major category of information.
5. Create one folder named "images" inside your main folder.
6. Keep each level to 5 to 10 items.
7. Develop a plan for maintenance and updates.
8. Put contact information (name, address, telephone, and fax numbers) on each page.
9. Include an e-mail link on each page.
10. Add new content weekly.
11. Check all links weekly.
12. Use a consistent look and feel.
13. Put navigation on each page.
14. Use no more than three images per page.
15. Put no more than two screens of information on each page.
16. If you must use more than two screens of information, provide a menu at the top of the page.
17. Design for 72 dpi, 256 colors, RGB, and 640x480.
18. Load time for a page should not exceed 30 seconds.
19. Test all pages on the two most commonly used browsers Netscape and Explorer—and on both a PC and a Mac.
20. Linked text should not exceed 20 percent of a passage.

2. Develop the content
3. Insert images and sounds
4. Insert links and frames.

Once you've created your Web site you will need to post your files on a server. You can either use your school's server, server space provided by your Internet Service Provider, or one of the free Web hosting sites. Do be careful when designing your site to follow the Web design guidelines in the highlight box on page 209.

Physical educators can post information related to their curriculum, rules, assessment procedures, the benefits of physical education, homework assignments, and other relevant information for parents. In addition, they can create learning activities and post them on the Web for student use. Coaches can post player information, schedules, scores, statistics, and scholarship information. Physical educators also can create online instruction or courses for their students using additional software such as Web CT (www.webct.com) and Blackboard (www.blackboard.com). These programs include online chat spaces, student progress tracking, grade maintenance and distribution, course calendars, student home pages, and search engine links.

Summary

The Internet can provide you with hours of enjoyment as well as the opportunity to secure vast amounts of information. However, it is always important to double check information and to ensure that the information you are reading is from a reliable source. A common feature of many Internet sites is "Frequently Asked Questions." This is a list of questions and answers about the site, and it provides a good introduction to the site. For those of you who are ready, try the next step and create your own web page.

Turn on your computer and start surfing, searching, and developing!

Reflection Questions

1. Do you think the benefits of access to the World Wide Web for physical education-related activities is worth the time, effort, and money invested in Internet access?
2. Which of the Web-based activities would best meet of the needs of your students? Why?

Projects

1. Design a Web-based activity for one of your classes. Be sure to align it with the content standards.
2. Create your own Web page.

Chapter 9

Computer Assisted Instructional Software

Students in gymnastics class are about to learn a new skill—the roundoff—and develop their individual floor exercise routines. The teacher has set up learning stations around the gymnasium. There are skill practice stations, fitness development stations, and a video station that demonstrates the roundoff. There also is a computer station where students learn to develop floor exercise routines, type in their routines, and see them in action.

Instruction software enhances the learning process by setting up a direct interaction between student and computer. The computer allows students to proceed at a rate that is meaningful to them. And it is forever patient, providing corrective feedback when needed and positive feedback when appropriate.

More than 30 research studies have found that the average learning time is reduced for 50 percent of the students who use multimedia instructional programs. Several studies also have shown 23 to 70 percent greater mastery in students who use interactive technology as compared to students who use more traditional methods (Levin & Meister, 1986; Niemiec, Blackwell & Walberg, 1986; Gu, 1996; Kulik, 1994). Students also show greater motivation and enjoyment when they use multimedia programs—they are actively involved and their attention is focused (Wilkinson, Pennington, & Padfield, 2000). Multimedia programs can be used for full-class presentations, small-group tutorials, and student projects. It is not unreasonable to expect

Why Use Instructional Software in Physical Education?

- Provides students with the "why."
- Introduces students to motor skills techniques before they actually practice them.
- Provides simulation, problem-solving experiences, and practice with offensive and defensive situations that would not otherwise be available.
- Provides a logical sequence from simple to more complex concepts.
- Provides unlimited practice, review, and remediation.
- Provides immediate feedback and reinforcement quickly and efficiently.
- Helps create a richer, more varied instructional setting.
- Meets a variety of student needs.
- Provides information, calculates answers, manages student progress, and prints out results.
- Programs are more easily updated than are other types of instructional material.
- Programs promote cooperation and collaboration among students, and good teachers can capitalize on these opportunities.

that the textbooks of tomorrow will be multimedia interactive.

Before you use computer-assisted instructional software in your class, you need to do four things:

1. Identify the instructional objective(s) of the lesson or unit.
2. Determine the most appropriate teaching strategy, including instructional materials, for meeting the objectives of the lesson or unit.
3. If the instructional materials include technology, select the software that will best help students meet the objective(s).
4. Decide how best to incorporate instructional technology into the lesson.

Steps 1 and 2 are common procedures for planning any lesson. While you might consider any number of teaching strategies and instructional materials, there are several reasons for selecting instructional software. Once you decide to use software, you must select the specific software program and plan the lessons.

This chapter will introduce you to a variety of instructional software, give you tips on how to evaluate them, and provide you with ideas for incorporating them into your lessons.

Instructional Software

There are several different types of instructional software on the market, including drill-and-practice programs, tutorials, analysis, reference, educational games, and simulations. When selecting software to review, follow the steps in the highlight box below. Then, use the assessment criteria on page 215 during the review process. To help you narrow your search, descriptions of each type of software and examples for physical education are provided in the following sections. Most programs cost between $25 and $100 per computer, although some are more expensive. All programs are available for Macintosh and Windows and can be used, at least partially, for grades 4 through 12, unless otherwise noted. Software vendors are listed in Appendix A.

Drill-and-Practice Programs

Drill-and-practice programs can help students memorize facts, such as the rules of a sport. These programs provide computer-directed instruction, so the learner merely answers questions. The basic format of drill-and-practice software is as follows:

Selecting Instructional Software for Review

1. Analyze needs.
2. Specify requirements.
3. Identify promising software.
4. Read relevant reviews.
5. Preview software.
6. Make recommendations.
7. Get post-use feedback.

The student reads and responds to the questions presented by the program. The program then evaluates the student's response to each question, provides immediate feedback, and presents a summary performance report. Some drill-and-practice programs include graphics and video. Drill-and-practice software has always been a very low level use of the computer, and today these programs pale in comparison to other programs. However, as a drill medium, the computer has some advantages. Just make sure the content of the program is important and is something students truly need to memorize. An example of this type of software follows.

Muscle Flash (Bonnie's Fitware). Muscle Flash (see Figure 9.1) is a flash card program designed to teach students the names of muscles. It displays a graphic of a single muscle and asks the student to identify it. Students receive feedback on the accuracy of their responses. There are five levels: Primary Muscle Flash, Elementary Muscle Flash, Middle Muscle Flash, Senior Muscle Flash, and College Muscle Flash. For older students, the program also can ask the muscle's origin, insertion, location, and function.

Tutorials

Tutorial software combines text, graphics, and video to introduce new concepts and it provides an opportunity for the students to interact with the program by answering questions. More sophisticated programs offer learners several options after each question is presented: enter an answer, review the topic, have the question asked differently, or select additional topics to explore. The program may even be able to evaluate the

Software Review Sites

http://www.superkids.com/
http://clearinghouse.k12.ca.us/

Reviewing Software

- The objectives are clear.
- The content is accurate.
- The program keeps track of how well students are doing.
- The program is easy to use.
- The program offers second chances when users respond incorrectly to questions.
- The program provides motivation.
- The program runs correctly (no bugs).
- The content moves from lower level objectives to higher level skills.
- Graphics are clear and appropriate.
- Sound is used to enhance program.
- The program makes effective and appropriate use of the computer as an instructional tool.
- The pace of the material can be controlled by the teacher or the student.
- The level of difficulty can be controlled by the teacher or the student.
- The student can easily access the program's Help function.
- Students are actively involved with the program.
- The program's instructional strategies are based on research findings.
- The presentation is free of any objectionable stereotyping.
- Inquiry processes are well integrated into the software package.
- The program's feedback responses are appropriate, informative, and timely.
- The program encourages two or more students to interact with one another.
- Program documentation is comprehensive, clear, and consistent with observed program behavior.
- It meets Student Interoperability Frameworks (SIF) compatibility.
- It is available in both Macintosh and Windows formats.

learner's performance and automatically adjust the difficulty level of future questions accordingly.

Bowling Tutorial (Bonnie's Fitware). This program is designed to teach students how to score in bowling. It includes rules, symbols, and scoring for spares and strikes. Bowling Tutorial also allows student interaction through self-check questions and the scoring of a sample game.

Softball Basic Strategy Tutorial (Bonnie's Fitware). This program presents the basics of defensive softball strategy,

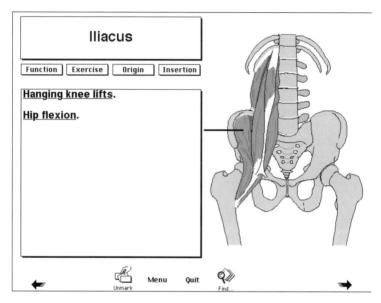

Figure 9.1   A screen from Muscle Flash (Bonnie's Fitware).

including base coverage for infield and outfield hits. Students interact by clicking on the base where they would throw the ball in a given situation. The software provides the students with feedback and an opportunity to select another base.

Analysis Software

Analysis software adds another level of interaction. Students input real or factitious data directly or through probes, and the software conducts the analysis. Four types of analysis software are used in physical education: nutritional analysis, risk assessment, exercise planning, and data collection.

Nutritional Analysis.   Many nutritional analysis programs are currently available. These programs ask the user for age, weight, height, gender, and amount of physical activity, and then calculate the individual's nutritional needs. The user records the types and amounts of foods he or she eats daily, and the program creates a report that lists calories ingested, the nutrient values for all foods, and the total of all nutrients ingested. You can use these reports to determine if the student has met the recommended dietary allowances (RDA) and whether the number of calories ingested was excessive.

Some programs allow the user to indicate the type and length of activity performed. The software then determines the number of calories expended for a specified amount of time and the relationship between caloric intake and caloric output. For the educational setting, I recommend DINE Healthy (DINE Systems). It exposes poor nutritional and fitness behaviors through its analysis of daily food intake and physical activity. Appropriate menus and exercises are recommended for a healthier lifestyle. The software serves as the student's personal trainer for fitness and nutrition. It is especially effective for students who desire a reduction in body fat, cholesterol level, and blood pressure.

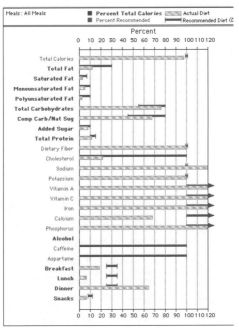

Figure 9.2   A screen from DINE Healthy (DINE System).

Risk Assessment. Risk assessment programs ask the user to input data regarding his or her lifestyle. Questions include height, weight, gender, age, cholesterol level, blood pressure, smoking habits, alcohol usage, physical activity habits, family medical history, nutritional information, and use of seat belts. Based on the data received, the program determines the individual's life expectancy, cardiovascular disease risk, and/ or cancer risk. There are several shareware programs for risk assessment; as well as web-based software at sites such as http:/ /www.bodybalance.com/hra/.

Exercise Planning. Exercise planning software can help a student develop an individual workout plan based on his or her current fitness level and physical activity goals. In addition to desktop/notebook versions, there also are software programs in this category that fit on a handheld or palm computer.

UltraCoach (Multi-sport Athletic Training Software), a desktop/ notebook Windows-based program, can provide students with a personalized workout program for cycling, running, swimming, inline skating, weight lifting, and/or aerobics, plus cross-training programs. It keeps track of all workouts, equipment, and routines, and gives feedback using graphs, charts, and reports. For heart rate monitor users, it will produce heart zone training for warm-up, workout, and cool down based on manually entered data or data transferred from a Polar heart monitor. The program ensures that students do not overtrain, and therefore can reduce the chance of injury.

Workout Log (Waverly Software Design), another exercise planning program, was designed for the Newton operating system. It tracks and analyzes workout information, helps the user design his or her own custom workout template, allows the user to add unique data to any log entry, records special events, tracks wear and tear on fitness equipment, summarizes workout data, and produces a variety of reports and graphs. Note that hardware for the Newton operating system is no longer being manufactured.

DietLog (HealtheTech) provides you with the opportunity to set personal nutrition and weight loss goals, track daily food consumption, and monitor progress on a palm computer (palm operating system). You can keep an accurate count of calories, carbohydrates, protein, fat, sodium, and fiber. A companion program is WeightLog which provides the opportunity to log, view, analyze, and graph your weight over time. The third component of this system is the ExerLog, which tracks exercise and calorie expenditure.

Fitness Planner (Vivonic) is available for both the Windows operating system and the palm operating system. The palm version offers a daily journal where you can enter what you eat and any exercise you perform in addition to viewing summary reports. On the desktop, you can set goals, determine nutritional needs, and develop an exercise plan. A Plan Wizard helps you establish your fitness plan. The software can record weight and other measurements such as cholesterol, blood pressure, and hours of sleep. It also can maintain your medical history.

Management Tips

1. Teach students to respect and properly care for the equipment.
2. Have students bring their own floppy disk or CD-R to school to use for physical education.
3. Have the students write their name and their teacher's name on the label of the floppy disk or CD-R.
4. Teach students to use reasonable names to save projects.
5. Teach students to save their projects every five minutes while they are working.
6. Have students keep floppy disks or CD-Rs in storage boxes.
7. If your computer has enough memory or you are working from a server, have students keep projects in folders labeled with their names.
8. Use a timer so students know how much time they can spend on the computer.
9. Assign students to specific computers.
10. Provide task cards for each computer assignment and have computer helpers available to trouble shoot problems.

Multimedia Workout (Human Kinetics) for Windows provides users with the tools to create an individualized exercise routine and diet plan and to track their progress. It consists of a muscle/ exercise data base with information about strength and stretching exercises that work selected areas, a workout planner where the user can track daily workout progress, a food data base the user can sort by 30 different nutrients, a food planner for analyzing and tracking nutrient and caloric intake, a recipe data base that contains the nutritional analysis for hundreds of recipes, and a personal progress log that graphs and tracks daily and weekly progress in weightlifting, cardiovascular fitness, body weight, percent body fat, and body measurements. This software brings together nutritional analysis and exercise prescription in one easy-to-use program.

Data Collection. Data collection involves the use of probes or videos to collect information for the computer to analyze. For example, eProbe (MSC Working Knowledge), designed for the eMate computer using the Newton operating system, allows students to use probes to collect and visually analyze complex scientific data. Probes for temperature, light, and voltage are included in the basic kit. Data samples are collected as either single values or as a continuous stream of data. The data are then easily converted into a table or graph for analysis. Students in physical education can measure body temperature before and after exercise and the intensity of light on grass and blacktop, for example, and analyze the results in terms of implications for physical activity settings. Other probe systems for desktop computers include PASCO Scientific Systems and Vernier probes. The motion detector probe has many possible applications in physical education. Software for using sensors with the palm operating system also is under development.

Motion Measurement is the term used in biomechanics to describe the collection and analysis of two-dimensional and three-dimensional data. The data are collected using reflective markers, so that the movement is automatically recorded and

Interdisciplinary Lesson: Physical Education/ Science/Math/Computer Multimedia Project

Instructional Unit: Swimming/SCUBA.

Cognitive Concepts: Exercise physiology and biomechanics.

Facility: Swimming pool.

Supplies: SCUBA gear such as tanks and regulators, masks, snorkels, fins, boots, and gloves.

Interdisciplinary Concepts:

Physical education—application of swimming skills in the lifetime activity of SCUBA.

Diving physiology—effects of diving and pressure on the human body and its various systems.

Diving physics—gas laws and the connection between scientific laws and safe diving.

Navigation mathematics—navigation and orienteering. Gain insight into the geometry concepts used by everyone from divers to pilots to locate their position and direction.

Scientific laws—Boyle's law, Dalton's law, Henry's law, buoyancy.

Life science—marine life encountered by scuba divers.

Human physiology—effects of scuba diving on body temperature, senses, circulation system, respiratory system, oxygen debt in muscles, and balance or equilibrium.

Multimedia project—students work in small groups to do research, design experiments, and present their findings. Each student team prepares a project proposal for their desired topic. Completed projects are presented at the end of the term.

analyzed by high-end computer systems. At the lower end, the performance is videotaped and the video is transferred from the camera to the computer allowing the user to identify (usually through a mouse click) the location of joints in each frame. The data then are analyzed for factors, such as displacement, velocity, and acceleration. When videotaping for the purpose of quantitative analysis, be sure to:

- videotape the motion at right angles to the camera
- physically move the camera back and use the zoom lens to frame the subject

- limit camera motion (including panning)
- create a field of view two to three times larger than the subject
- if the video will be used for slow-motion replay then zoom in on the subject (Knudson & Morrison, 1997).

It also is very important to know the number of frames per second at which the video was recorded and the length (in inches) of a physical object in the field of view. These are the two variables that allow for the analysis of the data. The three programs described below should be used at the high school level.

Measurement in Motion (Learning in Motion) is another tool-based program that encourages open-ended exploration. It focuses on biomechanics and the analysis of movement. Students use video clips (included with the software or created on their own) and analyze measurements (e.g., body position, body rotation, stride length, height of knees/ankles, height of jump, position of ball release, arc of ball, and speed of swung). The software is accompanied by a teacher's manual that includes instructions for using the measurements along with five practice activities. Student worksheets also are included.

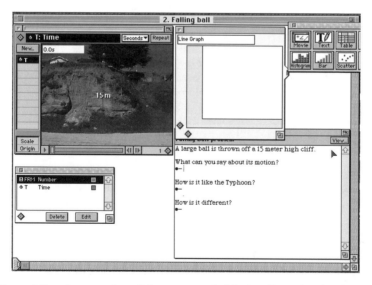

Figure 9.3   A screen from Measurement in Motion (Learning in Motion).

Teaching Biomechanics

Biomechanics is the science of how and why movement occurs, and whether it is efficient. The Elements of Physical Education class covers the principles of gravity, stability-balance, Newton's Law of Motion, force, types of motion, levers, projectiles, application of force and absorption of force. Students work in groups of four at learning stations as they study these principles. Each station has a task card that challenges students' motor, problem solving, and movement analysis skills. The textbook Moving for Life is used at one station, where the students read several paragraphs and answer two questions. At other stations, the students experiment with different motor skill techniques in order to determine the biomechanical principles involved. A computer station allows students to interact with the concepts, check their understanding with a quiz, and see the motion being studied.
–Carolyn Thompson, Bell Gardens High School

The NEAT system allows you to capture and analyze full motion video on any Windows-based PC. This system provides several graphic tools (line, circle, semi-circle, rectangle, parallelogram, angle, grid, pencil, back swing trace, and follow thru trace) for isolating and highlighting positions on the video screen. The graphics appear over the video as it plays or advances frame by frame. The system also allows for the simultaneous playing of several video files. Users can select two, three, or four window mode.

The Peak system is another Windows-based motion analysis program. Its modular design allows users to select only those specific applications that they need. The Peak Motus Basic Video System collects video data at a maximum of 25 (PAL) or 30 (NTSC) pictures per second. The use of reflective markers are optional, and the system can provide two-dimensional and/or three-dimensional data as needed.

Reference Software

Reference software provides users with the opportunity to explore and retrieve information relevant to their learning. It

223

runs the gamut from electronic encyclopedias, to medical CD-ROMs, to sport-specific software. In many of these programs, students enter search words and are presented with a number of related documents, graphs, tables, pictures, sounds, animated graphics, video clips, three-dimensional interactive tours, and/or interactive activities. Hypermedia (similar to the hyperlinks on the World Wide Web) frequently is used with reference software; it allows for interactive linking. Thus, access to reference software is non-linear. Users can skip certain information and target the specific information they need.

MicroSoft's Bookshelf. This seven-"book" CD-ROM includes The American Heritage Dictionary, Columbia Dictionary of Quotations, The Original Roget's Thesaurus, Hammond World Atlas, The World Almanac, The People's Chronology, and The Concise Columbia Encyclopedia. Students can search for information across all seven books simultaneously. The Concise Columbia Encyclopedia is especially helpful to students in physical education, since they can search for information on various sports and health issues. Other electronic encyclopedias include World Book Multimedia Encyclopedia–Deluxe Edition (World Book), which includes three-dimensional models of human anatomy and an online component for current downloads from the World Book Web Site, Encarta Encyclopedia (MicroSoft), Britannica CD (Britannica), and Grolier Multimedia Encyclopedia (Grolier).

Awesome Athletes (Sports Illustrated). This Windows-based program uses a fun approach to teach students about the greatest athletes of all times. There are photos and facts about 250 athletes. Live action videos are combined with interviews. In addition, there are a number of games that test sports knowledge.

ESPN Let's Play Tennis (Intelliplay). This program provides step-by-step live action instruction to help your students execute better strokes and learn the essentials of successful on-court strategy. Students see top athletes in action, in full motion or one frame at a time. Students can learn the serve, baseline play, approach shots, half and full volleys, lobs, and overhead stokes. Other titles in this series include: Golf (driving, irons, sand shots, shots from trouble areas, special short shots, and putting); Lower Your Score with Tom Kite (full swing, driving, and putting techniques); Football (passing, catching, passing patterns, offensive lineman skills, defensive lineman skills, and running back skills); Baseball (pitching, catching, batting, defense); Interactive Soccer (skills and strategies); Let's Play Baseball (offensive and defensive strategies); Let's Play Basketball (offensive and defensive skills and strategies); Let's Go Skiing (step-by-step instructions for straight running, wedge movements, wedge turns, wedge christy, advanced wedge christy, and open parallel maneuvers); and Let's Play Beach Volleyball (stretching, digging, spiking, setting, passing, serving, blocking, and offensive and defensive strategies).

Interactive Guide to Soccer (SISU). Essentially an electronic encyclopedia on soccer, this CD-ROM provides instruction on the history, rules, game, motor skills, officiating skills, and tactics. It also includes a question-and-answer section where students can test their soccer knowledge, and a glossary of 150 soccer terms. SISU produces a similar CD-ROM entitled Interactive Guide to Volleyball. These programs were designed for the community college level student, but they can be used at the high school and even the middle school level.

Golf Tips (DIAMAR). This CD-ROM comes in two formats: Golf Tips: Breaking 100, and Golf Tips: Breaking 90. Both provide tips and techniques from the best golf instructors from around the world. Both are organized in four sections—5-Day Lesson, Analyze Your Trouble Areas, Build Your Own Golf Workshop, and Play the Hole—and are designed to provide a comprehensive instructional package. The Breaking 100 program is recommended for middle school students and the Breaking 90 program for high school students.

The 5-Day Lesson, Analyze Your Trouble Areas, and Build Your Own Workshop cover the same material but in different ways. The 5-Day Lesson covers more than 50 topics in a sequential, instructor-led form. Each day builds on the skills and techniques learned the previous day.

In Analyzing Your Trouble Areas, students can focus on a specific problem with a particular aspect of the golf game. For example, the software will organize a series of lessons around playing out of hazards.

In Building Your Own Workshop, the student designs his or her own workshop and customizes the learning. The student chooses the lessons he or she wants to pursue—such as hitting from a bunker—and clicks on related topics of interest as he or she progresses through the lesson. The CD includes 360-degree video clips, video clips (slow and normal motion), audio coaching cues, and photography sequences to assist with instruction.

Finally, Playing the Hole provides students with the opportunity to play a championship par five hole to test their knowledge of

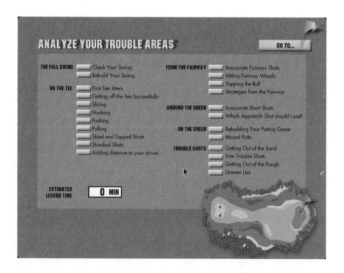

Figure 9.4   A screen from Golf Tips (Diamar).

Sample Instructional Stations for Golf

1. Videotape golf stroke
2. Review video of golf stroke*
3. Use Measurement in Motion to analyze golf stroke*
4. Practice putting
5. Practice driving
6. Practice golf stroke with peer feedback
7. Practice putting
8. Practice driving
9. Use Golf Tips software to review golf stroke
10. Practice golf stroke

* Do not start groups at stations two or three

golf strategy and club selection. This virtual reality simulation of an actual hole enables the user to specify average score, choose a club, and then play the hole customized to his or her skill level. The user receives feedback from the pros on club choices and strategies.

Rock Climbing (Media Mosaic). This program uses animation, videos, and photographs to provide detailed instruction on rock climbing. More than 200 topics, ranging from the fundamentals, to belaying, to more advanced climbing techniques such as climbing faces, cracks, corners, overhangs, and steep faces, are covered. Students choose the topics they wish to explore using a graphic user interface in the design of a rock climb. A similar program from this producer—Mountain Biking—provides detailed instruction on the sport and covers beginning to expert skill levels. Students can choose when and how to learn difficult techniques by exploring more than 300 animations, videos, and photographs.

1996 U.S. Olympic Team (Archimedia Interactive). This Windows-based program provides a comprehensive look at every aspect of the 1996 games. There are video clips, photographs, and text covering the athletes and the competition.

Olympic Gold (S.E.A. Multimedia). This Windows-based software provides a 100-year history of the summer Olympic games. It includes video, photos, and in-depth articles. Also included are individual and country-wide statistics relating to medals, times, and records.

What Is a Bellybutton? (IVI). Designed for students in grades K-3, this CD-ROM answers personal health questions youngsters in this age group typically ask. It includes animated characters, funny sounds, and lots of surprises to maintain the interest of younger students.

Welcome to Bodyland (IVI). This program provides the user with the opportunity to visit 12 lands within the Bodyland Theme Park. The various lands refer to body parts, and include the nose, tummy, eyes, skin, ears, heart, lungs, hair, bones, mouth, palms, and head. Information is provided in each of the different lands, and students can visit Discovery Towers, where they are encouraged to play a game to find out how much they know about their bodies. Designed for the elementary school student, this CD-ROM is a nice follow-up to What Is a Bellybutton?

My Amazing Human Body (DK). My Amazing Human Body is designed for students between the ages of 6 and 10. It presents information on human anatomy, health, nutrition, and much more. Students learn about their skeleton, organs, and body systems as they follow the activities of a specially created three-dimensional skeleton host. Activities include Build Me a Body, where students answer multiple-choice questions to earn bones and organs; What Am I Made Of, where kids examine, manipulate, and learn about 35 body parts; and Me and My Day, where students determine the events of the skeleton's day by selecting activities and meals. In Secret File, students record information about themselves such as favorite foods, height, and weight, as well as developmental milestones.

Body Voyage (Forest). Body Voyage data were compiled from a real human body that was dissected into more than 1,800 sections. Video clips, text explanations, and a fly-through display body images. Users can manipulate and zoom in at varying levels of anatomical depth by dissolving through layers of skin, muscle, and bone.

Body Park (Virtual Entertainment). Body Park is a place where kids from all over the world come to visit, learn, and have fun. It involves Professor Frankenslime, a mad scientist who is trying to turn real people into plastic dummies. The students are told that Frankenslime has only succeeded in turning one person—Harvey—into a plastic dummy so far. The students are encouraged to play a game that adds magic body parts to Harvey until he becomes a whole person again. In addition to playing the game, the software includes interesting information, facts, experiments that can be performed online or with real materials, health and safety tips, and entertaining music with educational lyrics. This program is available only for Windows.

Ultimate 3-D Skeletal System (DK) . This CD-ROM provides a medically accurate, three-dimensional digital skeleton. The software identifies every bone, shows every muscle attachment, pronounces every word, manipulates in three-dimensions every bone in the human body, and shares a wealth of information pertaining to bones and the skeletal system. The three-dimensional images are derived from an x-ray scan of real bones. The detail of images is extremely fine; every small pit and crevice can be screen. The name of each part of the skeleton is heard and viewed as the cursor is placed on it. The "Amazing Facts" section provides interesting information related to the bones and the "Extra News" section allows bones to be viewed from unusual angles. A quiz tests knowledge of the names of particular bones. Students may copy text, graphics, or an entire screen to the clipboard of their computer. An index allows access to any part of the program at any time. A teacher's guide offers

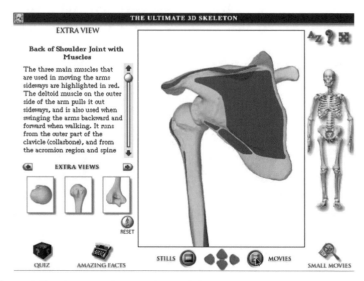

Figure 9.5   A screen from Ultimate 3-D Skeletal System (DK).

supplemental activities and ideas for classroom use.

A.D.A.M.: The Inside Story (A.D.A.M.). Targeted for grades four through eight, this software takes students on a multimedia journey through the 12 major systems of the human body. Students can cut away and restore structures; choose anatomical views, image size, gender, and skin tone; and search for and highlight structures. In the Family Scrapbook section, a modern-day Adam and Eve guide students on a system-by-system voyage into the body. The couple narrates stories and animations, and medical experts discuss a variety of topics ranging from heartburn to snoring and from coronary artery disease to osteoporosis. The in-depth teacher's guide provides interdisciplinary activities, anatomical system overviews, homework activities, summaries of the animation and videos, lists of key terms, and detailed illustrations of each system. Note: An optional fig leaf is available at installation for covering genitals and female breasts.

A.D.A.M. Essentials (A.D.A.M.). Designed for high school

students, this CD-ROM contains a multimedia reference program on the fundamentals of human anatomy and physiology. The 12 body systems are described along with each of their functions. There are more than 4,000 anatomical structures in approximately 100 medically accurate layers, along with 38 narrated animations on the inner workings of the body that include pronunciation of structure names. Students can participate in interactive puzzles and build different body structures. A complete teacher's guide with lessons for all body systems is included. Note: Genitalia can be covered using a fig leaf at the time of installation.

How Your Body Works (Mattel). This CD-ROM focuses on the 12 major body systems. It shows how the different organ systems function and describes what can happen if something goes wrong. It uses video clips, voice, illustrations, text, and music. It has a very unique graphic user interface—a laboratory where students click on different objects (for example, a video cassette recorder/monitor to see video clips). A teacher's guide with detailed supplemental materials including student

Figure 9.6   Adam: The Inside Story and Adam Essentials.

Figure 9.7   A screen from How Your Body Works (Mattel).

worksheets accompanies this program.

The Total Heart (IVI). The Total Heart provides a comprehensive guide to heart health and heart disease. It includes all the information in the 400-page print version, plus animation, graphs, pictures, video clips, three-dimensional visualizations, audio, and illustrations. It provides information about the anatomy of the heart and circulatory system along with explanations of a wide range of cardiovascular diseases and conditions, symptoms, possible causes, medications, and treatment options. This CD-ROM also includes practical advice on lifestyle, diet, and other preventive measures. Students can search for the information by typing the name of the topic in the "find box" or they can click on related information until they find what they are seeking.

BodyWorks (Mattel). This is another strong anatomy and physiology program. It includes text, video, three-dimensional models, and animation, and it provides a complete overview of all major human body systems. A Health, Fitness, and Living guide is provided for individual assessment, goal setting, and monitoring. The program also has a Virtual Doctor (Dr. BodyWorks) interface. A special health section provides information on first aid, general fitness, sport injuries, and common illnesses. Students can test their knowledge of anatomy by playing BodyBasics, a game show for one or two players. The teacher's activity guide includes support materials, an overview of the program, and suggestions for individual projects and quizzes. The program also provides online access to the BodyWorks home page. Note: This program contains explicit, realistic drawings of female and male sexual organs as well as detailed information on reproduction.

BioMechanics Made Easy (Bonnie's Fitware). This program instructs students on analysis of movement. It provides a reference section on each of the biomechanical principles (i.e., stability, projection, levers). In addition, there is a simulation section where students apply their knowledge in "real-life" situations and their performance is monitored and recorded.

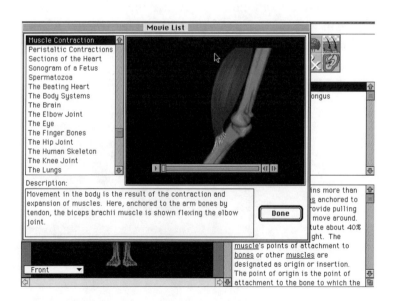

Figure 9.8   A screen from Body Works (Mattel).

Instructional Games

Instructional games usually contain very definite rules for how questions will be answered or problems will be solved. A score keeping element, designed to increase student motivation, separates games from other types of computer-assisted instruction. Some educators may prefer not to encourage competition in learning; however, most of these programs can be set up so students compete against themselves or against a standard.

Football Rules Game (Bonnie's Fitware). The Football Rules Game uses a game-like setting to teach and/or reinforce touchdown rules. The game can be played by an individual or by two teams. The ball is kicked off by one team, and the receiving team gets the ball at the 25-yard line. The offense has four opportunities (questions) to move the ball across the next quarter line. The team can choose to answer a 5-yard, 10-yard, or 15-yard question. A correct answer moves the ball the number of yards indicated. If the team crosses the quarter line, they get a first down and four more opportunities to advance the ball. Otherwise, the other team gets possession of the ball and the chance to answer questions. This program is available only for the Macintosh.

Figure 9.9 A screen from Bonnie's Fitware football rules game. Students select 5-, 10-, or 15-yard questions to answer. If their answer is correct, the ball advances that many yards.

Softball Rules Game (Bonnie's Fitware). The Softball Rules Game is similar to the Football Rules Game. It uses a game-like setting to teach and/or reinforce softball rules. Students choose a single, double, or triple question. After three outs (incorrect answers), the other team gets a turn at answering the questions. Automatic outs are included with the single questions to prevent students from selecting only the easier questions. This program is available only for the Macintosh.

Links 386 (Access Software and Picture Perfect Golf). Links 386 for windows is one of many golf simulation games on the market. These programs reinforce correct club selection, stance, and reading of the course as you play the game from tee to cup and make all the shots you would on a course. With the addition of PC Golf, you actually can use a short (26-inch) club as the input device instead of a mouse. PC Golf consists of a durable plastic base unit (8" wide, by 6" long, by 1.5" high) that contains light sensors, a microprocessor, and a golf ball graphic. The sensors in the base pick up the lighted club head image and measure club head speed, club face angle, and club path in order to determine the direction and distance of your shot.

Simply connect PC Golf to an IBM compatible personal computer, install the software, and then tee-up to play Pebble Beach, Mauna Kea, or Big Horn. Although programs like this are considered educational games because of the score keeping feature, they also can be considered simulations, since many aspects of the software parallel the true game of golf.

Alley 19 (Starplay Productions). This Macintosh-based program allows bowling on computer through use of the mouse. It can be played with others or on a network. Students learn the game of bowling, rules, and scoring through the on-screen simulation. It also provides students with an opportunity to simulate the motor skill technique used for various "pick-ups." A booklet contains information on installation and quick start, option menu, screens, network play, high score contest, rules of bowling, and troubleshooting.

Simulations

Simulations are the most sophisticated form of computer-assisted instruction. The computer is programmed with a definite number of rules related to an event. These are accompanied by extensive graphics to enhance the illusion of the actual situation. An event is presented, and based on the user's interaction with the program, different results are obtained. Simulations are ideal for teaching problem solving and decision making, especially in situations where the real event can be dangerous or expensive. The strength of simulations is that they simplify circumstances in order to highlight special conditions and create realistic problem solving environments. A weakness is that they may be oversimplified and some details may be omitted, giving the user a false impression of what the reality is like. Simulations also may provide a false sense of accomplishment, since a high score on a simulation does not guarantee a high score in the real situation.

MacHeart Monitor Simulation (Bonnie's Fitware). MacHeart Monitor Simulation teaches students how to program the Polar Vantage Heart Monitor. It provides information and practice on each of the four major functions, followed by a simulation that allows users to check for understanding prior to experimenting with the actual heart rate monitor. This Macintosh program is good for students and teachers.

Body and Mind (Fitness Lifestyle Design). Body and Mind is designed to help students practice real-life tasks in developing a fitness plan. The program allows students to simulate and model alternative fitness plans and to receive immediate feedback on the outcomes of their choices. The program immediately displays the consequences of adding or deleting exercises or changing the overload variables.

Sim Athlete (Bonnie's Fitware). Instructs students on how to develop their own practice plan. SimAthlete provides a reference section on each of the motor learning principles. It also has a simulation section where students can assume the role of a coach and develop a practice plan for an athlete. If they create an effective practice plan, their athlete performs well. If their plan is ineffective, then their athlete performs poorly. The scores for the simulation are recorded so teachers can monitor student progress.

Using Instructional Software

Once you have selected the appropriate software for the learning objective, you must determine how best to incorporate it into the lesson. Of course, it is important that you feel comfortable using a computer for your own purposes before you try to use one for instruction with students.

Your first experience using instructional software may simply involve typing notes into a word processing or presentation document and projecting the information onto a screen through a projection system or television set. (This use of the computer can help to increase your technology comfort level but it does not address the requirements of the fourth step listed at the start of this chapter—selecting the best method of incorporating computer-assisted instructional software into a lesson.)

You have at least four options for using instructional software. The first three require one computer (although for the third method a few more would be better); the last option requires a computer lab. For Method 1, you connect the computer to a projection system or to several 25-inch monitors. This method is used for class activities, with class members taking turns reading the tutorial part of the software. During the question-and-answer phase of the program, individual students are called on to answer questions, or, better yet, a cooperative learning strategy called "numbered heads" is used—students work in groups of four and collaborate within their groups to determine the correct answers to randomly asked questions. This is called numbered heads because each student is given a number from one to four, and the teacher calls out a number instead of a student's name. This technique should be used only when you want to cover a small piece of information with the entire class at the beginning of a lesson. It is not recommended for an entire class period.

Method 2 requires that you set up learning stations, including one computer station. A few management tips for student use of the computer will facilitate the process. Students work in cooperative learning groups of four students each rotating from one station to the next. Each student should be assigned a role—for example, navigator (controls the movement through the software), encourager (reinforces the contributions of the other individuals in the group), expander (elaborates on answers given by other members), and summarizer (brings closure to group learning). Method 2 is used most commonly in physical

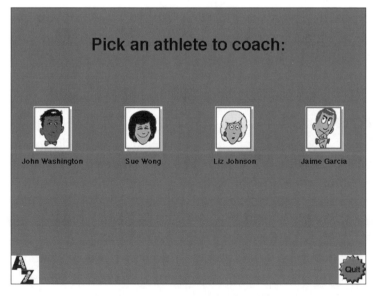

Figure 9.9   A screen from SimAthlete (Bonnie's Fitware).

education because it allows for a high percentage of time on task and keeps students physically active during most of the lesson. However, the actual amount of time spent with the computer is rather limited, so students should be directed to either follow task cards, respond to a series of questions, or conduct specific research. This method also can be structured to provide additional computer opportunities for those students who have medical excuses.

Method 3 is similar to Method 2, in that it uses one computer station. However, in this method, the groups that are not using the computer are preparing to do so. For example, students prepare their tumbling routines on paper, then use the computer to input their routines and view a visual representation. Students then can evaluate and refine their routines. Another example of this method is the Orienteering Program in which students learn, in expert groups, various elements needed for orienteering. The computer program simulates an actual experience. Method 3 should be used only when students have time to prepare for what they will be doing on the computer.

In Method 4, each student or pair of students must have access to a computer, and each computer must be supplied with the software, either individually or by a network. There are three situations in which Method 4 is recommended: The first is when the objective for the lesson requires the use of the software for an extended period. The second is when students have computer lab time during the school day, separate from their other classes, and the lab teacher is open to using a variety of software (including physical education software) to teach students computer skills. Finally, the lab setting can be used when students create multimedia projects during out-of-school time or technology class. These projects may be specific to physical education or they might be interdisciplinary in nature. All uses of technology bring your students closer to meeting the technology standards for K-12 students.

Sample Lesson Plan Using Software

This lesson provides an example of how computer-assisted instruction software, specifically simulations, can be used effectively in a physical education class.

Lesson Time: One week on outdoor education with an additional eight days of follow-up to allow each group to have time on the computer (the follow-up time can be when students are working on other projects, or in conjunction with a science or social science class).

Environment: Classroom or gymnasium.

Computer Requirements: Macintosh or Windows.

Software: Orienteering: A Tutorial and Simulation.

Distributed By: Bonnie's Fitware.

Grade Level: Grades 5-12.

Class Size: 40 students.

Curriculum Goal: Demonstrate application of orienteering skills.

Computer Skill: Improve inputting skills and increase basic knowledge about computer operations.

Introduction: Outdoor education is often overlooked by physical education teachers. Using the computer, students can learn about hiking, navigating, and safety without ever having to leave a classroom or gymnasium. Orienteering: A Tutorial and Simulation is particularly effective in teaching students the skills related to orienteering. It also requires students to use higher-level thinking skills as they plan and execute their route through the control points.

Materials Needed: For this lesson, the teacher will need 1 copy of Orienteering: A Tutorial and Simulation from Bonnie's Fitware, and 10 copies of the accompanying information booklet. Other resources on orienteering will provide enrichment.

Preparation: The students participate in a cooperative learning jigsaw activity in order to learn the basic information about orienteering. Each student is assigned to 1 of 10 heterogeneous groups. After several preliminary team-building activities, the teacher gives a short introduction to orienteering, the software program, and the jigsaw activity. Each group is then given time to decide who will specialize in each of the following areas: taking a bearing, map reading, safety issues, and planning a route. Once students make their selections, double expert groups are formed for each area of specialization (two groups of five students each work on taking a bearing, etc.).

Double Expert Group Activity: Each expert group reads through the information on their area and makes note of the important points. The expert groups are responsible not only for the orienteering content but also for how to use that knowledge in the orienteering program. Students who finish early may secure additional information from other available resources. Once all members of an expert group have learned their material, they prepare a presentation for their home groups.

Home Group Activity: Team members return to their home groups and present their information. During this time, each group has a limited amount of time to experiment with the software. Students should not be expected to successfully complete the entire route; they simply should become familiar with the program. At this point, the students will be very dependent on one another for the knowledge they have gained in their expert groups.

Concluding Group Activity: A quiz is given on the last day of the week, after all experts have completed their presentations and all teams have had the opportunity to experiment with the software. Students are evaluated on both individual and team quiz scores. In addition, during the next couple of weeks, as teams have their time on the computer, they are assessed on how well they complete the orienteering simulation.

Summary

Instructional software—including drill-and-practice, tutorial, analysis, reference, educational games, and simulation programs —is available to physical educators. And, even though we would like to see more high-quality instructional programs, there is much that we can do with the software that is available. Our students will benefit from learning health-related cognitive concepts, viewing model skill performances, interacting with sport related experiments, and investigating up-to-date fitness information.

Make sure you are using all of the instructional resources available to you, including instructional software.

Reflection Questions

1. Why do you think there are fewer instructional software for physical education compared to other subject areas?
2. Which strategy will you use when incorporating instructional software in your lessons? Why did you choose this strategy?

Projects

1. Design a lesson plan involving one of the software programs described in this chapter. Be sure to align the lesson with one or more of the National Standards.
2. Outline a software program you would like to see designed. Be sure the objectives of the program align with the design. Consider submitting your outline to a software publisher for review.

Chapter 10

Assessing Student Learning

Jeremy Thompson works in a small K-8 school. Because he is the only physical educator, he has the same students for nine consecutive years. At the beginning of each school year, Jeremy videotapes his students, digitizes the images, and stores them in individual electronic portfolios. The older students videotape themselves and transfer the images to their portfolios. They also review their images through the years and write essays describing their progress. They analyze their strengths and weaknesses, and indicate how they can improve their performance.

A quality physical education program provides meaningful learning experiences for all students. Physical educators in such programs assess student learning, analyze assessment data, and use the assessment analysis to plan future learning experiences. However, because many physical educators teach hundreds of children every week, documenting their learning can be a real challenge. What they need is an efficient and effective means for recording and analyzing assessment data.

Technology can help. Some aspects of computer-assisted assessment were described in Chapters 5, 6, and 9 in the sections on fitness assessment, spreadsheets, grading programs, programmed instruction, and motion analysis. This chapter focuses on more authentic assessment methods, including using technology to assess authentic learning, create projects, and maintain portfolios.

Assessing Authentic Learning

"Authentic assessment" requires students to apply skills, knowledge, and attitudes to real-world situations. These authentic tasks tend to motivate students, since the value of their work goes beyond the demonstration of competence in school, and relates to their actual lives and futures. If your standards are written so that they are observable, measurable, and require evidence of students' ability to create new knowledge or apply skills in new situations, then the development of assessment tools is a relatively easy task. The key to assessment is that there is a match between an assessment tool and each standard.

The Rubricator software program (Strategic Learning Technologies) is designed to assist with this process. Rubricator is a template for designing performance assessments and indicators aligned with standards and rubrics (description of qualitative levels of performance on a specific task) aligned with indicators. It also is an organizer for assessing content standards, performance tasks, performance checklists, scoring rubrics, and self-reflection questions/statements. This is a one-of-a-kind program that will no doubt be replicated by another company in the near future. In the meantime if you want a comprehensive tool to assist with assessing authentic learning, this program is for you.

Student Projects

In Chapters 3 and 4, we considered student use of videocassette recorders and camcorders for student projects. In this chapter, we will look at student projects that involve the use of the computer. Projects require students to create products from their research. Students find projects very motivational, since projects often provide them with an opportunity to select their own topic for study, use skills associated with their primary intelligence, and demonstrate creativity. Projects also promote self reliance and reflection, since students must assume responsibility for determining when their projects are complete and ready for display.

A number of physical educators across the country are beginning to require their students to create multimedia projects. However, their situations vary widely. Some physical educators have only one computer in their department, others have one computer per teacher, while still others have access to complete computer labs. Their instructional strategies also vary. Some teachers have students rotate through a series of learning stations, one of which involves the use of a computer. Other teachers have students create their own projects using different media (e.g., one group uses the computer, one group uses a video camera, one group uses markers and chart paper). Still others have students create multimedia projects—by themselves, in small groups, or as a class project. Many of these projects, especially the multimedia ones, can become quite large and require more storage than a 1.4MB floppy disk can hold. A Zip drive (100MB), CD-R (600MB) drive, or CD-RW (600MB) drive may be required. The most viable option today is large hard disks on network servers.

Student projects, or project-based learning, allows teachers to assess student learning and provides feedback for students. Moursund (1998) has defined several key elements for project based learning:

- Learner-centered lessons: Students should have a choice in the selection of the projects.
- Authentic content and purpose: The project should be linked to real world work.
- Challenging: The project should require students to put forth an extra effort.
- Product for presentation or performance: Once completed, the project should be presented to the teacher, other students, parents, and possibly even the community at large.

- Collaboration and cooperative learning: Whenever possible, projects should be developed in groups to facilitate collaboration and cooperation skills.
- Teacher facilitation: The teacher should assume the role of advisor, or the "guide on the side," as opposed to the "sage on the stage."
- Rooted in constructivism: The individual learner should construct his or her own knowledge by building on current knowledge. Thus, each group may require different information to complete its project, depending on the group members' current understanding and the depth of the project.
- Explicit educational goals: Students should be expected to learn specific technology skills as well as cognitive, social, and psychomotor skills related to physical education during activity.
- Incremental and continual improvement: Students should receive ongoing encouragement to improve their projects and not to be satisfied with their first efforts.

In order to ensure that your students' projects include the key elements, consider the 12-step project design process in the highlight box on page 247. Each step is crucial in order to ensure continual learning and improvement.

The possibilities are endless when students use computers to develop their projects. They can combine text, still images, digitized sound, and digitized video clips. In addition, various software programs—from presentation software, to animation software, to authoring software—can help them bring the entire project together.

Still Images

A variety of methods for accessing still images have been introduced in previous chapters: scanning (Chapter 2), using digital cameras (Chapter 4), using painting and drawing programs (Chapter 6), and downloading graphics from the

Project Design Steps

1 Set criteria for the project and let students know your expectations.
2. In small groups, students brainstorm and determine the type of project, the subject, and the audience.
3. Students write a proposal to present their ideas.
4. Students confer with the instructor regarding their proposal.
5. Students present their proposals to the entire class and revise them based on feedback from the group.
6. Students create a script and storyboard for their projects.
7. Students confer with the instructor regarding their script and storyboard.
8. Students conduct research using the Internet, CD-ROMs, and books.
9. Students complete their projects.
10. Students confer with the instructor regarding their projects and make revisions based on teacher feedback.
11. Students demonstrate their projects to the entire class and revise them based on feedback from the group.
12. Students add their projects to their personal portfolios.

Internet (Chapter 8). When scanning images or using graphics secured from Internet, it is important to keep copyright laws in mind. Often, the use of an image in a student project is not considered a violation of copyright law; however, students should be taught how to properly reference the image (see Chapter 8), and the distribution of the project should be limited.

Scanners are easy to operate; they are much like copy machines. The scanning process is controlled by the software that comes with the scanner, which is connected to the computer. The image to be scanned is placed on the bed of the scanner, and you click on a button in the software program—typically labeled Preview—to begin the process. Once the preview scan has been completed, you will be prompted to designate a location in which to save the image. You also will choose the format in which you wish to save the image. That decision should be based on how you plan to use the image. For posting on the Internet, choose "gif" for graphics, and "jpeg" for photos; for inclusion in authoring and presentation programs, "pict" for the Macintosh

247

and "bmp" for the Windows operating system are good choices. The second decision you will need to make concerns compression. The more the compression (making the file smaller), the lower the quality. You and your students will need to experiment with different compression schemes in order to determine what works best for you. You now click on a button in the software program—typically labeled Scan—to complete the process.

Images secured from digital cameras are especially effective for student projects. Students can take the pictures themselves and can manipulate them (resize, eliminate unnecessary sections, etc.). Most pictures taken with a digital camera are stored as jpeg files. To convert these to a different format you will need an image processing program, such as Adobe Photoshop, Adobe Photoshop Light, Adobe PhotoDeluxe, or GIF Converter.

Drawing and painting software offers those with artistic abilities the option of creating their own images. Painting programs create images pixel by pixel, or dot by dot. Drawing programs create images object by object (i.e., squares, triangles, and ovals). The primary advantage of drawing and painting programs is that—because the images created are original—there is no need to be concerned with copyright issues. Another advantage is that students have the opportunity to express themselves and their learning through another medium.

The fourth method of securing still images is to download them off the Internet or a CD-ROM. There are many locations on

How Copyrighted Material May Be Used

- Student multi-media creations.
- Faculty-produced curriculum materials.
- Distance learning—provided that only their students access it.
- Demonstrate multi-media creations at professional symposia.

the Internet and many CD-ROMs that contain royalty free clip art, either for free or for a nominal price. These images are intended for use in electronic projects. Other images can be secured from the Internet or a CD-ROM by taking what is known as a "screen dump." On the Macintosh, this is accomplished by holding down the Option, Shift, and 3 keys simultaneously to capture and save an image to the hard drive. For the Windows environment, this is accomplished by pressing the Print Screen key.

Digitized Sound

Sound is an important component of multimedia tutorials and presentations. Sounds can be secured from the Internet or a CD-ROM, digitized using your computer, or created by your computer. The process of securing music clips from the Internet or a CD-ROM is very similar to securing images. Certain sounds, like clip art, are distributed for free or for a nominal price for use in electronic projects. You also can use a regular tape recorder to capture the sound coming from the computer, play it back, and digitize it as described in the following paragraph. Some computers can actually digitize the sound as it is played. (This is another area in which to be cautious about copyright issues.)

Fair Use Guidelines for Educational Multimedia

- Motion Media - up to 10% or 3 minutes whichever is less.
- Text - up to 10% or 1000 words whichever is less.
- Poems - up to 250 words. Three poem limit per poet; five poem limit per anthology.
- Music - 10% or 30 seconds, whichever is less.
- Photos/Images - up to 5 works from one author; up to 10% or 15 works, whichever is less, from a collection.
- Data base information - up to 10% or 2,500 fields or cell entries, whichever is less.

Digitizing Audio

1. Turn on audio cassette recorder or CD player.
2. Place audio cassette or CD in recorder or player.
3. Press play on the audio cassette recorder or CD player.
4. Double click on audio digitizing software.
5. Use fast forward/rewind on the audio or track button on the CD player to select a segment to capture.
6. Press play on the audio cassette recorder or CD player.
7. Click record button on the computer screen.
8. At the end of the segment, click stop button on the computer screen.
9. Select File-Save to save the audio clip to your disk.

Audio digitizing is the process of converting a sound from analog to digital format so that it can be manipulated, saved, and used in electronic projects. Digitizing sound requires a sound source (tape cassette, CD), a microphone attached to the computer or a line port so that a cable can connect the sound source to the computer, and software, such as SoundEdit (Macromedia) or SoundJam(Sound Step) to digitize and manipulate the sound. Sampling rates determine how often an analog audio signal is cut up to make a digital audio clip. The higher the number of samples per second (5K, 7K, 11K, or 22K), the more lifelike the digitized sound—and the more memory it will require. Whenever possible, digitize sound at 22K in order to maximize the quality. You can always reduce the sampling rate when you compress the sound for storage. A great compression format for sound is MP3.

Finally, you can program your computer to produce musical notes with different pitch, rhythm, and volume. You can use musical software such as MusicShop, or authoring software such as HyperCard can be programmed to create the sounds. There also is a device called a MIDI interface that connects musical instruments with MIDI ports to the computer. The instrument, such as an electric keyboard, is played and the interface software digitizes the music as it enters the computer.

250

Digitized Video

Digitized video is the ultimate addition to electronic projects. You can obtain digitized video clips from the Internet, CD-ROM, or digital video camera. You or your students also can digitize (convert analog video to digitized video) their own video clips. The quality is not quite as high as with digital video (transferring digital video from a digital video camera to the computer via a firewire cable), but it will do the job.

A video digitizing card (e.g., Dazzle) is necessary to convert the analog video into digital video. The input source for digitized video is any analog medium, such as a video camera, videocassette recorder, videodisc player, or broadcast television signal from an antenna, cable, or satellite. A cable connects the video source to the video card, and a second cable connects the audio ports on the video source to the video card. Software distributed with the video card controls the computer display. Most digitizing programs also allow the user to cut, copy, paste, and alter the clips. If this is an area of interest for you, then it is a good idea—and it will be cheaper—to purchase the video card when you purchase your computer. Examples of these programs include Avid ePublisher (Avid) for Windows, MovieMaker (MicrosSoft) for Windows ME, and iMovie

Digitizing Video

1. Turn on video cassette recorder.
2. Place video in VCR.
3. Press play on the VCR.
4. Double click on video digitizing software.
5. Use fast forward on the VCR to select a segment to capture.
6. Once you find the segment you want, use the rewind on the VCR to return to the starting point.
7. Press play on the VCR.
8. Click record button on the computer screen.
9. At the end of the segment, click stop button on the computer screen.
10. Select File-Save to save the video clip to your disk.

Suggested CD-ROM Video Compression Settings

Video codec: Sorenson Video
Resolution: 320x240
Frames per second: 15
Keyframes: 75
Data rate (Kbps): 100
Audio codec: IMA 4:1
Bit rate: 16
Resolution: 22.05kHz
Channels: Stereo or Mono

(Apple) for the Macintosh. Note that you will need a good hard drive with at least 7,500 rpm (revolutions per minute), a large storage capacity, an access time of less than 10 milliseconds, and a sustained data transfer rate of three MB per second.

Panoramic Pictures

Using a program like QTVR Authoring Studio (Apple) or Photovista (MGI), a series of linear pictures can be stitched together in a panoramic picture (three-dimensional image). Dragging the mouse up moves you closer, dragging the mouse down moves you away, dragging the mouse to the right turns your view to the right, and dragging the mouse to the left turns your view to the left. Students can create panoramic pictures for inclusion in their projects.

Software

There are four types of software that can be used to create student projects. They are presentation, animation, authoring, and web authoring tools. Presentation software, such as PowerPoint (Microsoft), provides the user with a template on which to create an electronic slide show. Students can incorporate text, graphics, videos, and/or sound on each slide. In addition, they can choose the type of transition and the timing between the slides.

Animation software allows the user to combine a large number of still images in sequence to create a moving image. This is the same process used for animated cartoons. Animation is much more effective than a still graphic, yet it requires much less memory than a digitized video. Computer programs such as LifeForms (Credo Interactive) are available to help you with the process. The process involves creating the first and tenth frames to be used in the animation. The program then fills in the second through ninth frames, adjusting for the changes that take place. Continue the process for the rest of the sequence, and you end up with an animation segment for your program.

Authoring software, such as HyperStudio (Knowledge Adventure) and Director (MacroMedia), let you bring together in one package text, still images, animation, sound, analog video, and digital video. While presentation and animation software allow for a linear presentation, authoring software uses buttons or "hot spots" that let the user use a variety of pathways (known as hypermedia) to move through the program. Buttons are most commonly used to link one screen to another, but they can provide for other actions as well. The action is determined by the designer, and might include playing sounds, displaying images, asking questions, playing video clips, checking for correct answers, displaying animations, or performing calculations—almost anything that you can imagine.

Suggested Web Movie Settings

Video codec: Sorenson Video
Resolution: 192x144
Frames per second: 7.5
Keyframes: 75
Data rate (Kbps): 5
Audio codec: QDesign Music 2
Bit rate: 16
Resolution: 22.05kHz
Channels: Mono

Multimedia Projects in Physical Education

At the end of each school year, I conduct an eight-week Technology in Physical Education instructional unit for my eighth grade students. During this unit, the students select one sport that is unfamiliar to them to research. They use HyperStudio to create multimedia projects that demonstrate their learning, and they practice the skills related to the sport. This instructional activity assesses student progress toward National Standard One as the students work on their motor skills for the new sport, and National Standard Two as they apply motor learning and biomechanical principles.

–Carol Chesnutt, 1997 NASPE Southern District Middle School Teacher of the Year

Project-based learning involves creating a product for presentation to others. What better way to share one's product than by posting it on the World Wide Web! This can be accomplished in several ways. Some of the programs mentioned above—including PowerPoint, HyperStudio, and Director—create files that can be posted on the Web using a "plugin." The second method is to use a Web authoring program, such as Claris HomePage or Adobe PageMill, to create web pages (see the Web section in Chapter 8). If your school does not have its own server for posting work, you can use one of several existing Web sites where student work can be posted for free.

Whichever software program is chosen, it is imperative that a storyboard be designed first. The storyboard is a paper display of what the project will look like once it is finished. I have found it most helpful to give students a stack of 3x5 or 5x8 cards. They use one card per anticipated screen. Each card illustrates the general layout of the screen, including sketched illustrations and written text. When creating a Web site, write the name of the particular file on the card. Instruct students to be as detailed as possible at this stage.

Developing Projects in Physical Education

Project-based learning can be used as an end of the year activity, with students researching and presenting information on a unique sport.

Web Design Guidelines for Students

1. Start small.
2. Add material gradually.
3. Create one main folder for your entire site.
4. Create a separate folder inside the main folder for each major category of information.
5. Create one folder named "images" inside your main folder.
6. Keep each level to 5 to 10 items.
7. Develop a plan for maintenance and updates.
8. Put contact information (name, address, telephone, and fax numbers) on each page.
9. Include an e-mail link on each page.
10. Add new content weekly.
11. Check all links weekly.
12. Use a consistent look and feel.
13. Put navigation on each page.
14. Use no more than three images per page.
15. Put no more than two screens of information on each page.
16. If you must use more than two screens of information, provide a menu at the top of the page.
17. Design for 72 dpi, 256 colors, RGB, and 640x480.
18. Load time for a page should not exceed 30 seconds.
19. Test all pages on two browsers—Netscape/Explorer—and on two platforms—Macintosh/Windows.
20. Linked text should not exceed 20 percent of a passage.

Sites for Posting Student Work

GeoCities: http://www.geocities.com/
Teacher Web: http://www.teacherweb.com/
Tripod: http://www.tripod.com/
One Stop: http://www.onestop.com/

Other methods for creating projects related to physical education, include:

• Interdisciplinary projects where physical education is the content, language arts is the process, and technology is the means.

• Homework assignments where students work on their projects during out-of-school time and use computers in the media center or computer lab during after-school hours.

255

Students need not limit their projects to sports. They might focus on one of the following topic areas:

- Tumbling/gymnastics routines
- Weight training
- Proper methods for stretching
- Healthy hearts
- New games
- Dance routines
- Motor learning concepts
- Biomechanic concepts
- Historical perspectives
- Sports nutrition
- Sports medicine
- Rules of the game
- Sport strategy
- Motor skills

Electronic Portfolios

A student's portfolio is similar to an artist's portfolio, and can contain a wide range of materials (e.g., plans, projects, scores) that indicate progress toward the identified grade level standards. Too often, when physical educators first begin to use portfolios, they have their students create collection portfolios that include everything they have done throughout the year. However, the goal of portfolios is actually for each student to develop a performance portfolio—a purposeful collection of work that demonstrates that student's efforts, new learnings, emerging insights, progress, and achievement over time. Some of the work will be from earlier in the year and some from later in the year. Most of the work should be selected by the student; however, some teachers like to designate certain required items. Typically 6 to 10 pieces of work are selected for each student's portfolio. Most portfolios also include an end-of-the-year reflective essay, in which the student comments on his or her progress during the year.

At the end of the year, the portfolio provides the teacher and student with concrete information for discussion of his or her progress and the setting of goals for the next year. During the end of the year conference, the teacher should ask students to explain the connection between the grade level standards and the pieces of work they selected to demonstrate their learning. This process will help students understand how learning occurs. Students also may be asked to share their work with their parents during end of the year parent conferences. In many schools, the teacher takes a secondary role during these conferences, while students explain their own progress to their parents. This is also an opportunity for students to reflect on their work and celebrate their learning (Mohnsen, 1997).

Electronic portfolios are an extension of the paper portfolio. Students can store text, graphics, video clips, and audio clips along with complete multimedia projects. The electronic version provides both students and teachers with a means of tracking and accessing large amounts of data from a variety of formats in a short period of time. For example, video is ideal for documenting growth in physical education, but it can be cumbersome to store videotapes and time consuming to access a particular clip, unless the images are digitized and stored in an electronic portfolio. Once digitized, students can view pre- and post-clips and write an essay describing the differences and how they illustrate personal growth. Other items commonly placed in an electronic portfolio include motor skill rubrics, fitness scores, biomechanical analysis of skills, social rubrics, and personalized motor and movement learning plans.

Physical education classes across the United States range from 20 to 80 or more students per class. Physical educators who wish to use electronic portfolios often are faced with time constraints and limited access to computers. For individualized portfolios to be successful, a physical educator must have access to at least one computer for every eight students, or access to a computer lab. In the former case, students form eight groups and rotate through a circuit (see Chapter 9 for more information on circuits). The circuit's computer station contains a computer for each student. Physical education teachers with access to a computer lab send their students to the lab on a rotational basis. In the lab, students enter data into their personal portfolios. At the end of the year, the electronic portfolio provides the teacher and student with concrete information to use in discussing progress and setting goals for the following year.

Portfolio Software

Students can use one of three methods to create electronic portfolios. They can use authoring software, discussed earlier in this chapter. This method requires that students create not only the work that goes into the portfolio, but also the structure for collecting that work. They can use one of several generic electronic portfolios on the market that are used by a number of subject-area teachers—GradyProfile (Aurbach & Associates),

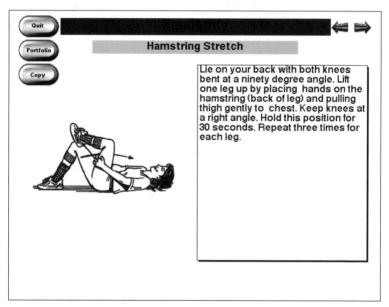

Figure 10.1   A screen from Health-Related Fitness Tutorial/Portfolio - Tutorial Stack (Bonnie's Fitware).

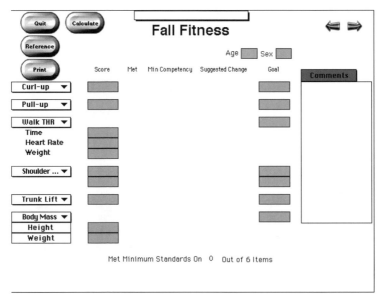

Figure 10.2   A screen from Health-related Fitness Tutorial/Portfolio -
Portfolio Stack (Bonnie's Fitware).

The Portfolio Assessment Kit (Super School Software), or The
Portfolio Assessment Toolkit (Forest). All of these programs
are capable of capturing illustrations and writing samples,
evaluations and observations, student reflections, self-
assessments, and parent observations. The third method involves
using portfolio templates specifically designed for physical
education. Currently, three such templates are on the market,
and there are plans for additional sport-specific versions.

Health Related Fitness Tutorial/Portfolio (Bonnie's Fitware).
The Health Related Fitness Tutorial/Portfolio is a two-stack
program (see Figures 10.1 and 10.2). The first stack is a tutorial
on health related fitness that incorporates Hypermedia so
students can locate specific areas of interest. It includes cognitive
concepts related to principles of fitness, safe versus dangerous
exercises, training protocols, taking one's pulse, and warm-up/
cool-down procedures, along with a variety of exercises for each
fitness area. The second stack is an electronic portfolio where

Figure 10.3   A screen from Volleyball Complete (Bonnie's Fitware).

students enter fitness scores, selected exercises, caloric input/ output, drawings or video clips, journal entries, and fitness plans. The program is set up to record fitness scores for pull ups, push ups, modified pull ups, flexed arm hang, curl ups, back saver sit and reach, shoulder stretch, trunk lift, mile run, pacer, body mass index, and skinfold.

Volleyball Complete (Bonnie's Fitware). This portfolio (see Figure 10.3) relates each of the eight subdisciplines of physical education (exercise physiology, motor learning, biomechanics, psychology, motor development, aesthetics, sociology, and historical perspectives) to the teaching of volleyball. This is a two-stack program, similar to the Health Related Fitness Tutorial/Portfolio. One stack is a tutorial, and the second stack is a portfolio. Using the tutorial stack, teachers and students can access and interact with information on volleyball skills, techniques, strategies, training, and teamwork. Then, using the portfolio stack, students enter journal writings, interactive activities, rubrics for volleyball skills, and video clips. This two-stack sport concept will continue to expand, with additional titles added each year (swimming and bowling are already on the drawing board). In addition, there is a comprehensive portfolio that can be used as a collection device for the best examples from the various sport-specific portfolios.

Physical Education Portfolio (Bonnie's Fitware). This portfolio (see Figures 10.4 and 10.5) is formatted around the eight subdisciplines of physical education. Students can enter fitness scores, journal entries, and video clips. It also contains rubrics for basic movement (run, hop, skip, etc.) and motor (throw, catch, kick, etc.) skills. Students simply select their level of competency.

Using Portfolios in Physical Education

Electronic portfolios are relatively new. Typically, each student is given (or purchases) a floppy disk (or uses a CD-R, CD-RW, Zip disk, or folder on a server or the Internet)

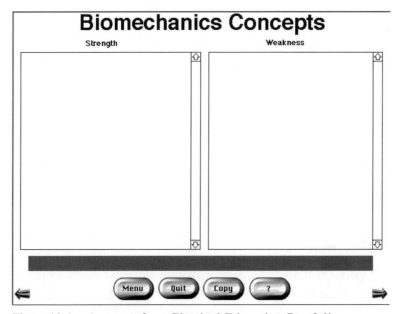

Figure 10.4   A screen from Physical Education Portfolio (Bonnie's Fitware).

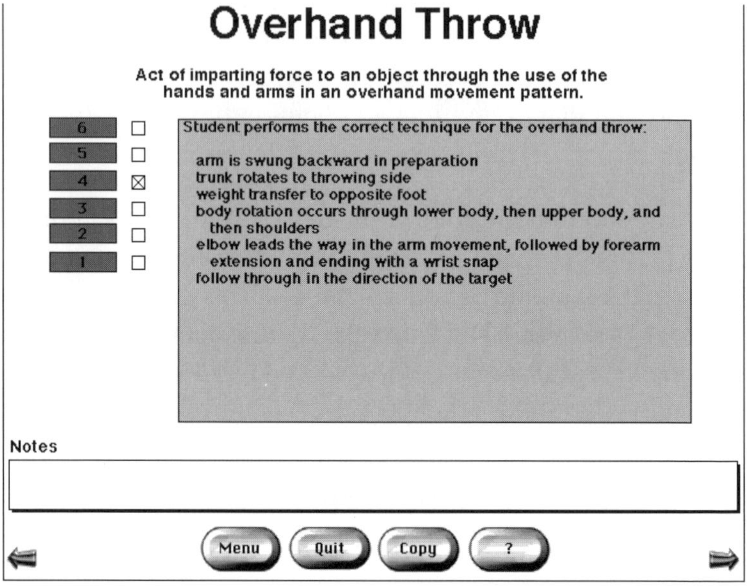

Overhand Throw

Act of imparting force to an object through the use of the
hands and arms in an overhand movement pattern.

6	☐
5	☐
4	☒
3	☐
2	☐
1	☐

Student performs the correct technique for the overhand throw:

arm is swung backward in preparation
trunk rotates to throwing side
weight transfer to opposite foot
body rotation occurs through lower body, then upper body, and
   then shoulders
elbow leads the way in the arm movement, followed by forearm
   extension and ending with a wrist snap
follow through in the direction of the target

Notes

(Menu) (Quit) (Copy) (?)

Figure 10.5   A screen from Physical Education Portfolio
(Bonnie's Fitware).

that contains his or her portfolio. Then, in either a
computer lab setting or as part of a circuit, students use a
computer to enter information into their portfolios. Some
physical educators require that their students work on their
portfolios during time outside physical education—during
school breaks, after school in the media center, or at home
if they have access to a computer. When time and access
to computers is limited, teachers often will create task
cards to ensure that students use their computer time
efficiently.

Summary

The educational community as a whole continues to move
toward more authentic types of assessment, and it is
imperative that physical educators do the same.
Technology can facilitate the monitoring, documentation,
262

Portfolio Assessment

The fitness center is a converted wood shop with one-third of the room devoted to exercise equipment, one-third to tables and chairs, and one-third to computers. The students are assigned to one of three groups, and each group is assigned to one of the three areas in the fitness center. The students (wearing heart monitors) rotate through a number of aerobic stations (e.g., climber, rower, stair stepper, ergometer, and treadmill). The different stations provide variety for the workout and teach students that there are a number of ways to participate in an aerobic activity (related to National Standard 4).

At the table and chair station, the students read from their Moving as a Team textbook and prepare their answers to the question, "What are the key elements of warm-up?"

At the computer station, students boot up the Mac Health Related Fitness Tutorial/Portfolio (Bonnie's Fitware) software. Students had entered their fitness scores and set goals for the year previously. Today, students click on the schedule section and enter their answers to the warm-up question. Task cards help students complete these tasks. At the end of each year, students create their own fitness plans using their electronic portfolios. They select exercises from the data base of information and copy them into their electronic portfolio stack. Then they videotape themselves performing the exercises, digitize the images, and place them into their stack. Finally, the students fill out their fitness schedules, noting their one-week fitness plans.

–Karen Mendon,1995 NASPE SW District Middle School Teacher of the Year

and storage of assessment items. In this chapter we examined the role of technology in multimedia projects and electronic portfolios that allow students to demonstrate and improve their learning in the content area of physical education. In the next chapter, we will look at how technology can improve the quality of teaching.

Reflection Questions

1. What do you consider the benefits of multimedia projects and electronic portfolios to be for your students?

2. What are some items you might have students include in an electronic portfolio to demonstrate their understanding and performance related to the standards?

Projects

1. Practice digitizing audio and video clips.

2. Design an instructional unit that culminates with students creating their own multi-media projects.

Chapter 11

Using Technology To Improve the Instructional Process

Jane Garcia slips a videotape, recorded during her last class by one of her students, into the videocassette recorder and sits down to observe herself. She takes out her palm computer to collect data on her teaching as she watches. After reviewing her lesson, she has the software analyze her teaching behaviors and produce a print out of areas that need improvement.

In previous chapters, we looked at how technology can be used to improve student learning. In this chapter, we turn our attention to the ways technology can be used to improve teacher effectiveness. Several of the technologies discussed thus far can assist with preservice training as well as with professional development. Physical educators—like students—can use CD-ROMs and the Internet to increase their knowledge, for example. And, just as there are assessment tools for students, there are technology-based assessment tools that teachers can use to improve their performance. Finally, teachers can create "professional portfolios" similar to student portfolios to demonstrate their teaching effectiveness. In fact at many colleges and universities, electronic portfolios are required prior to the student teaching experience.

Information Related to Teaching

There are two categories of information that will be of specific interest to physical educators. The first is current research related to pedagogy and physical education concepts. Some of this information can be accessed from the same sources that students use (see Chapters 8 and 9); other sources are designed specifically for physical educators. The second category is related to lesson planning. It includes instructional materials and student assessment tools. Both types of information are available on CD-ROMs and the Internet.

On the research side, the Sport Information Resource Centre (SIRC) is the largest resource center in the world. It collects and disseminates information in the area of sport, physical education, physical fitness, and sports medicine. Every month, SIRC scans more than 1,200 magazines and journals ranging from the practical Runner's World to the scholarly Research Quarterly for Exercise and Sport as well as other published material. SIRC then produces the SPORT Database, which contains bibliographic references to more than 360,000 magazine articles, books, theses, conference papers, and other published research from around the world. More than 235,000 citations also are available. Using the SIRC CD-ROM, you define your search topic by identifying the important words and related terms for each concept. Although this is a very expensive resource (more than $1,000), you may find that your central office, city library, or local university has a copy.

The Internet is an excellent resource for research pertaining to many physical education topics. But, heed the same advice you give your students when conducting research on the Internet: double check all pieces of information and investigate the credentials of the individuals who conducted the research and posted the results. When doing research on the Internet, follow the searching strategies outlined in Chapter 8.

On the lesson plan side, Movin' On (software designed by Anne Edwards-Turnacliff and Lee Tillotson) can help physical educators manage elementary physical education activities. The activities in Movin' On were collected by experienced physical educators; however, you can personalize the program and add to the activities it contains. The program includes equipment, instructional units, academic skills, and game applications, along with exercises and suggested references. Users can search for lessons by type of equipment, instructional unit (including several thematic units), academic skills, and/or game applications. At the end of the year, the software can provide you with a summary of your lessons. Everything can be printed, so if you want a hard copy of something you can create one.

Preservice Training

Preservice training typically occurs in the college/university setting. And, although there are schools that provide curriculum via the Internet, most still provide the majority of their undergraduate instruction on-site. However, even with on-site courses, technology is often utilized as a means of sharing information, keeping open the lines of communication, and training young professionals to use technology. Let's take a look at each of these areas.

Many professors create their own home pages with hyperlinks to each of the classes they teach. On the main page of each course, they often post the course syllabus, homework assignments, lecture notes, and links to related information. Some instructors have even gone so far as to include sample tests on their Web pages; students answer the questions and then receive their scores and other helpful feedback.

Electronic mail has increased communication throughout the educational community, and the interaction between instructor and student at the college level is no exception. Students can use e-mail to ask follow-up questions about lecture material. And, during student teaching, e-mail allows for three-way communication among the student teacher, cooperating teacher, and university supervisor. Student teachers can e-mail their lesson plans simultaneously to both their cooperating teacher and university supervisor. After receiving timely feedback from both advisors, students can adjust lessons before teaching them.

Finally, most undergraduate teacher training programs require some form of instruction on the use of current technologies in education. This often takes the form of a course offered either by the education or physical education department. It typically covers word processing, data bases, spreadsheets, grading software, instructional software, Internet skills, and the creation of a multimedia project. Such courses are beneficial, but interacting with professors via e-mail, accessing Web sites, and using technology in their other coursework also can be very helpful. A few universities require students in the teacher preparation program to purchase and use heart monitors throughout their undergraduate work. This provides an additional experience in using technology in physical education.

Professional Development

Inservice training typically is conducted by local colleges/ universities, professional associations, and/or regional educational institutions (district offices, local educational agencies). These agencies award college credits or salary points for teachers. However, physical educators (especially those with coaching responsibilities) often have found it difficult to attend professional development workshops. Today, training can take place via the Internet, allowing educators to learn at their convenience. The number of virtual colleges and training centers on the Internet is growing by leaps and bounds. Virginia Tech (Blacksburg, VA), for example, offers a Masters Degree program in physical education via the Internet.

Orange County Department of Education: Online Courses for Physical Education

California Physical Education Framework, National Standards, and Fitnessgram
Middle School Physical Education - Instruction Unit 1
Middle School Physical Education - Instruction Unit 2
Middle School Physical Education - Instruction Unit 3
High School Physical Education - Instruction Unit 1
High School Physical Education - Instruction Unit 2
High School Physical Education - Instruction Unit 3

In another example, the Orange County Department of Education provides a number of online learning experiences each year that are designed specifically for physical educators. Information about the courses is distributed nationally through flyers and journal articles. Each course consists of 16 learning modules (three units) that can be completed any time between October 15 and May 15. Class sizes have ranged from 5 to 50 students per course.

The Orange County Department of Education begins each of its online learning opportunities by sending an e-mail message to the participants. The message welcomes students to the course and provides an Internet address that they can click on to get to the course syllabus. The syllabus provides participants with the objectives, a list of the 16 modules, course assessments, and textbook references. The participants are asked to read the syllabus and then click on Module 1. The first module does not include any physical education content. It simply congratulates participants on their web navigating skills and provides instructions for joining the class listserv. Participants are asked to send an e-mail message that introduces themselves to their classmates. Participants then select one or two study partners, based on the areas of interest and timelines for completing the course.

Online Course Objectives

Participants will be able to:
- describe the development of National Standards
- describe the four areas of quality physical education.
- develop a plan to implement quality physical education
- describe the Fitnessgram test program
- correctly administer the Fitnessgram test battery to students.

Online Modules

Modules	Content	Internet Skills
Module 1	Introduction	Listserv
Module 2	Reform	Web sites
Module 3	Education Codes	Bookmarks
Module 4	Environment	Virtual auditorium
Module 5	Curriculum	Accessing Web sites
Module 6	Goal 1	Accessing Web sites
Module 7	Goal 2	Virtual auditorium
Module 8	Goal 3	Search tools
Module 9	Instruction	Virtual field trip
Module 10	Support Materials	Virtual auditorium
Module 11	Assessment Tools	Audio
Module 12	Portfolios	File transfer
Module 13	Fitness Testing	Search tools
Module 14	Fitness Tests	Videoconferencing
Module 15	Endurance	Video
Module 16	Muscular Fitness	Chat software

Online Course Assessment

1. Description of the development of the California Framework or National Standards (10%).
2. Implementation plan for each section of quality physical education (50%).
3. Description of Fitnessgram test program (10%).
4. Videotape your administration of fitness tests (30%).

Participants are informed that at any time throughout the course they can interact with the entire class, their study partners, or the instructor when they need assistance or want additional information. In fact, many lessons require participants to discuss ideas and concepts with their teammates. Most modules consist of both an Internet skill and physical education content. Both are taught simultaneously and in support of one another. This strategy provides participants with real-life reasons for learning about the Internet, since in many cases the student must use the Internet to access the physical education content.

Several times throughout the year, virtual auditorium—or chat sessions—are offered. These sessions provide an opportunity for the participants and the instructor to discuss issues and concepts in real time. They also provide an opportunity for guest speakers to share information and respond to questions from the students.

The first time an online course was offered by the Orange County Department of Education, the instructor maintained a journal of reflections (see highlight box on page 272). As can be seen from the comments, the course was a learning experience for the instructor as well as for the students! Online courses appear to meet the lifelong learning, lifestyle, and sharing/social needs of the participants. However, in order to truly understand a professional development experience via the Internet, you must experience one for yourself.

Assessing Teacher Performance

Over the years, student teacher and teacher evaluation has shifted from subjective to objective evaluation. Researchers have demonstrated the relationship between increases in student learning and process variables such as time on task, amount and types of feedback, use of class time, and the number of successful completions of a task. These variables can be measured and the feedback provided for use in improving teaching effectiveness. A supervisor can collect these data live or from a videotape (see Chapter 3) of the lesson. Taping lessons facilitates unbiased evaluation and enables both the teacher and supervisor to review the lesson as often as necessary.

There are three methods for recording teaching behaviors during observations: pen-and-paper tallying, portable computers, and palm

Instructor's Comments During Third Week

The virtual auditorium experience was fantastic! However, I will need to learn a whole new approach for class management, since I can't go stand between two students who are having a side conversation. I continue to be amazed at how the technology improves communication between the participants. By having them copy me on their correspondence, I can monitor whether or not they are understanding concepts.

Instructor's Comments Toward End of Course

I see even more clearly that the facilitator has to plan his/her preparation and instruction time as if the class were live. It still takes the same, if not more time, to prepare for the class, and I have noticed a tendency to forget that, since the course is not "live." The actual flow of the class has gone well; however, I still feel a need to control the learning situation for each participant—but I am getting better. The frustration has been using the virtual auditorium. I am guaranteed that it is working and then we arrive for a session and can't get in. The beginners think that they are doing something wrong, and the rest of us are just plain frustrated. It will be better when I can set this all up using our own equipment.

Participant's Comments at Start of Course

I am slow signing up for this list [listserv] because I don't really know what I am doing. I have already put well over 10 hours into this class and I am only on Module 2! I signed up for this class to learn about the topics to be covered and also to learn how to use a computer, the online service, the World Wide Web, and the Internet. So far, this class is fulfilling my desires. Please be patient with me if I am not where I am supposed to be at certain times. Most likely, I'll be here at my computer trying to figure out how to do what I'm supposed to do to get where I want to go.

Participant's Comments at End of Course

Just a note to say thanks for offering the class. Have learned much and enjoyed even more. It was interesting to hear what is happening in the rest of the United States. The listservs helped some, but the workshop was even more enlightening. I hope that more of our teachers will participate next year.

computers. The use of computers makes the process of recording, storing, analyzing, and printing data more efficient. It also allows for the simultaneously collection of data on a number of different variables. The following sections describe the software that is available.

Observation, Analysis, and Recording System

Observation, Analysis, and Recording System (OARS), used at the University of Virginia, records frequency and duration data in as many as 10 categories (behaviors or events). You can create an unlimited number of your own categories, and several common categorical systems (e.g., Flanders, Galloway, Blumburg) are predefined and ready to use. Prompts are provided on the screen to label each category being observed and to indicate which categories are active during recording. Comments can be entered at any time during the recording session through the keyboard; they are recorded as part of the session event log. One hundred lines of summary comments also can be entered at the end of each session. The print out includes a graphic

National Board Certification

National Board Certification is a way for the teaching profession to define and recognize highly accomplished practice. A certificate awarded by the National Board for Professional Teaching Standards attests that a teacher has been judged by his or her peers as one who meets high and rigorous professional standards. He or she has demonstrated the ability, in a variety of settings, to make sound professional judgments about students' best interests and to act effectively on those judgments (http://www.nbpts.org/seeking/).

The National Board has developed an innovative, two-part assessment process to determine whether a teacher possesses the attributes of accomplished teaching based on the National Board's standards. One component of the assessment is done at a teacher's school. A teacher shows evidence of good teaching practice by preparing a portfolio. The portfolio contains videotapes of classroom teaching, lesson plans, samples of student work, and written commentaries in which the teacher reflects on what he or she is doing and why. The second component of the assessment includes exercises that take place at an assessment center. Candidates spend one day at the assessment center. Exercises are designed around challenging teacher issues and include evaluating other teachers' practice, interviews, and exams in a teacher's field (http://www.nbpts.org/seeking/faqs.html).

summary of all categories across time and a sequential, time-coded log of events. The program is menu driven, user friendly, and complemented by a comprehensive, step-by-step how-to manual available on diskette or in paper format.

The Evaluator

The Evaluator is a Windows-based program that measures time on task and frequency related behaviors. Specific behaviors to be measured are established ahead of time by the observer. Data are collected during the actual observation. Reports can be viewed or printed immediately after the observation in chart or graph form.

Computerized Observation System (COS)

COS (Prospect Sales and Marketing) is a Windows-based duration and event recording data base program that automates the observation process. The data collected during observations are stored in the system data base. After the observation is completed, the data can be viewed on the screen (see Figures 11.1 and 11.2) or sent to a printer. Comparison charts are available for all events and categories. The system charts up to 10 observations. The user can set threshold levels for each category.

CASAIL-PEC

Computer Assisted Systematic Analysis of Instructor and Learner Behavior: Physical Education and Coaching edition (CASAIL-PEC) for the Windows operating system was created by Daniel Frankel. CASAIL-PE was designed to help student teachers, supervisors, teachers, and coaches evaluate instructional efficacy, lesson density, and learner behaviors in an accurate, fast, and relatively effortless manner. It features several data collection formats, such as:

-Academic Learning Time in Physical Education Settings (ALT-PE) variables (e.g., waiting, transition, management, lecture, demonstration).

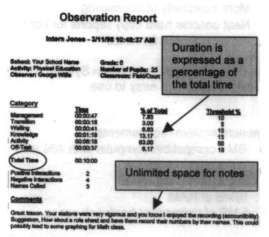

Figure 11.1   Sample screen from Computerized Observation System.

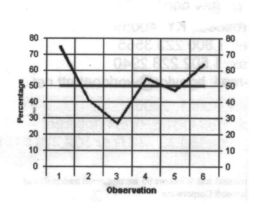

Figure 11.2   Sample screen from Computerized Observation System.

-Opportunities for Response (tallying of successful and unsuccessful learner on-task experiences).

-Feedback (e.g., positive, negative).

-Modeling (e.g., by instructor, student, correct/incorrect).

-Attention to safety issues (e.g., positive/negative).

-Instructional Space (e.g., soccer field, basketball court).

Likert scale data collection also is included in CASAIL-PE.

Summary

Recent studies have shown that the teacher accounts for 51 percent of the learning that goes on in school. This chapter has addressed four ways that technology can be used to improve the effectiveness of the teacher. They include software designed to increase teacher understanding of concepts, effective preservice training, inservice professional development designed to maintain teacher effectiveness and to keep teachers abreast of new strategies and techniques, and assessment tools designed to provide teachers with feedback on their instructional effectiveness.

So far in this book, we have focused on "what is." In the next chapter we will address "what can be."

Reflection Questions

1. In what other ways can you imagine using technology in teacher preparation programs and teacher inservice programs?
2 What would be the advantage of National Board Certification? Have you considered applying for National Board Certification? Why or why not?
3. Have you ever considered taking a course via the Internet? What would you see as the advantages? What would you see as the disadvantages?

Projects

1. Imagine that you are applying for National Board Certification in physical education. Arrange to have yourself videotaped (by an adult or student) during one of your classes. Then, take the time to review the tape and reflect on your teaching practices. Think about what worked, what didn't work, and what you would do differently next time.
2. Select a topic of interest related to pedagogy or physical education content, then conduct an Internet search to bring yourself up-to-date on the topic.

Chapter 12

The Future of Technology in Physical Education

The year is 2015. The place is the gymnasium of Middle School USA, and a physical education class is about to begin. As the students walk across the gym, they turn to face a biometric device that conducts a retina scan and documents their presence. The students begin their warm up and fitness exercises, following a model who demonstrates each exercise on a large flat display panel on the gym wall. The students have been learning tennis for the past several weeks, and today they will focus on the correct technique for the tennis serve. There are five learning stations set up around the gymnasium. The students, working in groups of four, rotate from one station to the next.

At Learning Station 1, students view a hologram of an Olympic athlete demonstrating the correct technique for the serve. The students, racquets in hand, mimic the hologram in order to connect the visual image and kinesthetic feeling to their brains. At Learning Station 2, a computer digitizes the students' images as they replicate the tennis serve and provides them with immediate feedback on their technique. At Learning Station 3, students have the opportunity to hit a "real" ball. A recording device captures their image as they practice serving. Before proceeding to the next station, a computer again provides them with feedback. At Learning Station 4, students have an opportunity to question a tennis pro, via a video conference, about her serving technique and practice schedule. Learning Station 5 brings together all the skills the students have been working on during the last several weeks. The students use a virtual reality program that provides them with competition customized to their level of experience and ability. At the end of class, the students pause momentarily on their way out of the gym to allow the teacher's computer to upload data (vital signs, calorie expenditure and heart rate data collected during the instructional period, and movement data from the serving activities) from the sensors each student wears. The teacher's computer analyzes the information and forwards a copy of the results to the student's e-mail account and to the teacher for review.

Fifteen years ago, most physical educators could not imagine using a computer in any part of their program, and none of us could foresee the role computers would play in our personal and professional lives. As we look to the future and hear wondrous stories of what technology will be like in the new millennium, we need to remember how far we have come and how far we still have to go.

In this chapter, I will review the 1993 and 1998 versions of the future (Using Technology in Physical Education, Editions 1 and 2) and note how far we have come. Then, I will again attempt to look into the crystal ball and predict the future from the 2001 perspective. However, since it is not only the advancement of the technology but its use by physical educators that will determine the future, I also will examine how these devices may be used in physical education programs tomorrow.

The Future: 1993 Version

In the first edition of this book, I addressed four areas of growth in technology—pen technology and voice recognition, distance learning, student response keypads, and virtual reality. Each area was reviewed along with its application for physical education. Each of the following sections contains a passage from the first edition, followed by information on that technology's current level of sophistication and use in physical education programs.

Pen Technology and Voice Recognition

Usually we use a keyboard, mouse, or touch screen to communicate with our computers. The new pen technology allows us to communicate with our computers by writing on a special surface; the software for pen technology is becoming so sophisticated that it can interpret our handwriting. The next step will be voice recognition—we will communicate with our computers simply by speaking to them. This will be especially convenient for physical educators who are out on the field and want to input information. They will be able to speak into a small microphone and the message will be transmitted to the computer back in the office.

Pen technology in the form of a stylus has become the primary input device for handheld and palm computers. And the age of voice recognition is here with products such as NaturallySpeaking Deluxe (Dragon Systems) and ViaVoice Gold (IBM). The programs still require time and patience to set up, and there are glitches from time to time. The voice recognition products haven't yet found their way to the physical education field, but have been used by persons with disabilities to record information. Although they still require fast computers to work effectively, prices are coming down daily and capability is fast approaching everyday use.

The next step in voice recognition technology will be interpretative telephony. This is the ability of the voice recognition system to translate the language spoken into a second verbal language. This type of system will allow a physical educator to communicate with every child in his/her class in his/her native language. Imagine the instructional and safety implications when working with non-English speaking students.

Distance Learning

Distance education instructors conduct class sessions in front of a video camera. The video is then uplinked to a satellite and downlinked to subscribing schools' satellite dishes. This provides teachers and students in many different geographic areas with the benefits of hearing from an expert on a given subject or seeing a model lesson or demonstration of a skill. You can even call in and ask questions while the program is on the air. If the time is inconvenient for you, you can videotape the program and show it later. This type of staff development will become the norm in the future.

This type of professional development is the norm today. The United States Department of Education, along with numerous regional educational agencies and private agencies, commonly conduct distance learning seminars for educators. In addition, Chapter 11 illustrated how the Internet has become an even more viable option for distance learning—both for teachers and for students (see Chapter 8). The future for this technology is wide open—the only question that remains is, "Will it, along with the Internet, completely replace regular on-site learning for teachers and students?"

Student Response Keypads

Future students will carry around their own handheld computers. In the meantime, student response keypads (which are about the size of a small television remote control) allow student interaction with the teacher. Up to 255 keypads can be connected to one computer, allowing you to conduct ongoing quizzes during instruction and receive instant feedback on your presentation.

Student response keypads never really infiltrated the K-12 educational setting, and I for one, have never seen their use in physical education. However, we seem to have jumped quickly to the feasibility of the handheld computers. The eMate was making its way into the schools before Apple dropped its support for the Newton Operating System, and other student notebook computers are now making their way into the hands of students. What we are talking about here is miniaturizing computers. And, we are seeing that happen as we watch the size of the computer diminish from laptop, to notebook, to handheld, to palm. Futurists predict that within the first quarter of the new millennium, information storage will be so compact that all the information a well-informed person can consume in a lifetime—all the books, manuals, magazine and newspaper articles, letters, memos, reports, greeting cards, notebooks, diaries, ledgers, bills, pamphlets, brochures, photographs, paintings, posters, movies, TV shows, videos, radio programs, audio records, concerts, lectures, phone calls, etc.—will be stored in an object no bigger than a book and potentially as small as a fat fountain pen (Perelman, 1992).

Virtual Reality

Virtual reality envelops the user in an artificial world. Through special interfaces (such as gloves and a helmet), the user receives from the computer the sensory illusion of being in a very different environment. This artificial world is felt through tactile stimulators in the gloves and seen through a screen mounted in the helmet. The user interacts with this world by gesturing with the gloves or moving the helmeted head, and the computer responds appropriately to those gestures.

Virtual Racquetball Game by Autodesk is available for use in labs and at conferences. The user becomes immersed in a computer-generated three-dimensional racquetball court. With computer-interface racquet in hand and helmet in place, the user plays a racquetball game against an opponent, in interaction with a computer.

This prediction wasn't hard to come by, since virtual reality was a reality by 1985, when a programmer developed such a system so he could learn to juggle. The sophistication of virtual reality systems has increased over time. Currently, there are four categories of virtual reality: desktop systems (navigating through three-dimensional on a monitor), partial immersion (navigating through three-dimensional on a monitor with enhancements such

Sport Simulators/Virtual Reality

The High Cycle (Autodesk) is a stationary bike augmented with a head mounted display and headphones, allowing users to experience riding through a desert landscape or along a bike path next to a lake. The computer monitors the speed of the pedal rotation, and travel in the visual display reflects that speed. Designers used force feedback to simulate variations in the slope of the road and type of terrain in the virtual environment. So, as the user pedals up a hill, there is an increase in the resistance on the rear wheel, which in turn requires more effort to pedal. A mechanical encoder measures the rotation of the handle bars and passes the information back to the computer, which then calculates the scene shown in the display.

Virtual Hoops (CCG MetaMedia), a basketball simulation that pits the user against a computer generated opponent, takes simulations to the next level. The user, fitted with a glove, stands in front of a large-screen display that shows his or her image in a basketball court environment. When the virtual basketball appears on the screen, the user grabs it and begins shooting at the virtual basket. At the same time, the user is challenged onscreen by a virtual defender. The virtual defender is programmed to block shots and to steal the ball. The computer monitors the movement of the player's hand and calculates whether or not a basket is made.

The PGA Tour Gold (Electronic Arts) provides players with a virtual reality version of golf that is played using a 3DO machine (a super powered video game system). The game uses fully digitized images of golfers, three-dimensional courses with accurate elevations, and a special golf club interface. Players plot their strategies, adjust for obstacles on the course, and play 18 holes of golf from a stationary position.

as gloves and three-dimensional goggles), full-immersion systems (head gear, gloves, and bodysuits), and environmental systems (externally generated three-dimensional, but with little or no body paraphernalia).

Partial and full immersion applications that require head gear, gloves, and other external devices are becoming available at prices that are considerably less than the research models. Head gear—including viewers—is becoming lighter and less obtrusive, with even greater resolution and accuracy. Gloves are providing more precision at lower prices. These devices let you play certain VR-compatible games, such as "Virtual Reality Ninja" (http://www.manleytoyquest.com) and those listed in the highlight box on page 282.

Although virtually reality applications have become more common, very few schools use them as instructional tools. However, I believe it is an emerging technology that will have a significant impact on the future of physical education. If you are looking for financial assistance from grants and foundations in order to incorporate technology into your physical education program, then virtual reality is your ticket.

The Future: 1998 Version

In the second edition of this book, I addressed seven areas of growth in technology. Each of the following sections contains a passage from the second edition, followed by information on that technology's current level of sophistication and use in physical education programs.

Identification Units

There are several new biometric identification devices on the market. The Fingerprint Identification Unit scans an image of a fingerprint and saves it in a data base. Then, it matches the print copy against the user's finger as he or she logs in. Other biometric devices scan faces, retinas, voice, and even blood.

Primarily designed for use in security systems, these devices have a place in physical education. They can be used to identify an individual taking a computer-generated test on-site or online. No doubt we also will see these devices becoming the attendance takers of the future. I can see students looking into a camera, as described at the beginning of this chapter, or placing their index finger on a pad or screen as they enter the locker room. Eliminating the traditional roll call will provide additional time for instruction.

The sophistication of these devices has continued to develop with an emphasis on fingerprint readers, retina scanners, and facial scanners. Already several companies, including Biometric Identification, have developed attendance taking devices using finger print readers. These are currently used in major businesses, but the potential for schools as a time-saving device are unlimited.

Flat Panel Display

Display monitors are becoming larger, thinner, and better each year. Fujitsu currently sells a 42-inch, gas-plasma flat panel display. The monitor, which can also display computer images, is only four inches thick. Unfortunately the cost, as of 1998, is $17,500.

Flat panel display units will decrease in cost and be used in physical education much like television monitors are used today. However, the quality will be much better and the equipment will take up less space. Panels will display fitness lessons, cognitive concepts, and model demonstrations. An Internet connection will allow an entire class to take electronic or virtual field trips to Olympic Training Centers or other sporting venues.

The cost is coming down and this technology still holds much promise for the area of physical education. Already, flat-panel displays for computers are a realistic purchase for many. And, it is only a matter of time before we see large panel television/display screens come down in price.

Three-Dimensional Animation

Three-dimensional animation is finally coming of age. It seems that every month a new three-dimensional product hits the market with a claim to be the best, fastest, and most lifelike. For example, Biped (Kinetix' Character Studio) is a new plug in program for 3-D Studio MAX. It allows the user to create realistic human movement simply by placing footsteps—much like chalking steps on the floor in a dance class. The software

284

automatically generates appropriate walking, running, or jumping movements with the correct foot and leg rotation.

These three-dimensional animation programs allow students to create original routines for dancing, tumbling, and gymnastics. In addition, they can be interactive in real time with on-screen simulations for self-defense and orienteering activities. These programs also provide programmers with the tools to produce higher quality software for use in physical education.

Three-dimensional animation programs also can be used to design new facilities, including playgrounds. Landscape Structures, a playground equipment company, already provides buyers with a two-dimensional working site plan of a new playground that provides a top view layout of the equipment in the proposed site. It includes the actual size and minimum use zones. At this stage, the buyer makes adjustments in the arrangement of the equipment and reconsiders any component choices. Then, the computer generates a high-quality three-dimensional color rendering of the playground, enabling the buyer to verify the design.

Three-dimensional animation programs have continued to develop and improve. Educational-level programs, such as Poser and LifeForms, bring the technology into the hands of students. Poser (Fractal Design) is a figure design and animation tool that allows the user to create lifelike drawings and animations of human figures in action—dancing ballet, climbing a cliff, exercising, etc. You simply create a pose, go to a new position on the time line, change the pose and let the software generate all the in-between motion.

Life Forms (Credo Interactive) allows you to create three-dimensional animations for choreography, movement planning, and physical education. In addition to its animation feature, Life Forms provides you with the tools for applying finishing touches such as textures and colors. You can even export the animations as QuickTime movies, or other file formats.

Movement Tracking

As mentioned earlier in this chapter, body suits, or exoskeletons, take virtual reality to another level. Electromagnetic movement tracking technology lets the user move around in three-dimensional space and see the corresponding changes of view while tracking the position of moving objects. For example, The Gypsy ($19,995) uses an exoskeleton with potentiometers at the joints. The Gypsy can be set up in minutes and it does not require a controlled environment. It requires only one suit and a single analog to digital converter card that connects to a personal computer. Movement of the individual is then monitored on the computer.

Movement trackers have the same potential for physical education as other virtual reality options—skill improvement, strategy sessions, and game play. Although it will be many years before this particular application becomes a reality in physical education, it will revolutionize physical activity as we know it today.

Today we are seeing more and more sensors used for tracking motion. There are even sensors that can be placed in shoes to monitor motion. And, real time swing analyzers (CyberScan) for golf, baseball, tennis, and hockey are now available at reasonable ($300-500) prices.

Nanotechnology

Nanoparticles—just one one-thousandth of a micron in size—will be 1,000 percent stronger than traditional materials. Nanotechnology—the development of applications using new composite materials made of nanoparticles—will have a wide variety of applications in defense, medicine, sports, and recreational industries.

As mentioned earlier in this chapter, miniaturization is the name of the game. Nanotechnology takes this one step farther. Nanotechnology will help make your clothes "smarter." Future sport fabrics will contain tiny heating and cooling tubes, making

Teacher With a Vision

I am teaching at a brand new state of the art technology school, and have found the use of technology in my curriculum to be the best motivation I have ever had in trying to get students to do "academic" type work in "physical education" class. My students are using heart rate monitors with computer interface, using digital cameras—still and video—to do projects based on fitness concepts or skill development. They are using the Fitness- and Activity- Gram software to track their individual progress. All of this has motivated my students to exercise at home daily, and everyone wants to take physical education all year (it is not a required class at the middle school level in the state of Florida).

I am constantly learning about the newest technology from listservs, other colleagues, and my students. I think the future of education is all about technology, and I hope to be a big part of it.

Daniel Jenkins Academy of Technology is a magnet middle school with a small number of high school students who are on campus every day, but are taking their classes completely online from teachers all over the country. They can take personal fitness or regular physical education from me, or online. This is the first school in the country to offer a program such as this. We are being followed by USA Today as well as several other news and government agencies to see if this is the type of program that should be offered to everyone.

Susan Searls
Daniel Jenkins Academy of Technology
Haines City, Florida

a thin jacket as warm as a parka, for example. Nanotechnology also may have a negative impact on physical education: With the development of ultra-tiny micromachines that can travel in the blood vessels of the human body and do repair work, people may become less concerned about preventive health behaviors.

There are now "jackets that grow warmer when the temperature drops, sweat socks that resist bacteria and odors, T-shirts that ward off ultraviolet rays" (Minerd, 2000). This type of clothing allows for safer and more comfortable enjoyment of physical activities. We are even seeing wearable computers that fit into our clothing and jewelry.

Nanotechnology also has impacted the three-dimensional fax movement. The nanobox passes plastic back and forth, laying down patterns of molecules much like a regular fax lays down ink on paper. However, the nanobox, using different "toners," can add circuits, antennas, keypads, speakers, microphones, etc. to the product (Port, 1999). Imagine the day when you no longer have to wait for a replacement part to fix a piece of equipment; instead it will be faxed to your nanobox.

Ultra-tiny micromachines for medical purposes are still seen as the number one use of nanotechnology., And, to that end, President Clinton allocated $500 million dollars for research in the year 2001.

Expert Systems

Expert program software will compress knowledge about a particular topic. It will arrange information in a branching configuration, so that possibilities can be discarded one at a time until a correct answer is found. In other words, this software will lead an individual through a step-by-step problem-solving process.

Expert programs will help teachers and students analyze and improve motor performance, assist coaches with game strategies, help individuals identify health problems and improve health practices, and advise people on the kinds of leisure time experiences they need to balance their lives. Coaches will be able to ask questions such as, "If the defense does this, what should the offense do?" Or, if maximum strength is needed in a given movement pattern, "What exercise program should be applied?"

There are now expert systems that can diagnose human illnesses, make financial forecasts, and schedule routes for delivery vehicles. Some of these expert systems are designed to take the place of human experts, while others are designed to assist them. This area of technology, also known as artificial intelligence, will continue to expand and, much of that expansion will be in the area of education. Halal (2000) also is predicting that virtual assistants will be one of the applications for expert systems. "We envision the virtual assistant as a very smart program stored on your PC or portable device, that monitors all e-mails, faxes, messages, computer files, and phone calls in order to learn all about you and your work. In time, your virtual assistant would gain the knowledge to take over routine tasks, such as writing a letter, retrieving a file, making a phone call, or screening people" (Halal, 2000, p. 5). Primitive versions are already available in systems such as Wildfire and Portico. These programs can locate people by phone, take messages, and perform other simple tasks.

Holograms

A hologram is a collection of all possible views of a scene combined into a single plane of light-modulating patterns. A hologram can take the form of an another person or an object. In the future, you will actually experience a sensation when you come in contact with the holographic image, and the image will be capable of reacting to such stimuli.

Holographic images in physical education will be used primarily in model performances. Other uses will include simulations that involve an opponent (e.g., martial arts), and simulations that provide the opportunity to talk with holographic versions of experts. One futurist predicts, "Sometime in the next millennium our grandchildren or great grandchildren will watch a football game by moving aside the coffee table and letting eight-inch-high players run around the living room passing a half-inch football back and forth" (Negroponte, 1995).

The practical application of holograms is still in the future, but the vision and research continue.

The Future: 2001 Version

Each of the technologies described in the 1993 and 1998 editions have continued to evolve, and we can project that—like the computer—their growth will double every 18 months. New technologies also have emerged during the last three years, along with their potential applications for physical education. In this section, we will examine two of these new technologies and their potential for physical education.

Mapping of the Human Genome

On June 26th, 2000, nearly five years ahead of schedule, a "working draft" of the human genome was completed. This draft depicts the layout of 100,000 human genes along with the sequence of the nearly 3 billion DNA base pairs. This document and the refinement to follow will have a dramatic impact on molecular medicine, microbial genomics, forensics, and agricultural business. Gene therapy may, in fact, improve people's learning abilities and reverse the effects of aging on memory.

Certainly, anything that helps to improve learning and memory has a carry-over affect on physical education. But, the mapping of the human genome, also will have an impact on risk assessment. Folks prone to certain illness and disease will have fore- warning. This may have a positive impact on physical education as individuals are able to take more responsibility for their own health, or it may have a negative impact as individuals rely more on medical interventions to solve their health issues.

Instant Electronic Diagnosis of Illnesses

Small physiological sensors, attached to the body or available at "health" kiosks will allow for constant monitoring of an individual's health. Smart chips will provide a complete record of patient history from birth to death, replacing the papers that always seem to get lost when transferring between providers (Halal, 2000). Imagine this scenario at a health kiosk in a shopping mall:

> Place your arm in a tube on the left side of the chair. The tube and chair are connected to a computer that determines your height, weight, blood pressure, body fat, and blood chemistry. The computer has a floating camera attached, which allows close —even microscopic—inspection of the skin, eyes, mouth, etc. There also is a small mouthpiece for you to blow into; it monitors how your body is handling the air and analyzes a sample of saliva from your lips. When you insert your hand into a glovelike device at the end of the arm tube, it extracts (no needle, just pinpoint suction) two drops of blood from your finger and runs a complete spectrum of tests that once required multiple vials of blood (Wooten, 2000).

Much like the implications for the human genome project, this may have positive or negative effects on physical education. It all depends on whether individuals accept the additional responsibility for their own health or rely more on the medical profession.

Summary

Each of the advances discussed in this chapter—and more—will have a tremendous impact on society, education, and physical education. We must keep up with these advances to ensure that we find positive applications for them in physical education.

And the journey continues...

Reflection Questions

1. Can you think of other possible applications of cutting-edge technology that might be useful in the future of physical education?

2. What changes related to physical education instruction do you see occurring in the next several years?

3. Given the changes that technology introduce to the teaching of physical education, what do you see as the role of the physical educator in the future.

Projects

1. Write a one-paragraph letter to an administrator describing why you need a computer (this is an update of the letter you wrote at the end of chapter 1).

2. Prepare a list of resources (publications, Web sites) or activities that keep you up to date on important developments related to using technology in physical education.

Appendix A

Suggested Vendors

3Com Corporation
5400 Bayfront Plaza
Santa Clara, CA 95052-8145
800-638-3266
www.3com.com

Ablesoft, Inc.
8550-E Remington Ave.
Pennsauken, NJ 08110
800-467-3569
www.ablesoft-inc.com

A.D.A.M. Software
1600 Riveredge Pkwy. #800
Atlanta, GA 30328
770-980-0888
www.adam.com

Adaptec, Inc.
691 S Milpitas Blvd.
Milpitas, CA 95035
800-442-7274
www.adaptec.com

Adobe Systems, Inc
345 Park Ave.
San Jose, CA 95110
800-833-6687
www.adobe.com

Advanced Information
Box A, 1800 N. Stonelake Dr.
Bloomington, IN 47402
800-397-7725
www.ait.net

AIT
P.O. Box A
Bloomington, IN 47402-0120
812-335-7667
www.ait.net

AIMS Multimedia
9710 DeSoto Ave.
Chatsworth, CA 91311
800-367-2467
www.aims-multimedia.com

Alchemedia, Inc.
41 South Forks Avenue - 8H
Forks, WA 98331-2569
877-755-2331
www.alchemediainc.com

All-Pro Software
30 Maple View Ct
Madison, WI 53719
800-776-7859
www.allprosoftware.com

ALVA Access Group
436 14th Street, Suite 700
Oakland CA 94612
888-318-2582
www.aagi.com

AAHPERD
1900 Association Dr.
Reston, VA 20191
800-213-7193
www.aahperd.org

AlphaSmart, Inc.
20400 Stevens Creek Blvd, Ste. 300
Cupertino, CA 95014
888-274-0680
www.alphasmart.com

American Medical Screening
2923 N. 33rd Avenue
Phoenix, AZ 85017
602-269-0655

American Red Cross
431 18th Street NW
Washington DC 20006
202-639-3520
www.redcross.org

Apple Computer
1 Infinite Loop
Cupertino, CA 95014-6299
408-996-1010
www.apple.com

Assembled Solutions, Inc.
11 Cottage Grove Woods SE
Cedar Rapids, IA 52403
800-356-5361
www.asmsol.com

Associated Press Photo Archive
385 Science Park Rd.
State College, PA 16803
888-438-9847
www.ap.accuweather.com

Athletic Institute
200 Castlewood Dr.
North Palm Beach, FL 33408

Athletic Rules Study
PO Box 8413
Cedar Rapids, IA 52408
800-399-3013
www.rules-study.com

Aurbach & Associates
9378 Olive St., Suite.102
St Louis, MO 63132
800-774-7239
www.aurbach.com

Autodesk
111 McInnis Pkwy.
San Rafael, CA 94903
800-538-6401
www.autodesk.com

Avid Sports
55 Technology Dr
Lowell, MA 01851
978-275-0200
www.avidsports.com

Baudville
5380 52nd St. Se
Grand Rapids, MI 49512
800-728-0888
www.baudville.com

Benchmark Media
569 N. State Rd.
Briarcliff Manor, NY 10510-1542
800-438-5564

Bergh International
5428 Lyndale Ave South
Minneapolis, MN 55419
800-423-9685
http://www.borton.com/bergh.html-ssi

BioAnalogics Systems
7909 S.W. Cirrus
Beaverton, OR 97005-7151
800-327-7953
www.bioanalogics.com

Biometric ID
5000 Van Nuys Blvd., Suite 300
Sherman Oaks, CA 91403
www.biometricid.com/

Biometrics
637 S. Broadway, PMB 156
Boulder, CO 80303
800-522-6224
www.pccoach.com

Blackboard
1899 L Street NW, 5th Floor
Washington, DC 20036
202-463-4860
www.blackboard.com

Bonnie's Fitware
18832 Stefani Ave.
Cerritos, CA 90703
562-924-0835
www.pesoftware.com

Britannica
310 S. Michigan Ave.
Chicago, IL 60604
800-323-1229/800-621-3900
www.britannica.com

Brother International Corp.
100 Somerset Corporate Blvd.
Bridgewater, NJ 08007-0911
800-284-1937
www.brothereducation.com

Brown and Benchmark
25 Kessel Ct.
Madison, WI 53711
800-338-5371

Bullfrog Films
P. O. Box 149
Oley, PA 19547
800-543-3764
www.bullfrogfilms.com

Busy Body
4540 Beltway Dr.
Addison, TX 75001
1-800-HOME-FIT
www.busybody-fitness.com/

Cable in the Classroom
1800 N. Beauregard Blvd 100
Alexandria, VA 22311
703-845-1400
www.ciconline.org

Cambridge
PO Box 2153
Charleston, WV 25328-2153
888-744-0100
www.cambridgeol.com

Cardio Tech
255 N. Washington St, #202
Rockville, MD 20850-1703
800-543-2850
www.cardiotech.net

Casio, Inc.
570 Mt. Pleasant Ave.
Dover, NJ 07801
888-204-7765/800-435-7732
www.casio.com

CE Software
1801 Industrial Circle
West Des Moines, IA 50265
800-523-7638
www.cesoft.com

CeQuadrat, Inc.
691 South Milpitas Blvd
Milpitas, CA 95035
www.cequadrat.com

Chalkware Education Solutions
101 Norwalk Court
Vacaville, CA 95687
800-838-9058
www.iepware.com

Chancery Software Ltd
3001 Wayburne Dr., Suite 275
Burnaby, BC, Canada V5G 4W1
800-999-9931
www.chancery.com

Chariot Software
123 Camino De La Reina
San Diego, CA 92103
800-242-7468/619-298-0202
www.chariot.com

Chip Taylor
2 East View Drive
Derry, NH 03038
800-876-2447
www.chiptaylor.com

Chronomix Corp
650-F Vaqueros Ave
Sunnyvale, CA 94086
800-538-1548
www.chronomix.com

Competitive Edge Software
722 Oak Hill Rd.
Afton, NY 13730
888-237—6381
www.cesoftware.com

Computer Athlete
Dublin, OH 43017
614-761-1059
tile.net/vendors/computerathlete.html

Computer Outfitters
639 N. Swan Road
Tucson, AZ 85711
800-827-2567

Concept 2 Rower
105 Industrail Park Dr.
Morrisville, VT 05661
800-245-5676
www.concept2.com

Country Technology, Inc.
P.O. Box 87
Gays Mills, WI 54631
608-735-4718
www.fitnessmart.com

Cramer Software Group
P. O. Box 1001
Gardner, KS 66030
800-255-6621
www.cramersportsmed.com

Creative Health Products, Inc.
5148 Saddle Ridge Rd.
Plymouth, MI 48170
800-742-4478
www.CHPonline.com

Credo Interactive Inc
1140 West Pender St., Suite 1040
Vancouver, BC
Canada, V6E 4G1
604-291-6717
www.credo-interactive.com

Crystal Sportsware
105 Stone Lake Ct.
Yorktown, VA 23693
www.crystalsport.com

CSI Software
3120 S.W. FWY, Suite 300
Houston, TX 77098
800-247-3431
www.csisoftwareusa.com

CU See Me Networks
524 Amherst St.
Nashua, NH 03063
800-241-7463
www.wpine.com

Custom Design Systems
200 Daniels Way, 210
Freehold, NJ 07728
800-CDS-SALE

CyberScan
82 Walker Lane
Newtown, PA 18940
215-860-8082
www.cyberscan.com

Cybersports
PO Box 3216
Redmond, WA 98073-3216
800-846-3688
www.cybersportsusa.com

Dairy Council of California
1101 National Drive, B
Sacramento, CA 95834-1945
www.dairycouncilorca.org

DataViz, Inc.
55 Corporate Dr.
Trumbull, CT 06611
203-268-0030
www.dataviz.com

Dazzle Multimedia
47211 Bayside Pkwy
Fremont, CA 94538
888-436-4348
www.dazzlemultimedia.com

Destination Fitness
P.O. Box 10285
Eugence, OR 94401
800-624-4952
www.destinationfitness.com

DIAMAR Interactive
600 University St., #1701
Seattle, WA 98101
206-340-5975

Digital Image FX
One Research Dr.
Dartmouth Nova Scotia, Canada
B2Y 4M9
www.digital-fx.ca

DINE Systems
586 North French Rd.
Amherst, NY 14228-2103
800-688-1848
www.dinesystems.com

Disney Interacative
500 S. Buena Vista St.
Burbank, CA 91521-8464
800-688-1520
disney.go.com/education

DK Interactive
95 Madison Ave.
New York, NY 10016
800-342-5357
www.dk.com

Don Johnston
26799 W. Commerce Dr.
Volvo, Il 60073
800-999-4660
www.donjohnston.com

Dragon Systems
320 Nevada St
Newton, MA 02460
800-437-2466
www.dragonsys.com

Dynamix
9411 Philadelphia Rd
Baltimore, MD 21237
800-843-6499
www.dynamixmusic.com

Eastman Kodak
343 State St
Rochester, NY 14650
800-242-2424
www.kodak.com

EBSCO Publishing
10 Estes St.
Ipswich, MA 01938
800-653-2726
www.epnet.com

Edmark
6727 185th Avenue NE
Redmond, WA 98073-9721
800-426-0856
www.edmark.com

Educational Activities
P. O. Box 392
Freeport, NY 11520
800-645-3739
www.edact.com

Educational Software Institute
4213 South 94th St.
Omaha, NE 68127
800-955-5570
www.edsoft.com

Electronic Arts
209 Redwood Shore Pkwy
Redwood City, CA 94065
800-245-4525
www.ea.com

Electric Library
1000 Chesterbrook Blvd #111
Berwyn, PA 19312
800-304-3542
www.education.elibrary.com

ELMO
1478 Old Country Rd.
Plainview, NY 11803
800-947-3566
www.elmo-corp.com

Endeavor Software
40 Beach St
Manchester, MA 01944
www.endinfosys.com

Entertaining Fitness
2225 Broadway #B
Santa Monica, CA 90404
800-735-3315
www.karenvoight.com

Epson
3840 Kilroy Airport Way
Long Beach, CA 90806
800-463-7766
www.epson.com

ERIC
7420 Fullerton Rd, 110
Springfield, VA 22153
800-443-3742
www.edrs.com

ESHA
4263 Commercial SE, Suite 2000
Salem, Oregon 97302
800-659-3742
www.ESHA.com

ESPN Cable in the Classroom
P.O. Box 3016
Wallingford, CT 06492
800-565-0452
www.espn.com

Excelsior Software, Inc.
PO Box 3417
Greeley, CO 80633
800-473-4572
www.gradebook.com

Expert Software
802 Doublas Rd., North Tower, Suite 600
Coral Gables, FL 33134-3129
800-759-2562
www.expertsoftware.com

Extreme Software
704 228th Ave, NE, Ste. 813
Redmond, WA 98053
425-836-5448
www.extremesoftware.com

Farallon
3809 Teagarden St
San Leandro, CA 94577
800-859-7761
www.farallon.com

File Maker
5201 Patrick Henry Dr.
Santa Clara, CA 95054
617-494-1600
www.filemaker.com

Fitcentric Technologies
9635 Monte Vista Ave, St 201
Montclair, CA 91763
800-400-1390
www.fitcentric.com

Fitness Lifestyle Design, Inc.
2317 Eastgate Way
Talahassee, FL 32308
800-FLD-INCL

Fitness Reporter
5325 Elkhorn Blvd, Suite 116
Sacramento, CA 95842
916-338-7803
www.fitnessreporter.com

Forest Technologies
765 Industrial Drive
Cary, Il 60013
800-544-3356
www.ForestTech.com

Futrex Inc.
6 Montgomery Village Ave.
Gaithersburg, MD 20879
800-255-4206
www.futrex.com

Galactix Software
12834 110th Ave., NE
Kirkland, WA 98034
800-414-4268
www.galactix.com

Gamco Educational Systems
325 N. Kirkwood Rd., Suite 200
St. Louis, MO 63122
800-351-1404
www.gamco.com

Gartner Software Solutions
716 Newman Springs Rd.
Lincroft, NJ 07738
888-869-6070
www.gartnersw.com

GL Tech
2255-3 Loia Dr.
Rolling Meadows, IL 60008
800-346-5303
www.gl-tech.com

Glencoe/McGraw-Hill
8787 Orion Pl.
columbus, OH 43240
800-334-7344
www.glencoe.com

Global Village
1601 Clint Moore Road, Suite 200
Boca Raton, FL 33487
561-997-7202
www.globalvillage.com

Globalink
52 Third Ave.
Burlington, MA 01803
781-203-5000
www.lhsl.com

Grolier Publishing
P.O. Box 1795
Danbury, CT 06816
800-371-3908
teacherstore.grolie.com

Greenwood Electronic Media
88 Post Road West
Westport, CT 06881
203-226-3571
www.greenwood.com/gem

Handspring
189 Bernardo Ave
Mountain View, CA 94043
888-565-9393
www.handspring.com

Health Tech
433 Park Point Drive, Suite 120
Golden, CO 80401
1-800-345-4207
www.healtheTech.com

Health First
6811 Academy Parkway East
Albuquerque, NM 87109
800-841-8333
www.healthfirstusa.com

Her-Mar Inc.
PO Box 402916
Miami Beach, Fl 33140
800-327-8209

Hewlett Packard
3000 Hanover St.
Palo Alta, CA 94304-1185
800-752-0900
www.hp.com

HighWired.com
300 N. Beacon St
Watertown, MA 02472
www.highwired.com

HRS Publications
P. O. Box 70618
Eugene, OR 97401
800-261-8650
www.hrspublications.com/

Human Kinetics
P. O. Box 5076
Champaign, IL 61825-5076
800-747-4457
www.humankinetics.com

Hy-Tek
PO Box 12789
New Bern, NC 28562
252-633-5111
www.hy-tekltd.com

IBM Corporation
44 S. Broadway
White Plains, NY 10601
800-426-4968
www.ibm.com/education

Infogrip
1141 E. Main St.
Ventura, CA 93001
800-397-0921
www.infogrip.com

InLytes Productions
6101 E. Mescal St.
Scottsdale, AZ 35254
800-243-7867

Inprise
100 Enterprise Way
Scotts Valley, CA 95066
813-431-1000
www.inprise.com

Insight Software Solutions
P.O. Box 354
Bountiful, UT 84011-0354
www.wintools.com

Insignia Solutions
41300 Christy St.
Fremont, CA 94538-3115
www.insignia-solutions.com

Inspiration Software
7412 SW Beaverton Hillsdale Hwy.
Portland, OR 97225-2167
800-877-4292
www.inspiration.com

IntelliTools
1720 Corporate Circle
Petaluma, CA 94954
800-899-6687
www.intellitools.com

Interplay (MacPlay)
16815 Von Karman
Irvine, CA 92606
800-969-GAME
www.interplay.com

Intuit Corporation
2535 Garcia Ave.
Mountain View, CA 94043
800-446-8848
www.intuit.com

Iomega
1821 West Iomega Way
Roy, UT 84067
800-466-3422
www.iomega.com

Ipswitch
81 Hartwell Avenue
Lexington, MA 02421
781-676-5700
www.ipswitch.com

IVI Publishing
1380 Corporate Center Curve
Eagan, MN 55121
800-754-1484
www.ivi.com

Jackson Software
361 Park Ave.
Glencoe, IL 60022
800-850-1777
www.jacksoncorp.com

Jay Klein Productions, Inc.
2930 Austin Bluffs Pkwy.
Colorado Springs, CO 80918
719-599-8786
www.gradebusters.com

JB Software
4 Shinnecock Hills Ct
O'Fallon, MO 63366
847-452-3589
www.JBSoftware.net

Karen Westfall Productions
5899 S. State St.
Murray, UT 34107
800-566-2182

Kendall/Hunt Publishing
4050 Westmark Dr.
Dubuque, IA 52004-1840
800-228-0810
www.kendallhunt.com

Kimbo
P. O. Box 477
Longbranch, NJ 07740
800-631-2187
www.kimbo.com

Knowledge Adventure
19840 Pioneer Ave.
Torrance, CA 90503
800-545-7677
www.hyperstudio.com

LavaTech, Inc.
1615 Parkridge Circle
Crofton, MD 21114
www.lotusnotes.com

Learn Technologies Interactive
361 Broadway, Suite 600
New York, New York 10013
212-334-2225
www.learntech.com/learntech

Learning in Motion
500 Seabright Ave., Suite 105
Santa Cruz, CA 95062-3480
800-560-5670
www.learn.motion.com

Lego Dacta
555 Taylor Rd.
P. O. Box 1600
Enfield, CT 06083-1600
800-243-4870
www.lego.com

Lifestyle Software Group
2155 Old Moutrie Rd
St. Augustine, FL 32086
www.lifeware.com

LJC, Inc
7831 New York Ave
Hudson, FL 34667
800-226-9708
www.power51.com

Lotus Development Corp.
55 Cambridge Pkwy.
Cambridge, MA 02142
800-343-5414
www.lotus.com

Lucas Learning
PO Box 10667
San Rafael, CA 94912
www.lucaslearning.com

Lynx System Developers
175 N. New Boston St
Woburn, MA 01801
800-989-5969
www.finishlynx.com

Macromedia
600 Townsend St. Suite 310W
San Francisco, CA 94103
415-252-2000
www.macromedia.com

MacWarehouse
1720 Oak St.
Lakewood, NJ 08701
800-725-1450
www.warehouse.com

Mattel Interactive
6493 Kaiser Dr.
Freemont, CA 94555
800-358-9144
www.mattelinteractive.com

Maxis (part of Electronic Arts)
1710 Beau Rivase
San Pablo, CA 94806
510-233-2168
www.maxis.com

Media Mosaic
555 S. Renton Village, Suite 280
Renton, WA 98055
800-972-3766
www.mediamosaic.com

Metacreations
6303 Carpinteria Ave.
Carpinteria, CA 93013
800-846-0111
www.metacreations.com

CCG MetaMedia
460 West 34th Street 7th Floor
New York, NY 10001
212 268-2100

MGI
2105 South Bascom, Suite 300,
Campbell, California 95008
888-MGI-SOFT
www.mgisoft.com

MicroFit
1077-B Independence Ave
Mt. View, CA 94043
800-822-0405
www.microfit.com

Microsoft
One Microsoft Way
Redmond, WA 98052
800-426-9400
www.microsoft.com

MicroWarehouse
1720 Oak St.
Lakewood, NJ 08701
1800-367-7080
www.microwarehouse.com

Mindplay
160 W. Fort Lowell
Tucson, AZ 85705
800-221-7911
www.mindplay.com

Mini Mitter
20300 Empire Ave., B-3
Bend, OR 97701
800-685-2999
www.minimitter.com

Misty City Software
13625 Northeast 126th Pl., Suite 430
Kirkland, WA 98034-8738
800-795-0049
www.mistycity.com

MSC Working Knowledge
66 Bovet Rd., Suite 200
San Mateo, CA 94402
800-766-6615
www.krev.com

Multimedia Professionals Inc.
803 W. Broad St., Suite 520
Falls Church, VA 22046
www.mmpro.com

Neat Sports
7108 Fairway Drive, Suite 100
Palm Beach Gardens, Florida 33418
www.neatsys.com

Newlife Technologies
One Park West Circle, #303
Midlothian, VA 23113-4518
800-639-5432
www.newlifetech.com

Novel Products
P. O. Box 408
Rockton, IL 61072
800-323-5143
www.novelproductsinc.com

NTS Computer Systems
11491 Kingston St
Maple Ridge, BC V2X OY6
800-663-7163
www.dreamwriter.com

Nutridata Software
5150 E. Pacific Coast Hwy.
Long Beach, CA 90804
800-922-2988
www.nutridata.com

Olympus
Two Corporate Center Dr.
Melville, NY 11747-3157
800-347-4027
www.olympusamerica.com

Omron Healthcare, Inc
300 Lakeview Parkway
Vernon Hills, Il 60061
877 - 216 - 1333
www.omronhealthcare.com

Palm, Inc
5470 Great American Parkway
Santa Clara, CA 95052
www.palm.com

Palm Technology
306-N W. El Norte Pkwy
Escondido, CA 92026
www.palm-technology.com

Panasonic
2 Panasonic Way
Secaucus, NJ 07094
800-742-8086
www.panasonic.com

Pasco
10101 Foothills Blvd
Roseville, CA 95747
800-772-8700
www.pasco.com

Peak Performance
7388 S Revere Parkway 603
Englewood, CO 80112 USA
800-PIK-PEAK
www.peakperform.com

PenSport
1041 W. Bridge St., Ste 6
Phoenixville, PA 19460
888-223-1550
www.pensport.com

Perfect Solutions
15950 Schweizer Ct
West Palm Beach, FL 33414
800-726-7086
www.perfectsolutions.com

Philips
64 Perimeter Center East
Atlanta, GA 31146-7300
800-326-6586
www.philipsusa.com

Physical Genius
1105 Taylorsville Rd.
Washington Crossing, PA 18977
www.physicalgenius.com

Pierian Spring Software
5200 S.W. MacAdam Ave., #570
Portland, OR 97201
800-472-8578
www.pierian.com

Pinnacle Systems
280 N. Bernardo Avenue
Mountain View, CA 94043
888-484-3366
www.pinnaclesys.com

Pitsco Lego Dacta
913 East Jefferson
Pittsburg, KS 66762
316-231-0000
pitsco.com

Polar Electro Inc.
370 Crossways Park Dr.
Woodbury, NY 11797-2050
800-227-1314
www.polar.fi/index.html

Polhemus
40 Hercules Dr.
Colchester, VT 05446
800-357-4777
www.polhemus.com

PowerOn Software, Inc.
6525 W. Campus Oval, Ste 130
New Albany, Oh 43054
614-413-4000
www.poweronsw.com

PreciseSoftware Solutions
690 Canton St.
Westwood, MA 02090
800-310-4777
www.precise.com

Preferred Educational Software
9585 Woodgate Ln.
Byron, IL 61010
888-959-2016
www.pes-sports.com

Psion
150 Baker Ave
Concord, MA
800-997-7466
www.psioninc.com

Pro Power
6006 El Dorado Dr.
Tampa, FL 33615
800-732-2004
www.propower1.com

Pulse Metric
6190 Cornerstone Ct.. E. Ste 103
San Diego, CA 92121
www.dynapulse.com

Qualisys Motion Measurement
41 Sequine Dr.
Glastonbury, CT 06033
www.qualisys.com

304

Queue, Inc.
338 Commerce Dr.
Fairfield, Ct 06432
800-232-2224
www.queueinc.com

Real Networks
2601 Elliott Ave, Suite 1000
Seattle, WA 98121
www.realnetworkis.com

Reality Quest
1860 Lefthand Circle, Suite A
Longmont, CO 80501-6754
303-682-2689
www.theglove.com

Ricoh Corporation
5 Dedrick Pl
West Caldwell, NJ 07006
800-637-4264
www.ricoh-usa.com

Robert Widen Company
540 6th St. #F
Prescott, AZ 86301
800-862-0761

Royal Inc.
Intersports Books and Videos
790 W. Tennessee St.
Denver, CO 80223
800-525-9030

Satellite Information Systems
7464 Arapahoe Ave, Ste B-17
Boulder, CO 80303
www.siscommedia.com

Savvy Knowledge Systems
#701, 550 - 11th Ave. SW
Calgary, AB Canada T2R 1M7
800-230-5593
www.savvyknowledge.com

Scholastic Software
568 Broadway, 9th Floor
New York, NY 10012
800-724-6527
www.scholastic.com

Sharp Electronics
Sharp Plaza, Box 1
Mahwah, NJ 07430-2135
800-237-4277
www.sharp-usa.com

Sharper Image
650 Davis St.
San Francisco, CA 94111
800-344-4444
www.sharperimage.com

SIRS
P.O. Box 272348
Boca Raton, FL 33427-2348
800-232-7477
www.sirs.com

SISU Software
P. O. Box 2305
Renton, WA 98056
800-228-5385

The Skier's Edge Company
P. O. Box 2700
Park City, UT 84060
800-225-9669
www.skiersedge.com

Smart Technologies
1177 11th Ave. SW, Suite 600
Calgary, AB, Canada T2R 1K9
888-42-smart
www.smarttech.com

Softboard
7216 S.W. Durham Rd.
Portland, OR 97224
888-763-8262
www.softboard.com

Software Clinical Information
602 Park Point Dr., Suite 240
Golden, CO 80401
800-676-7793
www.healthetech.com

Softkey International
One Arthenaeum St.
Cambridge, MA 02142
800-845-8692
www.softkey.com

Sony
1 Sony Dr.
Park Ridge, NJ 07656
800-352-7669
www.sony.com

Sports Illustrated for Kids
Time & Life Building
New York, NY 10020
800-992-0196
www.sikids.com

Sports Software
PO Box 512683
Punta Gorda, FL 33951
www.sports-software.com

SportStat, Inc.
1217 Torington Dr.
Las Vegas, NV 89108
800-300-8010
www.sportstat-inc.com

Sprint Rothhammer
PO Box 3840
San Louis Obispo, CA 93403
800-235-2156
www.sprintacqusatics.com

Stagecast Software
805 Veterans Blvd., Suite 226
Redwood City, CA 94063
877-Stagecast
www.stagecast.com

Star Play
P.O. Box 19679
Boulder, CO 80308
www.starplay.com

Stereographics
2171 E. Francisco Blvd.
San Rafael, CA 94901
800-783-2660
www.stereographics.com

Strategic Learning Technologies
1355 Sherman Rd, Ste.F
Hiawatha, IA 52233
888-881-7979
www.sltech.com

Sunburst Technology
101 Castleton St.
Pleasantville, NY 10570-9971
800-321-7511
www.sunburstdirect.sunburst.com

Super School Software
1857 Josie Ave.
Long Beach, CA 90815-3432
800-248-7099
www.superschoolsoftware.com

SyberVision
One Sansome St., Suite 810
San Francisco, CA 94104
800-678-0887

TeachLogic,Inc.
22981 Triton Way, Ste-C
Laguna Hilla, CA 92653
800-588-0018
www.teachlogic.com

Terran
15951 Los Gatos Blvd, Ste.1
Los Gatos, CA 95032
800-577-3443
www.terran.com

- off

The Brain Store
4202 Sorrento Valley Blvd., Suite B
San Diego, CA 92121
800-325-4769
www.thebrainstore.com

TurboStats Software Co.
PO Box 144
Towaco, NJ 07082
800-607-8287
www.turbostats.com

Turner Multimedia
One CNN Center
Atlanta, GA 30348-5780
800-639-7797
learning.turner.com

Unicycling Society of America
P. O. Box 49534
Redford, MI 48240
800-783-2425
www.unicycling.org/usa

US Orienteering Federation
P. O. Box 1444
Forest Park, GA 33051
www.us.orienteering.org

Ventura Educational Systems
P. O. Box 425
Grover Beach, CA 93483
800-336-1022
www.venturaes.com

Vernier Software
13979 SW Millikan Way
Beaverton, OR 97005
www.vernier.com

Videodiscovery, Inc.
1700 Westlake Ave. North, Suite 600
Seattle, WA 98109-3012
800-548-3472
www.videodiscovery.com

Video Learning Library
15838 N. 62nd St
Scottsdale, AZ 85254-1988
800-383-8811

Virtual Entertainment
200 Highland Ave.
Needham, MA 02194
www.virtent.com

Virtual Technologies
5514 N. Davis Hwy, Suite 106
Pensecola, FL 32503
www.virtualtechnologies.com

Vivonic
5200 N.E. Elam Young Pkwy
Hillsboro, OR 97124
www.vivonic.com

VRex
85 Executive Blvd.
Elmaford, NY 10523
www.vrex.com

Wagon Wheels
17191 Corbina Lane, #203
Huntington Beach, CA 92649
714-846-8169

West Publishing Company
610 Opperman Drive
St Paul, MN 55164-0526

World Book
233 N. Michigan Ave.
Chicago, IL 60601
www.worldbook.com

Young American Bowling Alliance
5301 S. 76th St.
Greendale, WI 53129
www.bowl.com

APPENDIX B

Television Programmers

ABC
77 W. 66th St., 9th Floor
New York, NY 10023
www.abc.com

CBS
51 West 52nd St.
New York, NY 10019
www.cbs.com

The Disney Channel
3800 West Alameda
Burbank, CA 91505
www.disneychannel.com

Discovery Channel
7700 Wisconsin Ave.
Bethesda, MD 20814-3522
1-888-404-5969
www.discoveryschool.com

ESPN/ESPN2
Cable in the Classroom Dept.
935 Middle St.
Bristol, CT 06010
860-766-2000
www.espn.com

The History Channel
235 E. 45th St.
New York, NY 10017
www.historychannel.com

Lifetime
309 West 49th St.
New York, NY 10019
www.lifetimetv.com

NBC-TV
30 Rockefeller Plaza, 25th Floor
New York, NY 10112
www.nbc.com

Nickelodeon
1515 Broadway, 39th Floor
New York, Ny 10036
212-258-8000
www.teachers.nick.com

Public Broadcasting Service
1320 Braddock Pl.
Alexandria, VA 22314
www.pbs.org

Sci-Fi Channel
1230 Avenue of the Americas
New York, NY 10020
212-408-9168
www.scifi.com

The Learning Channel
7700 Wisconsin Ave.
Bethesda, MD 20814-3522
1-888-404-5969
www.discoveryschool.com

Turner Network Television
1 CNN Center
Atlanta, GA 30348-5366
www.tnt-tv.com

Suggested Journals and Magazines

Camcorder&Computer Video
4880 Market St.
Ventura, CA 93003-7783
805-644-3824

Converge Magazine
100 blue ravine Road
Folsom, CA 95630
916-363-5000
www.convergemag.com

Learning & Leading with Technology
480 Charnelton St.
Eugene, OR 97401
541-346-4414
www.iste.org

Mac Home Magazine
703 Market St., Suite 535
San Francisco, CA 94103
415-957-1911
www.machome.com

MacWorld
P. O. Box 54506
Boulder, CO 80323-4506
303-665-8930
www.macworld.com

Media & Methods
1429 Walnut St - 10th Floor
Philadelphia, PA 19102
215-563-6005
www.media-methods.com

Mobile Computing
P. O. Box 850901
Braintree, MA 02185-0901
800-274-1218
www.mobilecomputing.com

PC Magazine
P. O. Box 54093
Boulder, CO 80322-4093
303 - 665-8930
www.zdnet.com/pcmag/

Pen Computing
PO Box 408
Plainview, NY 11803-9801
516-349-9333
pencomputing.com

T.H.E. Journal
17501 17th St, 230
Tustin, CA 92780
714-730-4011
www.thejournal.com

Technology and Learning
600 Harrison St
San Francisco, CA 94107
www.techlearning.com

Videomaker
PO Box 3780
Chico, CA 95927-9840
800-284-3226
www.videomaker.com

Glossary

Address: There are two main types of addresses on the Internet—the Uniform Resource Locator (URL), and the e-mail address.

Analog: Refers to an electronic device that uses a system of unlimited variables to measure or represent the flow of data.

Animation: A method for displaying several different frames in rapid succession to give the illusion of movement.

Application program: A set of instructions that tell the computer to perform a specific task. Also referred to as a program or software.

ASCII: An acronym for American Standard Code for Information Interchange. It is useful for exchanging information between different kinds of computer equipment and software programs, because it eliminates all program-specific symbols. Sometimes referred to as text.

Aspect ratio: Proportional width and height of a picture on screen.

Attachment: Any file or document that is attached to an e-mail message and sent to another mailbox.

Audio dub: Allows you to replace sound without disturbing the picture.

Audio mixer: Device used to blend multiple sound inputs into a desired composite output.

Authoring systems/languages: Programs used in developing computer-assisted instructional programs. They allow computer-based text, numbers, buttons, graphics, video, and audio to be integrated into an instructional program.

Avatar: A graphic representation of a real person in cyberspace.

Back up: To make a spare copy of a file or disk.

Bandwidth: A measurement of how much information can be carried over the Internet. The greater the bandwidth, the faster information is transmitted.

Bar code: A set of lines that represents a number.

Bar-code reader: A device that reads and interprets bar codes.

BASIC: Acronym for Beginners All-Purpose Symbolic Instruction Code. One of the more popular languages for personal computers.

Baud: The rate of character transmission speed over asynchronous communication devices such as modems.

Bit: A one (1) or a zero (0) that represents a set or unset switch in machine code. This is the smallest measurement of data.

Bookmark: A way of marking an Internet site so that you can easily visit it again.

Boot: To start up a computer.

BPS: Bits per second. The speed at which data are transmitted.

Browser: A program that enables you to navigate the World Wide Web.

Bug: An error in a program.

Button: A graphic element within an interface that represents an embedded action or function.

Byte: A group of eight bits, or one character (letter, digit, symbol).

Cable: Wires or cords used to link various pieces of equipment.

Cable modem: A device used to connect a computer to the cable television network for fast data transfer.

Cache: A high-speed memory area used to store data.

Capacity: The amount of data you can store; the total number of bytes that can be stored in memory or, more likely, on a disk.

Capture card: A piece of computer hardware that captures digital video and audio to a hard drive.

Cardioid: The most common type of unidirectional microphone.

CCD: Light sensitive computer chip in video cameras that converts images into electrical flows.

CD-I (compact disc interactive): A type of CD-ROM used on special players with built-in computer and TV capabilities.

CD-ROM: A disk that contains graphics, pictures, movies, or text information. It cannot be written to by a personal computer.

CD-R (CD Recordable): A type of compact disc that can record data.

CD-RW (CD Rewritable): Like CD-R, except that it can be erased and rewritten to.

Central processing unit (CPU): Performs the functions as instructed by the program, and controls the transfer of programs, files, and data within the computer system.

Chat: To have a conversation via computer linkups with other computer users.

Chat room: A location on the Internet set up to allow people to converse in real time by typing messages.

Click: To position a pointer on a particular part of the screen, then press and release the mouse button.

Clip art: A drawing that has been saved on a CD-ROM, hard drive, computer program, or floppy disk. The clip art can be imported into another program.

Clock speed: A measure of how fast a computer's microprocessor or brain can think—measured in millions of cycles per second, or megahertz.

Codec: Software that translates video or audio between its uncompressed form and the compressed form in which it is stored.

Compact disc (CD): A 4-3/4-inch optical disc that contains programs and files encoded digitally in constant linear velocity format. One CD can hold the equivalent of 270,000 pages of text.

Computer: The piece of hardware that houses the central processing unit.

Computer system: A complete computer setup, including the computer, monitor, keyboard, disk drive, and other peripherals.

Cookie: A small piece of text transferred to a Web browser through a server for the purpose of tracking the user.

Courseware: Instructional software and support materials used to deliver a course or instructional module.

Cursor: A blinking underline, rectangle, or other symbol that marks the user's location on the screen.

Data: Information or material that are created on and manipulated by a computer.

Data compression: Any method of condensing information so it can be stored in less space and/or transmitted in less time.

Data base: A collection of information stored as a computer file that is set up to allow people to easily retrieve that information.

Demodulate: To change analog data into digital data.

Desktop publishing: Using software to produce documents with elaborate control of the form and appearance of individual pages.

Desktop videoconferencing: A computer-to-computer form of live action interactive two-way video/audio communication.

Dial-up access: A service that allows the user, with a modem and a personal computer, to create an Internet connection via a phone line.

Digital: The storing of data in a series of numbers.

Digital Subscriber Line (DSL): Technology used to transmit digital data on regular copper phone lines. With DSL, analog voice phone calls and digital signals can coexist on the same wires.

Digital video: A technology that displays digital graphics and full-motion video.

Digitzer: Device that imports and converts analog video and/or audio images into digital data.

Directory: A list of the contents on a disk.

Disk drive: A hardware component that reads programs and files stored on a floppy disk and sends the information to the central processing unit.

Distance learning: Using some means, electronic or otherwise, to connect students with instructors/resources that can help them acquire knowledge and skills.

Document: An electronic file.

Double click: To position the pointer at a specific location on the screen, then press and release the mouse button twice in quick succession.

Download: To copy something from the Internet and save it to your computer.

Drag: To move something to a new location by positioning the pointer at a specific location on the screen, then pressing and holding the mouse button while moving the mouse.

Driver resource: A program in a system folder or directory that tells the computer how to work with a device (a printer, for example).

DVD-ROM: An alternative to a CD-ROM that will hold up to 10 times more content.

e-book: A flat panel computer display that is designed to resemble a book, but provides interactive graphics and searchable text features.

Electronic gradebook: Software designed to maintain and calculate student grades.

e-mail: Electronic mail that is sent via an online service or the Internet.

312

e-mail address: The Internet equivalent of a mailing address.

Emoticon: A "picture" created with computer keys. Used to reflect emotions in e-mail messages.

Encoder: A device that translates a video signal into a different format.

Ergonomics: Centers on how the total work environment—including equipment, furnishings, and tasks—affects worker comfort, health, and productivity.

Ethernet: The basic network layout within a wired LAN architecture that can run at a top speed of 100 Mbps.

Export: To save all or part of a document in a format other than the one in which it was created.

FAQ: Frequently asked questions about a certain topic.

Field: Each video frame is made up of two fields. One field is odd-numbered, horizontal lines of pixels and the other field is even-numbered horizontal lines.

File: A single, named collection of data—such as a manuscript or a list of addresses—that can be recalled by the computer.

File transfer protocol (FTP): One of several methods of transferring information from one Internet location to another.

Finder: An application that is always available on the Macintosh desktop. It is used to locate and manage documents and applications and to move information to and from disks.

Firewall: A combination of hardware and software designed to prevent unauthorized users from entering a company's data infrastructure from the Internet.

Firewire (IEEE1394 or i.LINK): A high-speed two-way bus used, among other things, to connect digital camcorders to computers.

Firewire cable: A single cable that carries audio and video data to and from a digital camcorder.

Flattening: A post-processing pass that "flattens" the Macintosh resource fork of a QuickTime movie and makes the file available for viewing on a Windows-based computer.

Flame: A message that insults or attacks another user.

Flash memory: Semiconductor memory that is slower than RAM but does not require electricity to preserve its contents. This makes it an ideal alternative to a hard drive for the storage of data. Flash memory is generally packaged in CompactFlash, SmartMedia or the PC Card format.

Floppy disk: A device used to store programs and files.

Focal length: Distance from a camera's lens to a focused image with the lens focused on infinity.

Folder: A holder of programs, files, or other folders on the Macintosh or Windows desktop.

Font: A type style.

Footer: A line in a document that can be set to repeat automatically at the bottom of each page.

Format: To prepare a blank floppy disk for its first use.

Frame rate: Number of video frames displayed each second.

Freeze-frame: A mode of video replay that stops and holds a video image.

FTP (file transfer protocol): A way of transferring files from one computer to another using common settings and procedures.

Full-motion video: A standard for video playback on a computer (30 frames per second).

Function keys: The keys that contain the letter F and a number. Function keys (or F keys) tell the computer to perform certain functions, depending on the software.

f-stop: Numbers corresponding to variable size of camera's iris opening and the amount of light passing through the lens. The higher the number, the less light that enters.

Generation loss: Degradation in picture and sound quality resulting from duplication of original master video recording.

GIF (graphical interchange format): A graphic file.

Gigabyte (GB): Approximately one billion bytes—specifically, 1,073,741,824 bytes.

GPS: Global Positioning System, uses the government's fleet of 24 satellites to pinpoint a position on the globe to within about 100 yards.

Graphical user interface: A visual metaphor that uses icons to represent actual items that can be selected or manipulated with a pointing device.

Graphics: Computer pictures.

Hard drive: A magnetic disk that stores information.

Hardware: The physical, electronic, and mechanical components of the computer system.

Header: A line in a document that can be set to repeat automatically at the top of each page.

Hertz: The measure of the speed (clock speed) at which the computer processes information.

Hierarchical file system: The feature that uses folders to organize files, programs, and other folders on a disk. Folders (which are analogous to subdirectories in other systems) can be nested in other folders to create as many levels in a hierarchy as necessary.

Home page: The main World Wide Web page for an online site; the first screen you see when you connect to a site on the Internet.

http (hypertext transfer protocol): The primary protocol for the World Wide Web; http allows linking between Web sites.

Hypermedia: An extension of hypertext that utilizes various types of media. All the various forms of data are organized so that a user can easily move from one to another.

Hypertext: Linking information together through a variety of paths or connections. Hypertext allows users to cross-reference related units of information in a manner similar to the human thinking process.

Icon: A symbolic, pictorial representation of any function, task, program, data, or disk.

IEEE 1394 (Firewire): A specification for a new, high-speed external bus used to connect computer peripherals.

Import: To bring into a document all or part of another document that has been stored in another format.

Input: Data that are entered into the computer.

Infrared communications: The use of infrared light to move data between two computers.

Integrated Services Digital Network (ISDN): A telecommunications network that allows for digital voice, video, and data transmissions. ISDN replaces the slow and inefficient analog telephone system with a fast and efficient digital communcations network.

Interface: Hardware that links the computer to another device, such as a printer.

Internet: A world wide network that allows computers to communicate with one another.

Internet address: An e-mail or other address that specifies a location on the Internet.

Internet appliance: Devices such as WebTV units, Web-ready phones, and hand held devices that give users access to the Internet and e-mail.

Internet Service Provider (ISP): An organization that lets users pay a fee to dial into its computers and connect to the Internet. ISPs generally provide an Internet connection, an e-mail address, and perhaps Web browsing software.

IP (internet protocol): A standard, agreed-upon way of coding and sending data across the Internet.

Jog/Shuttle: Manual control on some videocassette recorders that facilitates viewing and editing precision.

JPEG (joint photographic experts group): A graphic file known for its photographic quality colors.

Kilobyte (K): A unit of measurement equal to 1,024 bytes.

Kilohertz (kHz): A measure of audio samples per second. Higher sample rates yield better sound quality and larger file sizes.

Kiosk: A self-contained, stand-alone unit that houses an interactive laser disc system.

Laser: A device that allows light to be amplified and concentrated into a very narrow and concise beam.

Listserv: A subscription mailing list that allows users to send to and receive e-mail messages from other subscribers.

Load: To transfer programs from a storage device into the computer's memory.

Local area network (LAN): A system that connects two or more microcomputers, allowing users to share resources and communications.

Lux: A measurement of light. One lux is equal to approximately 10 foot-candles.

Megabyte (MB): A unit of measurement equal to approximately one million bytes—specifically, 1,048,576 bytes.

Megahertz (Mhz): One million cycles per second.

Memory: The amount of space either on a floppy disk or the computer's hard drive in which information can be saved.

Menu: A list of options on the screen.

Menu bar: The horizontal strip at the top of the screen that contains menu titles.

Menu title: A word or phase in the menu bar that designates one menu. Clicking on the menu title causes the title to be highlighted and its menu to appear below it.

Microprocessor: The set of tiny switches (circuitry) that process data in a computer.

MIME (Multipurpose Internet Mail Extensions): redefines the format of message bodies to allow multi-part textual and non-textual message bodies to be represented and exchanged without loss of information.

Modem: A device that allows a computer to communicate with other computers via telephone lines.

Modulate: To change digital data into analog data.

Monitor: The screen that is used to display the computer's output.

Mouse: An input device that controls a pointer on the screen. By moving the mouse and pressing its button, the user can draw pictures, select from lists, and move things around the screen.

MPEG: A high compression method for video and audio data. MPEG supports the CD playing of full screen/full motion video.

MP3: A method of compressing audio files into one-tenth of their normal size while still keeping near CD-quality sound.

Multimedia: An integration of text, graphics, animation, voice, music, or motion video into a program on a personal computer.

Network: A group of computers joined by data-carrying links.

Newsgroups: Internet discussion groups that focus on specific topics.

Online: Connected to an online service or the Internet.

Online service: A service that enables the user to dial in, connect to the Internet, and send and receive e-mail.

Operating system: Computer system software that facilitates using a computer to create programs and data files. It also controls the transmission and receipt of data to and from peripheral devices connected to the computer.

Output: The results of a computer operation (data on printed paper or a computer screen, or data stored on some magnetic media, for example).

Pagination: Automatic page numbering done by a word processing or desktop publishing program.

Pan: Horizontal (side to side) camera pivot.

Parallel interface: Allows the computer to send information in the form of complete bytes of information.

Paste: To clip sections of material from one file and put them into another file.

Peripheral device: A piece of computer hardware—such as a disk drive, printer, or modem—that is connected to the computer system.

Photo CD: A compact disc format designed by the Eastman Kodak Company to store and display photographs.

Pixel: A picture element.

Plug in: An application that allows a graphic browser to complete a given task or view a specific file (e.g., Shockwave).

Port: A socket on the back panel of the computer where the cable from a peripheral device, another computer, or a network can be connected.

Potentiometers: Sensors that measure changes in joint flexion/extension.

Presentation software: Programs designed to allow people to display pictures and text to support their lectures.

Printer: A device that is connected to a computer to allow printed output.

Protocol: A set rules for using the Internet.

Public domain software: Uncopyrighted programs available for copying and use by the public at no cost.

Push technologies: A system set up to send out information whether or not anyone requests it.

Radio frequency (RF) modulator: A device that transforms a television set into a computer display device.

Random access memory (RAM): Computer memory that temporarily stores programs, files, and data while they are in use.

Read-only memory (ROM): Computer memory that stores permanent information and instructions for the central processing unit.

Rendering time: The time it takes an editing computer to composite source elements so they can be played in full motion.

Resolution: The number of dots (pixels) on the screen.

Sample rate: The number of samples per second for audio.

Sample size: Audio sample sizes are generally 8-bit or 16-bit.

Save: To store data on a disk.

Search engine: A software program that helps the user find information on the Internet.

Serial interface (RS -232): Transmits information one bit at a time.

Shareware: Uncopyrighted software that anyone may use; each user is asked to pay a voluntary fee to the designer.

Simulation: A resemblance to the actual, without being the actual activity.

Slots: Long, narrow connectors inside the computer that allow for internal peripheral devices.

Snail mail: Regular postal service mail, as opposed to e-mail.

Software piracy: Illegally copying and using a copyrighted software package without buying it.

Spamming: Flooding a mailbox or a listserv with unsolicited messages (usually advertisements).

Speech synthezier: An electronic device, usually a computer chip, that passes words and sentences through a speaker.

Spreadsheet: A computer accounting program that organizes financial data by placing it in categories in a series of columns and rows.

Streaming: Movie or audio data that are visible in real time while they are downloading.

Superimposing: Titles or graphics appearing over an existing video picture.

System file: The program the computer uses to start up.

T-1: High-speed connection capable of transmitting information at 1.544 megabits per second (Mbps).

T-3: Connection capable of transmitting information over fiber-optic cable at speeds of up to 44.73 Mbps.

Test generator: Software designed to help teachers prepare and/or administer tests.

Tilde (~): A squiggly character sometimes used in Internet addresses.

Tilt: Vertical (up and down) camera pivot.

Touch screen: Type of input device designed to allow users to make selections by touching the monitor.

Uniform Resource Locator (URL): Connects the user to a specific place on the Internet; a web page address.

Upload: To save something from your computer to the Internet.

User name: The name used to log on to a network.

UUCP (Unix to Unix Copy Protocol): a protocol used by UNIX systems to copy files between remote dial-up sites.

Video Compression: Reducing the digital data in a file, by throwing away information that the eye can't see.

Video dub: Insert edit that records video without disturbing the existing audio.

Virtual reality: A computer-generated environment designed to provide a lifelike simulation of actual settings.

Virus: A program written with the purpose of doing harm or mischief to programs, data, and/or hardware components of a computer system.

Voice recognition: The capability provided by a computer and program to respond predictably to speech commands.

Wearable systems: Computer components worn on one's body or clothing.

Web site: The place where a home page and its associated files are located.

World Wide Web (WWW): The collection of "pages" available to the millions of computers connected to the Internet. These pages can be accessed by using a web browser. Web pages can include graphics, sound, movies, and text documents.

Word wraparound: The automatic continuation of text from the end of one line to the beginning of the next.

References

Aker, S. Z. (1992). *The Macintosh bible* (4th ed.). Berkeley, CA: Goldstein and Blair.

Ambron, S., & Hooper, K. (Eds.). (1990). *Learning with interactive multimedia*. Redmond, WA: Microsoft Press.

Anderson, D. I., & Sidaway, B. (1994). Coordination changes associated with practice of a soccer kick. *Research Quarter for Exercise and Sport 65*(2), 93-99.

Anglin, G.J. (Ed.). (1991). *Instructional technology: Past, present, and future.* Englewood, CO: Libraries Unlimited.

Aukstakalnis, S., & Blatner, D. (1992). *Silicon mirage: The art and science of virtual reality*. Berkeley, CA: Peachpit Press.

Barlow, D. A., & Bayalis, P. A. (1983). Computer facilitated learning. *Journal of Physical Education, Recreation, and Dance, 54*(9), 27-29.

Bassett, D.R. (2000). Validity and reliability issues in objectively monitoring physical activity. *Research Quarterly for Exercise and Sport, 71(2),* 30-36.

Bassett, D.R., Ainsworth, B.E., Leggett, S.R., Mathien, C.A., Main, J.A., Hunter, D.C., & Duncan, G.E. (1996). Accuracy of five electronic pedometers for measuring distance walked. *Medicine and Science in Sports and Exercise, 28,* 1071-1077.

Baumgartner, T. A., & Cicciarella, C .F. (1987*). Directory of computer software with application to sport science, health, and dance II.* Reston, VA: AAHPERD Research Consortium.

Benedetto, S. (2000). A primer for educators. *Syllabus, August 2000: 47-49.*

Blackall, B. (1986). *Australian physical education, book 1*. South Melbourne: MacMillan Company of Autralia.

Blackall, B., & Davis, D. (1987). *Australian physical education, book 2*. South Melbourne: MacMillan Company of Australia.

Boettcher, J. A. (1983). Dance education: Innovation through technology. *Journal of Physical Education, Recreation, and Dance, 54*(9), 40.

Bouten, C.V., Westeerterp, K.R., Verduin, M. & Janssen, J.D. (1994). Assessment of energy expenditure for physical activity using a triaxial accelerometer. *Medicine and Science in Sports and Exercise, 26,* 1516-1523.

Bull, G., Bull, G., & Sigmon, T. (1997). Common protocols for shared communities. *Learning and Leading with Technology, 25*(1), 50-53.

Burger, J. (1993). *Desktop multimedia bible*. Reading, MA: Addison-Wesley.

Burkett, L.N. (1994). A comparison of three methods to measure percent body fat on mentally retarded adults. *Physical Educator, 51(2),* 67-73.

Burrus, D. (1993). *Technotrends*. New York: HarperBusiness.

Burton, E., & Lane, C. C. (1989). Using computers to facilitate the integration of art, music, and movement. *Journal of Physical Education, Recreation, and Dance, 60*(7), 58-61.

Cannings, T., & Finkel, L. (Eds.). (1993). *The technology age classroom.* Wilsonville, OR: Franklin, Beedle and Associates.

Cassady, S. L., Nielsen, D. H., Janz, K. F., Wu, Y. T., Cook, J. S., & Hansen, J. R. (1993). Validity of near infrared body composition analysis in children and adolescents. *Medicine and Science in Sports and Exercise, 25*(10), 1185-1191.

Chiasson, G. (1997). SPORTDiscus and information utilization. *Quest, 49*(3), 322-326.

Cicciarella, C. F. (1987). *The Computer in measurement and evaluation of physical education and sport.* Mobile, AL: Purr-Spective Press.

Coleman, K.J., Saelens, B.E., Wiedrich-Smith, M.D., Finn, J.D., & Epstein, L.H. (1997). Relationship between TriTrac-R3D vectors, heart rate, and self report in obese children. *Medicine and Science in Sport and Exercise, 29,* 1535-1542.

Consumer Guide (1997). *Best buy book: The complete personal shopping guide.* Lincolnwood, IL: Author.

Corbin, C. B., & Lindsey, R. (1997). *Fitness for life.* Glenview, IL: Scott, Foresman.

Council for Physical Rducation for Children. (1998). *Physical activity for children: A statement of guidelines.* Reston, VA: NASPE Publications.

Dale, D., Corbin, C.B. & Dale, K.S. (2000). Restricting opportunities to be active during school time. *Research Quarterly for Exercise and Sport, 71(3),* 240-248.

Darden, G. (1999). Videotape feedback or student learning and performance: A learning-stages approach. *JOPERD, 70(9),* 40-45.

Darden, G. & Shimon,J. (2000). Revisit an "Old" technology: videotape feedback for motor skill learning and performance. *Strategies, 13(4),*17-21.

Davis, D., Kimmet, T., & Auty, M. (1986). *Physical education: Theory and practice.* South Melbourne: MacMillan Company of Australia.

Davis, S. (1987). *Future perfect.* New York: Addison-Wesley.

Dockterman, D. (1991). *Great teaching in the one computer classroom.* Cambridge, MA: Tom Snyder Productions.

Doering, N. (2000). Measuring student understanding with a videotape performance assessment. *JOPERD, 71(7),* 47-52.

Donnelly, J. (Ed.). (1987). *Using microcomputers in physical education and the sport sciences.* Champaign, IL: Human Kinetics Publishers.

Dougherty, N. J. IV (Ed.). (1993). *Physical activity and sport for the secondary school student.* Reston, VA: AAHPERD.

DuRant, R.H., Baranowksi, T., Davis, H., Rhodes, T., Thompson, W.O., Greaves, K.A., & Puhl, J. (1993). Reliability and variability of indicators of heart-rate monitoring in children. *Medicine and Science in Sports and Exercise, 25,* 389-395.

Epstein, L., Paluch, R., Coleman, K., Vito, D., & Anderson, K. (1996). Determiants of physical activity in obese children assessed by accelerometer and self-report. *Medicine and Science in Sports and Exercise, 28,* 1157-1164.

Ernst, M.P. (2000). Examination of research supported physical activity measurement techniques. *CAHPERD Journal/Times, 63(2),* 20-23.

Eston, R.E., Rowlands, A.V., & Ingledew, D.K. (1998). Validity of heart rate, pedometry, and accelerometry for predicting the energy cost of children's activities. *Journal of Applied Physiology, 84,* 362-371.

Finkenberg, M.E. (1997). The Internet in kinesiology and physical education. *Quest, 49*(3), 327-332.

Fleming, M., & Levie, W. H. (Eds.). (1993). *Instructional message design: Principles from the behavioral and cognitive sciences.* Englewood Cliffs, NJ: Educational Technology Publications.

Floyd, S. (1991). *The IBM multimedia handbook: Complete guide to hardware and software applications.* New York: Brady Publishing.

Franks, B.D., & Wood, R.H. (1997). Use of technology in health-related fitness programs. *Quest, 49*(3), 315-321.

Freedson, P. (1991). Electronic motion sensors and heart rate as measures of physical activity in children. *Journal of School Health, 61,* 220-223.

Freedson, P. (1989). Field monitoring of physical activity in children. *Pediatric Exercise Science, 1,* 8-18.

Freedson, P.S., & Miller, K. (2000). Objective monitoring of physical activity using motion sensors. *Research Quarterly for Exercise and Sport, 71(2),* 21-29.

Frey, D., & Adams, R. (1989). *!@%:: A directory of electronic mail addressing and networks.* Newton, MA: O'Reilly.

Friesen, R., & Bender, P. (1997). Internet sites for physical educators. *Strategies,* September/October 1997, pp. 34-36.

Gagne, R. M., Briggs, L .J., & Wager, W. W. (1992). *Principles of instructional design.* Fort Worth, TX: Harcourt Brace Jovanovich College.

Glavac, M. (1998). *The busy educator's guide to the world wide web.* London: NIMA Systems.

Goggin, N.L., Finkenberg, M.E., & Morrow, J.R. (1997). Instructional technology in higher education teaching. *Quest, 49*(3), 280-290.

Gomez, T. (2001). Avid's easy-to-use tool. *Camcorder and ComputerVideo, Jan. 2001,* 67-70.

Gray, J. (Ed.)(1989). *Dance technology: Current applications and future trends.* Reston, VA: AAHPERD.

Grosse, S. J. (1997). Send Your Students Out to Cruise. *Strategies,* September/October 1997, pp. 18-20, 29.

Gu, W. (1996). The experimental researching the teaching method of fundamental volleyball skills with an optimized combination of multi-media. *Journal of Guanghous Physical Education Institute, 16*(2):73-78.

Hackbarth, S. (1996). *The educational technology handbook: A comprehensive guide—process and products for learning.* Englewood Cliffs, NJ: Educational Technology Publications.

Haggerty, T.R. (1997). Influence of information technologies in kinesiology and physical education. *Quest, 49*(3), 254-269.

Halal, W.E. (2000). The top 10 emerging technologies. *The Futurist 2000 Special Report.* World Future Society.

Healey, J. (2000). *Future possibilities in electronic monitoring of physical activity.* Research Quarterly for Exercise and Sport, 71(2), 137-145.

Hennessy, B. F. (Ed.). (1996). *Physical education sourcebook.* Champaign, IL: Human Kinetics.

Henry, J. & Hubbard, S. (1997). *The evaluator.* Wichita, KS: Guerilla Software.

International Society for Technology in Education. (1998). *National educational technology standards for students.* Eugene, Or: Author.

Jackson, A.S. (1997). New Wine in Old Bottles: Observations of a Chronic Computer User. *Quest, 49*(3), 333-338.

Jambor, E. & Weekes, E. (1995). Videotape feedback: Make it effective. *JOPERD 66(2),* 48-50.

Janelle, C. M., Barba, D. A., Frehlich, S. G., Tennant, L. K., & Caurangh, J. H. (1997). Maximizing performance feedback effectiveness through videotape replay and a self-controlled learning environment. *Research Quarterly for Exercise and Sport, 68*(4), 269-279.

Janz, K.F. (1994). Validation of the CSA accelerometer for assessing children's physical activity. *Medicine and Science in Sports and Exercise, 26,* 369-375.

Janz, K., Golden, J., Hansen, G. & Mahony, L. (1992). Heart rate monitoring of physical activity in children and adolescents: The Muscatine study. *Pediatrics, 89,* 256-261.

Janz, K. Witt, J., & Mahoney, L. (1995). The stability of children's physical activity as measured by accelerometery and self-report. *Medicine and Science in Sports and Exercise, 27,* 1326-1332.

Jennings, R. (1992). *Windows 3.1 multimedia.* Carmel, IN: Que.

Kehoe, B. P. (1993). *Zen and the art of the Internet.* Englewood Cliffs: Prentice-Hall.

Kelly, L.E. (1987). Computer assisted instruction: Applications for physical education. *Journal of Physical Education, Recreation, and Dance, 58*(4), 74-79.

Kelly, L. E. (1987). Computer management of student performance. *Journal of Physical Education, Recreation, and Dance, 58*(8), 12-13 & 82-85.

Kelly, L. E. (1989). Telecommunications: Electronic mail. *Journal of Physical Education, Recreation, and Dance, 60*(7), 86-89.

Kirkpatrick, B., & Birnbaum, B. H. (1997). *Lessons from the heart: Individualizing physical education with heart rate monitors.* Champaign, IL: Human Kinetics.

Klesius, S. E. (1992). Instructional design features of three interactive videodiscs for physical education teacher preparation. *Research Quarterly for Exercise and Sport, 63*(1), A67.

Knirk, F. G., & Gustafson, K. L. (1986). *Instructional technology: A systematic approach to education.* New York: Holt, Rinehart and Winston.

Knudson, D.V. & Morrison, C. S. (1997). *Qualitative analysis of human movement*. Champaign, IL: Human Kinetics.

Kromhout, O. and Butzin, S. (1993). Integrating Computers into the Elementary School Curriculum: An Evaluation of Nine Project CHILD Model Schools. Journal of Research on Computing in Education, Vol. 26, No. 1, 55-69.

Kulik, J.A. (1994). Meta-analytic studies of findings on computer-based instruction. In E. Baker & H. O'Neil (Eds), *Technology assessment in education and training* (pp 9-33). Hillsdale, NJ: Lawrence Erlbaum Associates.

Lamb, A. (1993). *IBM linkway plus linkway live! Authoring tool: For presentations, tutorials and information exploration.* Orange, CA: Career Publishing Incorporated.

Lamb, A. & Johnson, L. (1997). *Crusin' the information highway: Internet in the K-12 classroom.* Emporia, KA: Vision Action Publishing & Consulting.

Laukkanen, R.M.T. & Virtanen, P.K. (1998). Heart rate monitors: State of the art. *Journal of Sport Science, 1998(16),* S3-S7.

Lavroff, N. (1992). *Virtual reality playhouse.* Corte Madera, CA: The Waite Group.

Leavitt, S. B. (1995). *Vision comfort at VDTs: Ergonomic positioning of monitors and work documents.* Glenview, IL: Leavitt Medical Communications.

Lee, T.D., Swinnen, S.P. & Serrrien, D.J. (1994). Cognitive effort and motor learning. *Quest 46,* 328-344.

Levin, H. M., & Meister, G. (1986). Is CAI cost-effective? *Phi Delta Kappan, 67,* 745-749.

Levy, J. R., & Bjellan, H. (1995). *Create your own virtual reality system.* New York: Windcrest/McGraw-Hill.

Locke, L.F. (1997). Minutes of the commodore club: Even Luddites chat on the Internet. *Quest, 49*(3), 270-279.

Lunsford, K. (2000). Hold everything: New DVD-RAM drives off more storage for less money. *Macworld, May 2000:85-89.*

Macfarlane, D. J., Fogarty, B. A., Hopkins, W. G. (1989). The accuracy and variability of commercially available heart rate monitors. *New Zealand Journal of Sports Medicine, 17*(4), 51-53.

McFadden, A. C., & Johnson, E. (1993). Training teachers to use technology: The Alabama plan. *Tech Trends,* Nov/Dec 1993, pp 27-28.

Meijer, G.A., Klass, R., Westerterp, H.K., & Foppe, T.H. (1989). Assessment of energy expenditure by recording heart rate and body acceleration. *Medicine and Science in Sport and Exercise, 21,* 343-347.

Melanson, E. & Freedson, P. (1995). Validity and reliability of a 3-dimensional accelerometer in estimating energy expenditure (abstract). *Medicine and Science in Sport and Exercise, 26,* S42.

Messerer, J. (1997). Adaptive technology: Unleashing the power of technology for all students. *Learning and Leading with Technology,* February 1997, pp 50-52.

Miller, D.I. (1997). Technology in biomechanics instruction. *Quest, 49*(3), 291-295.

Using Technology in Physical Education

Minerd, J. (2000). High-tech clothes. *The Futurist, 34(1)*, 12.

Mohnsen, B. S. (Ed.). (1999). *The new leadership paradigm in physical education: What we need to lead.* Reston, VA: NASPE.

Mohnsen, B. S. (Ed.). (1998). *Concepts of physical education: What every student needs to know.* Reston, VA: NASPE.

Mohnsen, B.(1998). California physical education web site. *CAHPERD Journal/Times, 60(6)*, 11.

Mohnsen, B. (1998). Professional development: When you want it and where you want it. *JOPERD, 69(2)*, 14-17.

Mohnsen, B. (1998). Search the web for personal and professional needs. *Teaching Elementary Physical Education, 9(2)*, 29-30.

Mohnsen, B. (1998). Technology and special events. *Teaching Elementary Physical Education, 9(1)*, 27-29.

Mohnsen, B. (1997). What's the ideal system? *Teaching Elementary Physical Education, 8(4)*, 14-15.

Mohnsen, B. (1996). California physical education home page. *CAHPERD Journal/Times, 59(2)*, 39.

Mohnsen, B. (1997). Authentic assessment in physical education. *Learning and Leading with Technology, 24(7)*, 30-33.

Mohnsen, B. (1997). Exercise physiology software. *Teaching Secondary Physical Education, 3(6)*, 24-25.

Mohnsen, B. (1997). Exercise physiology software. *Teaching Elementary Physical Education 8(6)*, 22-24.

Mohnsen, B. (1997). Social skills and technology: What's the connection? *Teaching Elementary Physical Education, 8(5)*, 20-22.

Mohnsen, B. (1997). Social skills and technology: What's the connection? *Teaching Secondary Physical Education, 3(5)*, 20-22.

Mohnsen, B. (1997).Stretching bodies and minds through technology. *Educational Leadership, 55(3)*, 46-48.

Mohnsen, B. (1997) What's the ideal system? *Teaching Secondary Physical Education, 3(4)*, 10-11.

Mohnsen, B. (1998). Professional development: When you want it and where you want it. *JOPERD, 69(2)*, 14-17.

Mohnsen, B. (1998). Search the web for personal and professional needs. *Teaching Elementary Physical Education, 9(2)*, 29-30.

Mohnsen, B. (1998). Technology and special events. *Teaching Elementary Physical Education, 9(1)*, 27-29.

Mohnsen, B. S. (1997). *Teaching middle school physical education.* Champaign, IL: Human Kinetics.

Mohnsen, B. S. and Mendon, K. (1997). Electronic Portfolios in Physical Education. *Strategies, 11(2)*, 13-16.

Mohnsen, B. S., & Schiemer, S. (1997). Handheld technology: Practical application of the Newton message pad. *Strategies, 10(5)*, 11-14.

Mohnsen, B. S., & Thompson, C. (1997). Using video technology in physical education. Strategies, 10(6):8-11.

Mohnsen, B. S., Chesnutt, C. B., & Burke, D. K. (1997). Multimedia projects for physical education, *Strategies, 11*(1), 10-13.

Mohnsen, B. S., Thompson, C., & Mendon, K. (1996). Effective ways to use technology. *Teaching Secondary Physical Education., 2* (1), 14-17.

Mohnsen, B.(1998). California physical education web site. *CAHPERD Journal/Times, 60*(6), 11.

Montoye, H.J., Kemper, H.C.G., Saris, W.H.M., & Washburn, R.A. (1996). *Measuring physical activity and energy expenditure.* Champaign: Human Kinetics, pp. 72-79.

Moursund, D. (1998). Project-based learning in an information-technology environment. *Learning & Leading with Technology, 25*(8), 4, 55.

Murray, K. T. (1994). Copyright and the Educator. *Phi Delta Kappan, 75,* 555.

National Association for Sport and Physical Education. (1995*). Moving into the future: National physical education standards: A guide to content and assessment.* St Louis: Mosby.

Negroponte, N. (1995). *Beingdigital.* New York: Knopf.

Nichols, J.F., Morgan, C.G., Chabot, L.E., Sallis, J.F., & Calfas, K.J. (2000). Assessment of physical activity with the Computer Science and Applications, Inc., Accelerometer: Laboratory versus field validation. *Research Quarterly for Exercise and Sport, 71(1),* 36-43.

Niemiec, R. P., Blackwell, M. C., & Walberg, H. J. (1986). CAI can be doubly effective. *Phi Delta Kappan, 67,* 751.

Noland, M. Danner, F., Dwalt, K., McFadden, M. & Kotchen, M. (1990). The measurement of physical activity in young children. *Research Quarterly for Exercise and Sport, 61,* 146-153.

Nunez, C., Gallagher, D., Visser, M., Pi-Sunyer, F.X., Wang, Z., & Heymsfield, S. B. (1997). Bioimpedance analysis: evaluation of leg-to-leg system based on pressure contact footpad electrodes. *Medicine and Science in Eports and exercise, 29*(4), 524-531.

OSHA(1991). *Working safely with video display terminals.* Washington, DC: Author.

Pambianco, G., Wing, R.R., Robertson, R. (1990). Accuracy and reliability of the Caltrac accelerometer for estimating energy expenditure. *Medicine and Science in SPort and Exercise, 22,* 858-862.

Patterson, J. (2000). *Scanner round-up.* Mac Today Magazine. July/August 2000:30-31.

PC Novice. (1997). *Computing dictionary.* Lincoln, NE: Author.

PC Novice. (1997). *PC Novice guide to gizmos.* (Vol. 5:12). Lincoln, NE: Author.

Pealer, L. N., & Dorman, S. M. (1997). Evaluating health-related web sites. *Journal of School Health, 67*(6), 232-235.

Pearson, I.D. (2000). The next 20 years in technology: Timeline and commentary. *The Futurist, 34(1), 14-19.*

Pearson, O. R. (1997). *Guide to personal computers.* Yonkers, NY: Consumer Reports.

Percival, F., & Ellington, H. (1988). *A handbook of educational technology.* NY: Kogan Page.

Perelman, L. J. (1992). *School's out: Hyperlearning, the new technology, and the end of education.* New York: Morrow.

Pimentel, K., & Teixeira, K. (1993). *Virtual reality: Through the new looking glass.* Carlsbad, CA: Windcrest Books.

Pitts, W.G. & Sheppard, R. (1999). 25 tips for video. *PC Photo, Sept. 99,* 70-73.

Port, O. (1999). 21 Bright Ideas for the 21st Century. Business Week Online. http://www.businessweek.com/1999/99_35/b3644007.htm. August 30, 1999.

Powers, S., Ward, K., & Shanely, R.A. (1997). Contemporary exercise physiology research in the United States: Influence of technology. *Quest, 49*(3), 296-299.

Rainey, D.L. & Murray, T.D. (1997). *Foundations of personal fitness.* Minneapolis/St.Paul: West Publishing Company.

Rothstein, A. L. (1981). Using feedback to enhance learning and performance with emphasis on videotape replay. *Sport Psychology,* 22-30.

Rotman, D. (2001). Nanotech goes to work. *Technology Review 104(1),* 62-68.

Rowlands, A.V., Eston, R.G. & Ingledew, D.K. (1999). Relationship between physical activity levels, aerobic fitness, and body fat in 8-to-10-yr-old children. *Journal of Applied Physiology, 86,* 1428-1435.

Rowlands, A.V., Eston, R.G., & Ingledew, D.K. (1997). Measurement of physical activity in children with particular reference to the use of heart rate and pedometry. *Sports Medicine, 24,* 258-272.

Sallis, J.F., Buono, M.J., Roby, J.J., Carlson, D., & Nelson, J.A. (1990). The Caltrac accelerometer as a physical activity monitor for school-age children. *Medicine and Science in Sport and Exercise, 22,* 698-703.

Schroeder, R. (1996). *Possitlbe worlds: The social dynamic of virtual reality technology.* Boulder, CO: Westview Press.

Silverman, S. (1997). Technology and physical education: Present, possibilities, and potential problems. *Quest, 49*(3), 306-314.

Simons-Morton, B.G., McKenzie, T.J., Stone, E., Mitchell, P., Osganian, V., Strikmiller, P.K., Ehlinger, S., Cribb, P., & Nader, P.R. (1997). Physical activity in a multiethnic population of third graders in four states. *American Journal of Public Health, 87,* 45-50.

Simons-Morton, B.G., Taylor, W.C., Huang, I.W. (1994). Validity of the physical activity interview and Caltrac with preadolescent children. *Research Quarterly for Exercise and Sport, 65,* 84-89.

Sinclair, G. D. (1983). Instructional management and the microcomputer. *Journal of Physical Education, Recreation, and Dance, 54*(7), 29-30 & 68.

Spindt, G. B., Monti, W. H., & Hennessy, B. (1991). *Moving for life.* Dubuque, IA: Kendall/Hunt.

Spindt, G. B., Monti, W. H., Hennessy, B., Holyoak, C., & Weinberg, H. (1992*). Middle school physical education textbook series.* Dubuque, IA: Kendall/Hunt.

Staff. (1990). A simulated space station inspires math and science students. *The Electronic School, 9*, A21-A22.

Staff. (1997). eMate 300. *MacWorld*, August 1997.

Stein, J. (1987). Physical education selective activities: Computerizing choices. *Journal of Physical Education, Recreation, and Dance, 58*(1), 64-66.

Stein, J. U., & Rowe, J. N. (1989). Computerized budget monitoring. *Journal of Physical Education, Recreation, and Dance, 60*(4), 84-87.

Stokes, R., Schultz, S.L., & Polansky, B.C. (1997). *Lifetime personal fitness.* Winston-Salem, NC: Hunter Textbooks.

Strand, B. & Roesler, K. (1999). Calorie education: A new plan of study in physical education. *Journal of Physical Education, Recreation, and Dance, 70(9)*, 46-52.

Strand, B., Walswick, P. & Sommer, C. (2000). Tracking children's caloric expenditure in physical education. *Journal of Physical Education, Recreation, and Dance, 71(5)*, 35-39.

Stroot, S., & Bumgarner, S. (1989). Fitness assessment: Putting computers to work. *Journal of Physical Education, Recreation, and Dance, 60*(6),44-49.

Sweet, M. (2000). MP3 makes WAVs (Smaller). *Smart Computing, October 2000:53-56.*

Taylor, M. S., & Saverance, D. P. (1990). Computers, physical education, and the year 2000. *Journal of Physical Education, Recreation, and Dance, 62*(7), 38-39.

Terbizan, D.J., Dolezal, B.A., & Albano, C. (1999). Heart rate monitor validity. *Medicine and Science in Sports and Exercise, 31,* S142 (Abstract).

Thornburg, D. D. (1992). *Edutrends 2010: Restructuring, technology, and future of education.* San Francisco, CA: Starson Publications.

Torp, L.T. & Sage, S.M. (1998). Problems as possibilities: Problem-based learning for K-12 education. Alexandria. VA: Association for Supervision and Curriculum Development.

Treiber, F.A., Musante, L., Hartdagan, S., Davis, H., Levy, M. & Strong, W.B. (1989). Validation of a heart rate monitor with children in laboratory and field settings. *Medicine and Science in Sports and Exercise, 21,* 338-342.

Trinity, J., & Annesi, J. .J. (1996). Coaching with video. *Strategies*, June, 1996, pp. 23-25.

Trost, S.G., Ward, D.S., & Burke, J.R. (1998). Validity of the Computer Science and Application (CSA) Activity Monitor in children. *Medicine and Science in Sports and Exercise, 30,* 629-633.

Trost, S.G., Ward, D.S., Moorehead, S.M., Watson, P.D., Riner, W., & Burke, J.R. (1998). Validity of the computer science applications (CSA) activity monitor in children. *Medicine and Science in Sport and Exercise, 30,* 629-633.

Turner, E. T. (1998). A concise guide for the teacher-coach to successfully observe and correct motor skills. *Journal of Physical Education, Recreation, and Dance, 69*(3), 7-9.

Ulrich, B.D. (1997). Technology as a scientific tool for studying motor behavior. *Quest, 49*(3), 300-305.

Van Winkle, W. (2000). The healthy home office. *Home Office Computing*, October, 2000, pp. 59-62.

Wajciechowski, J. A., Gayle, R. C., Andrews, R. L., & Dintiman, G. B. (1991). Polar Electro radio telemetry heart rate compared to ECG measurements. *Clincial Kinesiology, 45*(2), 9-12.

Ward, D. (1998). Grant writing do's and don'ts. *Technology and Learning*, June 1998.

Welk, G.J. & Corbin, C.B. (1995).The validity of the Tritrac-R3D activity monitor for the assessment of physical activity in children. *Research Quarterly for Exercise and Sport, 66*, 202-209.

Welk, G.J., Corbin, C.B. & Dale, D. (2000). Measurement issues in assessment of physical activity in children. *Research Quarterly, 71(2)*, 59-73.

Wendt, J. C., & Morrow, J. R. (1986). Microcomputer software: Practical applications to coaches and teachers. *Journal of Physical Education, Recreation, and Dance, 57*(2), 54-57.

Wilkinson, C., Hillier, R. F., & Harrison, J. M. (1998). Improving the computer literacy of preservice teachers. *Journal of Physical Education, Recreation, and Dance, 69*(5), 10-13,16.

Wilkinson, C., Pennington, T.R. & Padfield, G. (2000). Studentperceptions of using skills software in physical education. *Journal of Physical Education, Recreation, and Dance, 71(6)*, 37-40, 53.

Williams, C. S., Harageones, E. G., Johnson, D. J., & Smith, C. D. (2000). *Personalfitness: Looking good, feeling good.* Dubuque, IA: Kendall/Hunt.

Wittenburg, D. K., & McBride, R. E. (1998). Enhancing the student-teaching experience through the internet. *Journal of Physical Education, Recreation, and Dance*, March 1998.

Wooten, J.O. (2000). Health care in 2025: A patient's encounter. *The Futurist. July-August 2000*, pp. 18-22.

Yoder, S. (1993). Ergonomics forgotten or are we teaching carpel tunnel syndrome? *The Computing Teacher*, Dec/Jan 93/94, pp 30-31.

Zeigler, E.F. (1997). Surviving and thriving in a technological age: To cybernetize or decybernetize? *Quest, 49*(3), 339-349.

Zeni, A. I., Hoffman, M. D., & Clifford, P. S. (1996). Energy expenditure with indoor exercise machines. *JAMA, 275* (18), 1424-1430.

Zinn, W. J. (1994). Private newsletter distributed to patients.

Index

About the Author

Bonnie S. Mohnsen is the county coordinator in the areas of physical education and integrated technology for the Orange County Department of Education in Costa Mesa, California. She is also the owner and a programmer for Bonnie's Fitware, which develops affordable software for use in physical education. A former physical educator with experience at the elementary, middle school, high school, and college levels, Bonnie now spends much of her time giving presentations and writing articles on how other physical educators can improve their programs and use technology to make their teaching easier and more effective.

Bonnie received her PhD in physical education administration from the University of Southern California in 1984. In 1990, she established the California Physical Education Electronic Bulletin Board which served as a model for physical education web pages. Dr. Mohnsen has received grants for using computers in education, including a $100,000 IBM Partnership Grant for using technology to teach biomechanic concepts in physical education.

Bonnie is a member of the American Alliance for Health, Physical Education, Recreation, and Dance and the International Society for Technology in Education. Her favorite leisure-time activities include jogging, hiking, swimming, boating, reading, and computer programming.

Professional Development Seminars

Technology

- Using Technology in Health and/or Physical Education
- Multimedia Development for Physical Education
- Multimedia Development for Health Education
- Heart Monitor Training
- Creating Electronic Portfolios
- Palm Computer Training
- Software Training for HyperStudio, Director, Web Page Development, File Maker Pro, PowerPoint, and more!

Physical Education

- Standards-based Curriculum Development
- Alternative/Authentic Assessment
- Improving Your Physical Education Program
- The Future of Physical Education
- Teaching to the Standards
- Creating High School Career Pathways
- Cooperative Activities and Social Skill Development
- Setting up a Fitness Lab

We can also arrange to provide these topics through online training! All professional development will be customized to meet your needs.

Additional information at: www.pesoftware.com

Training Manuals

$40 per manual plus $4 for shipping and handling!

Innovative Fitness Activities
Order#BF54   ISBN 1-893166-27-9
One hundred-page training manual for grades 6-12 developed by Carolyn Thompson and used at the IED Seminar by the same name.

Building a Quality Phys.Ed. Program
Order #BF52   ISBN 1-893166-28-7
One hundred-page training manual for grades 6-12 developed by Bonnie Mohnsen and used at the BER Seminar by the same name.

Health /Physical Ed. Technology
Order #BF55   ISBN 1-893166-29-5
One hundred-page training manual for grades K-12 developed by Bonnie Mohnsen and used at the BER Seminar by the same name.

Quality Phys. Ed.: Tools, Tips, Tricks
Order #BF90   ISBN 1-893166-48-1
One hundred-page training manual for grades 4-8 developed by Karen Mendon and used at the IED Seminar by the same name. Focuses on social initiatives, fitnes activities, making equipment, and ideas for teaching golf and tennis.

Software catalog at: www.pesoftware.com

Books

Teaching Middle School Physical Ed.-$27 Order #BF33 ISBN 0-88011-513-0

This comprehensive guide gives you a blueprint for designing a quality physical education program. Teaching Middle School Physical Education is packed with exciting ideas and proven strategies that cover all aspects of teaching middle school physical education. In addition, the book includes sample programs for sixth, seventh, and eighth grade that illustrate how all of the elements of a successful program fit together. Plus, handy checklists, insightful anecdotes, and detailed examples that help you put the information into practice.

Using Technology in Physical Ed.-$25 Order #BF51 ISBN 1-893166-51-1

Using Technology in Physical Education is especially for technology novices in language that's free from high-tech jargon. It provides comprehensive information and practical classroom applications for fitness testing equipment, digital video, computers and peripherals, telecommunications, computer-assisted instructional and assessment software, and multimedia systems.

Instructional materials at:
www.pesoftware.com

Bonnie's Fitware
Order Form

Mail
Bonnie's Fitware
18832 Stefani Ave
Cerritos, Ca 90703-8441

Fax
(419)828-2144

eMail
sales@pesoftware.com

Online
www.pesoftware.com/ fitware/eorder.html

*Shipping/Handling Fees
Books - $5.00/book
Training Manuals - $4.00/manual
Task Cards - $4.00/set
Software - $3.00/disc
Site License - 4* cost of program

Name of Item	Item No.	Quantity	Price	Ext. Price

Sub Total _____
  Tax (8.0% in Calif.) _____
    Shipping/Handling* _____
Total _____

Shipping Information

Name: _____

Address: _____

City/State/Zip: _____

eMail: _____